OXFORD WORLD'S CLASSICS

THE HISTORY OF THE ENGLISH PEOPLE 1000–1154

HENRY OF HUNTINGDON was a child of the Norman Conquest, a true 'Anglo-Norman'. The son of an English mother and a Norman father, he was born *c.*1088, probably at Little Stukeley, his family home near Huntingdon. When he was about 12 he was taken by his father Nicholas, who was the archdeacon of Huntingdon and a canon of Lincoln cathedral, to be educated at Lincoln and to be brought up in the bishop's household. On his father's death in 1110 Henry succeeded to the archdeaconry and canonry, offices which he retained until his own death in the late 1150s. Although he was an active and conscientious archdeacon, he had time to write poetry and prose, and between 1123 and 1130, encouraged by a new bishop of Lincoln, he began his *History of the English People*, which he was to continue updating until his final years, completing the last book with the events of 1154. In the section of the *History* that covers the period between 1000 and 1154 the major theme is the Norman Conquest of England—its origins, its immediate impact, and its long-term consequences. As an English speaker, Henry was able to draw on English sources, written and oral. As a Norman, a member of the influential circle of successive bishops of Lincoln, he was well informed about contemporary political life. As a Latin poet and rhetorician, he had the literary skill to create a powerful narrative, embellished with memorable stories, such as Cnut and the waves and Henry I's death from a surfeit of lampreys.

DIANA GREENWAY is Professor of Medieval History at the Institute of Historical Research, University of London and a Fellow of the British Academy. Among her published works are studies of English noble families and the personnel of the English cathedrals in the twelfth and thirteenth centuries, and a full Latin text with translation of *Henry, Archdeacon of Huntingdon: Historia Anglorum: The History of the English People* (Oxford Medieval Texts, 1996). She is the co-translator, with Jane Sayers, of Jocelin of Brakeland's *Chronicle of the Abbey of Bury St Edmunds* in Oxford World's Classics.

OXFORD WORLD'S CLASSICS

*For over 100 years Oxford World's Classics have brought
readers closer to the world's great literature. Now with over 700
titles—from the 4,000-year-old myths of Mesopotamia to the
twentieth century's greatest novels—the series makes available
lesser-known as well as celebrated writing.*

*The pocket-sized hardbacks of the early years contained
introductions by Virginia Woolf, T. S. Eliot, Graham Greene,
and other literary figures which enriched the experience of reading.
Today the series is recognized for its fine scholarship and
reliability in texts that span world literature, drama and poetry,
religion, philosophy and politics. Each edition includes perceptive
commentary and essential background information to meet the
changing needs of readers.*

OXFORD WORLD'S CLASSICS

HENRY OF HUNTINGDON

The History of the English People
1000–1154

*Translated from the Latin,
with an Introduction and Notes, by*
DIANA GREENWAY

OXFORD
UNIVERSITY PRESS

OXFORD

UNIVERSITY PRESS

Great Clarendon Street, Oxford OX2 6DP

Oxford University Press is a department of the University of Oxford.
It furthers the University's objective of excellence in research, scholarship,
and education by publishing worldwide in

Oxford New York

Athens Auckland Bangkok Bogotá Buenos Aires Cape Town
Chennai Dar es Salaam Delhi Florence Hong Kong Istanbul Karachi
Kolkata Kuala Lumpur Madrid Melbourne Mexico City Mumbai Nairobi
Paris São Paulo Shanghai Singapore Taipei Tokyo Toronto Warsaw

with associated companies in Berlin Ibadan

Oxford is a registered trade mark of Oxford University Press
in the UK and in certain other countries

Published in the United States
by Oxford University Press Inc., New York

British Library Cataloguing in Publication Data

Data available

Library of Congress Cataloging in Publication Data

Data available

ISBN 978-0-19-955480-5

Typeset in Ehrhardt
by RefineCatch Limited, Bungay, Suffolk
Printed in Great Britain by
Clays Ltd, Elcograf S.p.A.

CONTENTS

THE HISTORY OF THE ENGLISH PEOPLE
1066–1814

INTRODUCTION

England 1000–1154

England in the early middle ages saw conflict and conquest, followed by assimilation, as successive waves of peoples came to her shores from Europe, first as raiders, then as conquerors, and finally as settlers who were gradually absorbed into a mixed population.

Migration from northern Germany and southern Scandinavia into the former Roman province of Britain, in the fifth and sixth centuries, led to the formation of a number of Anglo-Saxon kingdoms, which in varying degrees exhibited a synthesis of native Celtic and imported Germanic cultural elements. By the ninth century the smaller kingdoms had been incorporated into the four most powerful—East Anglia, Northumbria, Mercia, and Wessex.

Already in the eighth century the coasts of western Europe were being harassed and plundered by the Vikings, also called the Northmen, who were mostly Danes and Norwegians and came in sailing ships. In the ninth century they took the northern islands of Orkney, Shetland, and the Hebrides, created outposts on the east coast of Ireland, and invaded England. In the face of this invasion, only the West Saxon kingdom (Wessex) survived, as the kings of East Anglia, Northumbria, and Mercia were conquered and deposed. By a treaty soon after 886, the West Saxon king, Alfred the Great (871–99), conceded to the Viking leader, Guthrum, the region to the north and east of Watling Street (the familiar road, the A5), comprising East Anglia, the east and central Midlands, and Yorkshire. In this large area, which came to be known as the Danelaw, the Vikings settled and lived alongside the English population, but retained many of the laws and customs of their Scandinavian homelands. It was not until 954 that the last of the Scandinavian kings of York was driven out, and the king of Wessex was able to establish dominion over the whole of England. Peoples of diverse origins and cultures were now ruled by a single English monarchy.

All around, however, the Vikings continued to expand their interests, settling in Iceland, Greenland, northern Scotland, Man, west Wales, Ireland, and northern France, sailing down the Iberian coast to North Africa, and venturing as far as North America, while in the east they penetrated into Russia and Byzantium. A second series of increasingly intensive Viking campaigns began in England in 980. As the invaders threatened to overwhelm his kingdom, Æthelred II ('the Unready') (978–1016) made a marriage alliance in 1002 with a powerful neighbour in northern France, the duke of Normandy, by marrying the duke's sister, Emma. The Norman duchy was in origin another Scandinavian conquest, having been carved out of the French kingdom in 911 by Rollo, the leader of the 'Normanni', the Northmen (hence the name 'Normandy'). In the event, Æthelred's marriage into the ducal family did not prevent England's fall to the Viking invaders, and was to have a disastrous unforeseen consequence by creating a dynastic link that would give the Normans an interest in the succession to the English throne.

The determination and military expertise of a professional army under the leadership of the Danish king, Swein Forkbeard, proved too much for the weakened and demoralized forces of Æthelred. The country was overrun, and in 1013, when Æthelred fled to his wife's kindred in Normandy, Swein was acknowledged king of England. Swein's sudden death early in 1014 allowed Æthelred to return, and he held the kingship with difficulty until he died in 1016. For a while Æthelred's son Edmund Ironside and Swein's son Cnut shared the kingdom, but after Edmund's death in the same year, Cnut became sole king.

England was now to be ruled by Danish kings until 1042— successively by Cnut and his sons Harold I and Harthacnut. Cnut's reign was the longest (1016–35) and the most significant. He resolved to rule all his subjects, both Danes and English, and secured his position by ruthlessly eliminating his enemies and rewarding his supporters with no regard for their ethnic background. He took as his partner the English noblewoman Ælfgifu of Northampton, and continued the relationship after his marriage to Æthelred's widow, the Norman Emma: what might have been condemned as adultery by Church leaders was tolerated as a Danish custom. Although in his early years his closest associates were men of Danish origin, by the mid-1020s Cnut had promoted several Englishmen, including Godwine (father of the future king, Harold II), whom he made earl of Wessex. His executive and judicial orders were to apply to 'all the peoples of my whole kingdom, whether English or Danish'. His comprehensive law-codes recognized the variations of customs between the Danelaw, Wessex, and Mercia, but maintained the principle that the king was the supreme lawgiver and judge.

When Cnut's line died out with the death of his son Harthacnut in 1042, the old English royal dynasty was restored in the person of Edward the Confessor, son of Æthelred and Emma. Having spent much of his youth in the comparative security of Normandy, he had no close ties with the Anglo-Danish lords who controlled the English localities. He brought several Norman advisers with him, but fell under the influence of the English Earl Godwine, whose elder sons he made earls and whose daughter he married. There was conflict between Godwine's faction and the king's Norman companions, with plots and counter-plots. But Godwine's son and heir as earl of Wessex, Harold, maintained his supreme position among the English aristocracy until the childless Edward's death in 1066, and, contrary to Edward's earlier wish that Duke William of Normandy should be his successor, it was Harold who 'succeeded to the realm of England', as the Anglo-Saxon chronicler says, 'just as the king had granted it to him, and as he had been chosen to the position'. He was immediately challenged by the Scandinavian claimant, Harold Hardrada, king of Norway, who was attempting to reconstruct the empire of Cnut. Within days of the English victory over the Norwegians at Stamford Bridge, near York, King Harold heard that the expected Norman invasion had begun. William, duke of Normandy, was a descendant of the father of Emma of Normandy, and claimed to have had the Confessor's promise of the kingdom. He made good his claim at the battle of Hastings.

Of the two eleventh-century foreign conquests of England, that by the Normans had the more far-reaching consequences. The English and Scandinavian aristocracies were ousted, to be replaced by new landowners. Not all those who came with William the Conqueror were from Normandy: there were also men from other parts of France and the Low Countries—from Brittany, Poitou, Anjou, Maine, Burgundy, Picardy, and Flanders. The settlement of England by the victorious leaders, their kin, and their followers involved a massive redistribution of landed estates to the incomers. Intermarriage occurred between the invading groups, and with the English and Anglo-Scandinavians. English society was multicultural, multi-ethnic, and polyglot.

The English language survived, but was forced into a subordinate position to Latin as the language of governmental documentation and to French as the language of the royal court and the ruling class. English continued as the vernacular among the great majority of the population, but was modified by the introduction of French and Latin linguistic elements. It re-emerged in polite society, literature, and government in the later fourteenth century, but its complete triumph over Latin as the language of scholarship and formal record came later still, in the eighteenth century. Many of the literate class in the eleventh and twelfth centuries, like our author, Henry of Huntingdon, were trilingual, equally at home in English, French, and Latin.

The members of the new aristocracy soon settled into their lordships and protected them by building castles, guarded by knights. The greatest of the magnates held estates on both sides of the Channel. As in the pre-Conquest period, the king needed a collaborative relationship with the leading men in order to maintain the kingdom, but this relationship was strengthened by the imposition on the chief landowners of the duty to supply quotas of armed knights when required. For the peasantry, conditions remained much the same, whoever their landlords might be: most were tied to their lords' farms and led lives of servile labour. The establishment on the land of large numbers of knights, some of English descent, who owed military service to their lords, created a social stratum between magnates and peasants. From this knightly class were to be drawn the local officials upon whom, from the twelfth century onwards, the king's government in the localities depended more and more. This class later gave birth to 'the gentry'.

The leaders of the Church—the bishops and abbots—had been essential to Anglo-Saxon government, providing advice and bureaucratic expertise. The situation had been much the same in Normandy, so that although after 1066 most of the English higher clergy were replaced by men of continental origin, ecclesiastical control was still maintained over the central administration. However, the incoming bishops and abbots brought changes to the Church. In a programme of modernization, there was a great rebuilding of cathedrals, abbeys, and larger parish churches (the Anglo-Saxon minsters), and an acceleration of the process of dividing large parishes into smaller units, each with its own local church. New monasteries were founded with stricter observances, on the Norman style. Under reforming archbishops and bishops, the education and training of the clergy was improved, and by the middle of the twelfth century there existed a body of literate men who were employed as clerks in government at all levels—in the service of the king, the lay magnates, the bishops and abbots, and the many ecclesiastical institutions throughout England. Connections with Rome were strengthened, so that the English Church became receptive to the growing authority of the popes in matters of faith, discipline, and ecclesiastical law.

Quite soon after the Norman Conquest, the distinctions between Norman and English began to fall away, in much the same way that the distinctions between Danish and English had become blurred in the earlier eleventh century. Intermarriage played an important part in this process, but cannot entirely account for the way in which English laws and customs were adopted and the history of England and its saints came to be cherished by the ruling elite of the cross-Channel Anglo-Norman realm.

In fact, the adoption of English methods of government was the most practical way forward for the Norman kings. They encouraged the development of the administration they had inherited, which was more sophisticated and effective than existed in Normandy. The achievement of the Domesday Survey of 1086, a comprehensive inquiry into lands and rights, was possible only through the use of pre-Conquest institutions and practices. The old English unit of local government, the shire, was preserved, along with its chief officer, the sheriff, who continued to be responsible for tax collection and the maintenance of law and order. The primary town of each shire, from which the sheriff operated, was now usually defended by a newly built royal castle, at which some of the military duties of the knights were discharged. The role of the earl, who in the pre-Conquest period had tended to control an area comprising several shires, was reduced: the earls appointed by the Norman kings were generally confined to a single shire, and by no means every shire had an earl. Earldom was ceasing to be an office and on the way to becoming a hereditary title of honour. At the centre, royal government was conducted through the king's writing office (the chancery), his financial department (the exchequer), and his law courts (later to be known as the king's bench and the common pleas). The sheriff, in the various aspects of his duties, was responsible to these institutions. To give additional links between centre and locality, the Norman kings increasingly used the old English practice of sending out itinerant commissions of inquiry, and by the second half of the twelfth century the system of travelling judges had been built into the judicial administration.

England's wealth was largely derived from agriculture, in which the majority of its population of about 2 million was employed. The fertile lowland areas yielded mostly grain, while the output of the less fertile hills and some of the marshlands was predominantly wool. Exports of both these raw materials went to many parts of Europe, wool superseding grain in importance in the twelfth century, when the leading European cloth manufacturers in Flanders relied to a large extent on English supplies. Goods imported into England included furs from Scandinavia, wines from the Rhineland, and cloth from Flanders. The development of internal and external trade in the eleventh and twelfth centuries encouraged the growth of sea-ports and inland towns: there was a network of markets and fairs throughout the land, and an increasingly self-assertive, if small, merchant community.

Throughout the period 1000–1154 there were two principal problems threatening royal control of the English state. One was the instability brought about by uncertainty over the laws of succession to the kingship: the idea of hereditary right had not yet hardened into primogeniture, so that collateral royal kin might succeed if it was thought appropriate by the kingdom's chief men, and there was scope for designation of a successor by a reigning king. The other problem was the predatory ambition of some of the chief magnates, who sought to increase their own power at the king's expense. Often these two problems were interrelated, as aggressive magnates gave their support to rival claimants for the crown. The most notable example before the Conquest concerns the family of Godwine, which repeatedly challenged and diminished the Confessor's kingship, and actually gained the throne in the person of Harold.

The Norman Conquest introduced a further complication by uniting the duchy of Normandy with the kingdom of England under William the Conqueror (1066–87). His deathbed recognition of the right of his eldest son, Robert Curthose, to his patrimony of Normandy, but his designation of his second son, William Rufus, as heir to his acquired land, England, created tensions that erupted in open warfare in 1088. Rufus died without issue in 1100 and was succeeded by the Conqueror's third son, Henry I (1100–35). Curthose attempted to contest this, but was defeated and captured in 1106, and the duchy and the kingdom were reunited. Curthose's son, William Clito, had a strong claim and continued to threaten Normandy, aided by ambitious Norman barons, as well as powerful rulers—the king of France and the counts of Flanders and Anjou— who were all ready to profit from instability in the duchy. It was fortunate for Henry that Clito died childless in 1128.

There was great doubt, however, over the rightful succession to Henry I. The death of his only legitimate son in the wreck of the *White Ship* in 1120 left as his sole direct heir his daughter the Empress Matilda. In her widowhood she was sent by her father to marry the count of Anjou, in an alliance to secure the southern border of Normandy. But as a woman, and as the wife of an enemy of long standing, she was unacceptable to much of the Anglo-Norman baronage. On her father's death in 1135 she lacked immediate support, and was outmanoeuvred by Stephen of Blois, who was Henry I's nephew, being a son of his sister Adela, a daughter of the Conqueror. Stephen had the support of enough of the baronage and Church leaders to be made king, but his reign (1135–54) was dominated by struggle in defence of his kingship against those who favoured Matilda. As the two sides sought to crush their opponents and reward their supporters, there was much activity around the building, besieging, and surrender of castles, and the grant of earldoms and shrievalties.

The death in 1153 of Stephen's elder son, and only credible heir, brought the wars to an end in a treaty whereby Stephen recognized Henry of Anjou, son of Matilda, as his successor and heir to the kingdom by hereditary right. Henry already controlled Normandy and Anjou, and by his marriage to Eleanor of Aquitaine had acquired Aquitaine and Poitou. In 1154 he became king of England as Henry II, the master of a considerable cross-Channel empire.

Henry of Huntingdon

Henry of Huntingdon's *History of the English People* has been one of the most enduring and best-known of medieval chronicles. Thanks

to the survival of documentary records to supplement the hints he
gives about himself in his work, we can construct for him a biog-
raphy that is fuller than for almost any other medieval English
historian.[1]

He was born *c*.1088, probably at Little Stukeley, a small village to
the north-east of Huntingdon (now in Cambridgeshire). His father,
Nicholas, a clergyman, was a member of the Norman family of
Glanville, and was related, perhaps as a brother or cousin, to Robert
de Glanville, the founder of the English branch of the Glanville
family, who had gained various estates in Norfolk and Suffolk after
the Conquest. Nicholas became the first archdeacon of Huntingdon,
appointed *c*.1075 by the Norman bishop of Lincoln, Remigius,
whose origins, like those of the Glanvilles, lay in the coastal region of
Normandy just to the north of Le Havre (the 'pays de Caux'). As
archdeacon, Nicholas was also a canon of Lincoln cathedral: his
permanent monument is the magnificent Great Bible, in two volumes, which he gave to the cathedral.[2] Henry notes his father's death
in 1110, proudly and affectionately describing him as 'the star of the
clergy'.

At this period it was not unusual for members of the clergy, such
as cathedral canons and archdeacons, to marry. Nor was it unusual
for Norman men to marry English women, especially heiresses.
Although we do not know her name, we can be sure that the wife of
Archdeacon Nicholas was English: possibly she had inherited the
estate at Little Stukeley which was held for rent from the nearby
abbey of Ramsey. It would have been she who taught Henry to speak
English, his mother tongue.

The line of hereditary clergymen-squires at Little Stukeley continued for another three generations. Henry also married, but we do
not know his wife's name or origin. Their son, Adam of Stukeley,
also a clergyman, was the father of at least two sons. One of these,
called Master Aristotle, another clergyman, had a son, Nicholas of

---

[1] A fuller account of Henry's career, with references, will be found in *Henry,
Archdeacon of Huntingdon, Historia Anglorum: The History of the English People*, ed.
and trans. D. Greenway (Oxford Medieval Texts, 1996) (abbreviated below as HH),
pp. xxiii–lvii.

[2] Lincoln Cathedral MS 1 and Trinity College Cambridge MS B. 5. 2. See R. M.
Thomson, *Catalogue of the Manuscripts of Lincoln Cathedral Chapter Library* (Wood-
bridge, 1989), pp. xiv, 3, 212, and frontispiece; also C. M. Kauffmann, *Romanesque
Manuscripts 1066–1190* (London, 1975), no. 13 and pls. 30–3.

Stukeley, yet another clergyman, who was the last of the line. Nicholas held the family estate at Little Stukeley until *c.*1230, when, being unmarried and having no heir, he surrendered it to the landlord, the abbot of Ramsey.

At the age of about 12 Henry was taken by his father to Lincoln, to be educated at the cathedral by the schoolmaster Albinus, who had been recruited by Bishop Remigius from the flourishing cathedral school of Angers in France. Henry learned Latin grammar, including poetics and rhetoric, very much in the style of the contemporary literary culture of Angers and the Loire region, with its emphasis on poetry and rhetorical writing. During the period of his education he lived in the household of the bishop of Lincoln, Robert Bloet, who had been chancellor to King William II and was one of King Henry I's closest advisors. Here, as he recalls in 'On Contempt for the World', he saw life at the top, enjoying the luxury and ostentation of the French-speaking ruling class, and observing the glitterati of Anglo-Norman society—royalty and aristocracy, bishops, judges, and king's ministers.

On the death of Archdeacon Nicholas in 1110, Bishop Bloet appointed Henry to his father's archdeaconry of Huntingdon and the canonry of Lincoln—offices which Henry was to hold until his own death soon after 1156. Henry continued to be close to the bishop, accompanying him in the king's entourage. His detailed accounts of two deaths that occurred in the royal party in the last days of December 1122 and the first days of January 1123 suggest that he was an eyewitness: these were the deaths of Ranulf the chancellor and Bishop Robert Bloet himself, for whom Henry composed an epitaph in verse.

Bloet's successor as bishop of Lincoln was Alexander 'the Magnificent', just possibly an Englishman,[3] the nephew of the king's first minister, Bishop Roger le Poer of Salisbury. Recognizing Henry's potential as a writer, probably from the books of poetry that he had already written, Alexander commissioned him to write the *History of the English People*. Alexander is celebrated in the book in two panegyrical poems. In his company Henry attended the royal court in 1127–8 and 1130–3 and was present at several ecclesiastical councils in the 1120s, 1130s, and 1140s. As Alexander's representative he

---

[3] Henry calls him 'the highest and most splendid ornament . . . of our people' (below, I. 4). This may mean that Bishop Alexander was of English origin.

journeyed to Rome in 1139 to secure a papal privilege for Lincoln cathedral. While Henry was away, the bishop was arrested, along with his uncle, Bishop Roger of Salisbury, in one of the most notorious episodes of King Stephen's reign: for Henry this was a defining moment that ushered in a period of 'lamentation and terror'. Bishop Alexander himself visited the pope at least three times, twice in Rome, in 1125 and 1146, and for the last time in Auxerre, in the late summer of 1147. On the way to Auxerre he probably stayed at the abbey of Bec in Normandy, where he donated a copy of Henry's *History*, complete down to Christmas 1146. The heat in Auxerre brought on a sickness which worsened after his return to England: he died at Lincoln in February 1148. Henry's notice of this death includes a brief but perceptive character-sketch.

Robert de Chesney, Henry's colleague as a canon of Lincoln and archdeacon of Leicester, who succeeded as bishop, had no powerful connections in the political world. But as bishop he was required to attend national assemblies, and at least twice was probably accompanied in London by Archdeacon Henry. Thus Henry is the sole source for the London council of March 1151 and the London assembly of April 1152, when the bishops refused to crown Stephen's son Eustace.

At the local level, too, Henry was an active man of affairs. The archdeaconry of Huntingdon was his homeland, an area for which he felt a great affection and in which he took considerable pride. As squire of Little Stukeley he built the church of St Martin there and had it dedicated. At one point in the *History* he gives an almost lyrical description of the nearby fens—'the marshland . . . beautiful to behold, washed by many flowing rivers, adorned by many meres, great and small, and green with many woods and islands'.[4] Henry was well acquainted with the abbeys of the east midlands and fenland. He celebrates the region's saints—Rumwold at Buckingham, Neot at St Neots, Yvo at St Ives, Æthelred and Æthelberht at Ramsey, Cyneburh, Cyneswith, and Tibba at Peterborough, Guthlac at Crowland. He knew personally the successive abbots of Peterborough and Ramsey. When blood bubbled out of the walls of the church and cloister at Ramsey, while Geoffrey de Mandeville was holding the abbey as a castle during his rebellion of 1144,

---

[4] HH, 321, describing the fenland abbeys of the time of King Edgar (959–75).

Henry was one of those who saw and wondered at this sign of God's anger.

In a digression after recounting the events of the year 1010, Henry explains that the river Ouse, after flowing through Buckingham and Bedford, goes on to Huntingdon, an explanation that serves to introduce a description of Huntingdon—one of nine references in the *History* to the town or its vicinity. The place-name he correctly derives from 'the hill of the hunters'—it is far superior to Buckingham and Bedford, 'for the splendour of its site and for its beauty, as well as for its proximity to the said marshes and for the abundance of its wild beasts and fish' (below, II. 6).

Before the foundation of the bishopric of Ely, in 1109, in Henry's father's time, Cambridgeshire and the Isle of Ely had formed part of the archdeaconry of Huntingdon in the diocese of Lincoln. Henry shows local knowledge of Ely and an interest and pride in its patron saint, Æthelthryth (or Etheldreda). His father had been present at the inspection and reburial of her incorrupt body in the new Norman cathedral in 1106, and Henry himself knew of the miracle in which, in 1115 or 1116, St Æthelthryth appeared to a prisoner called Bricstan and freed him by breaking the irons that bound him: 'his shackles hang at the present time [*c*.1140] by the altar [of Ely cathedral], to be seen and touched with wonder by visitors' (VI. 3).

The slimmed-down archdeaconry to which Henry succeeded covered Huntingdonshire and Hertfordshire. Much of the latter county, however, belonged to the great abbey of St Albans and was exempt from the archdeacon's jurisdiction. In his account of the abbey, Henry acknowledges the antiquity of its highly privileged status and describes two ceremonies which he probably witnessed personally: the dedication of the Norman church by Bishop Robert Bloet of Lincoln in 1115, and the transfer of St Alban's remains to the new shrine in 1129 in the presence of Bishop Alexander.

There is abundant documentary evidence to suggest that Henry was a diligent archdeacon. Charters show him at work in his archdeaconry, supervising the clergy, the income, and the rights of parish churches, and settling disputes over tithes and boundaries. He was present on important occasions at many of the religious houses of the region—both outside his archdeaconry (Thorney, Thame, Vaudey, Crowland) and within it (Peterborough, Ramsey, Sawtry, St Neots, Markyate)—witnessing the foundations of communities,

attending the dedications of their churches, and giving his attest-
ation to solemn charters of various sorts.

As archdeacon he was also a canon of Lincoln cathedral. Henry
makes numerous references to the city in the *History*, and is especially interesting when commenting on the cathedral and its clergy,
on the successive bishops, and on political and military events in
Stephen's reign. He was present among assemblies of the dignitaries and canons of Lincoln on many occasions, as we know from
surviving archives. His name is entered in a list of canons drawn up
c.1132, from which we learn that when the Psalter was chanted
daily in the cathedral Henry's portion (which he was required to
chant personally or by proxy) was Psalm 78, 'Give ear, O my
people, to my law', a long, narrative psalm of which there are
echoes in his work.

The last event in the *History* is the coronation of King Henry II,
which took place on 19 December 1154. Henry appears as archdeacon several times in the mid- and late 1150s, and was certainly
still alive in October 1156, when he would have been about 68 years
of age. By 1164 or early 1165, however, he was dead, and the archdeaconry of Huntingdon was in the hands of his successor, Nicholas
de Sigillo. He therefore died sometime between 1156 and 1164.

The History of the English People

Purpose and content

As he states in the prologue, Henry wrote at the explicit direction
of Bishop Alexander (I. 4). This request was made not long after
Alexander's appointment to Lincoln in 1123. By *c*.1133 Henry had
finished the first version of his *History*, in seven books, with prologue and epilogue, covering the entire period from the legendary
naming and settling of Britain by the Trojan exile Brutus, down to
the year 1129. During the next decade he wrote two further books
(one on the English saints and their miracles and the other a collection of essays in letter form), and began the tenth, which dealt with
the period after 1135. He continued this final book as events
unfolded in the reign of Stephen, and went on revising and adding to
some of the earlier books until a little after 1154, the year in which
the narrative comes to an end with the coronation of Henry II. The

History satisfied a need: copies began to circulate while the book was still in process of composition.[5]

As envisaged by Bishop Alexander, the object was 'to narrate the history of this kingdom and the origins of our people' (I. 4). It was intended as a popular manual in one volume, written for 'the many—I mean the less educated' (V, preface). It was therefore written in simple Latin, with a strong story-line and plenty of dramatic incident, the completed work being arranged in ten books of roughly equal length, each making a unit that might be read—and read aloud—at a single sitting. Few laymen at this time were able to read and understand Latin. Largely the audience would have consisted of members of the clergy—in monasteries, cathedrals, and greater churches, and also in the households of king, nobles, and bishops.

The focus of the *History* is 'our people', that is, the English people, the inhabitants of 'this, the most celebrated of islands, formerly called Albion, later Britain, and now England'.[6] Henry clearly identified himself as English, and in this definition of England conveniently ignored the existence of non-English communities in the island—Welsh, Scots, Normans. He was happy to see himself as a successor to earlier English writers, especially Bede, who in the eighth century had recorded in Latin the history of the conversion of the English to Christianity, and the many annalists who over the years between the late ninth and the mid-twelfth centuries had compiled the various versions of the vernacular Anglo-Saxon Chronicle.[7] Henry was able to read and translate the Chronicle and make sense of English personal names and place-names. He took an interest in the history and topography of the English and Welsh towns and was the author of a poem celebrating them.[8] He may have been the first to list the shires and bishoprics.[9] He was interested in the sites of battles, and realized the historical significance of ruins.[10] His description of the four 'marvels' of Britain includes an account

[5] I have identified six different versions, which correspond to copies taken in *c.*1133 (versions 1 and 2), *c.*1140 (version 3), *c.*1147 (version 4), *c.*1149 (version 5), and *c.*1155 (version 6). See HH, pp. lxvi–lxxvii.

[6] Ibid. 13.

[7] Bede, *The Ecclesiastical History of the English People*, ed. J. McClure and R. Collins (Oxford World's Classics, 1994); *The Anglo-Saxon Chronicle*, ed. and trans. D. Whitelock, D. C. Douglas, and S. I. Tucker (London, 1961).

[8] HH, 21.

[9] Ibid. 17–19.

[10] Ibid. 15 'Dormecestre' [Castor], 93 Pevensey.

of Stonehenge that is the first surviving written record of that great prehistoric monument and of its name.[11]

The *History* is based on the idea that there was a continuity in English history and identity, even though the land had suffered repeated invasions by other races—first the Romans, second the Picts and Scots, third the Angles and Saxons, fourth the Danes, and fifth the Normans. Following Old Testament models, including his special psalm (Psalm 78), and using ideas in Bede, Henry saw the invasions as five punishments or plagues inflicted by God on a faithless people. Even the fifth and final invasion, the Norman Conquest, which is the subject of the three most important books of the *History* (printed below as parts II, III, and IV), did not ultimately disrupt the continuum of English history. At first it looked as if the English had ceased to be a people, but by the time of the battle of the Standard, in 1138, the glorious past victories of the Normans, including the conquest of England, had been enthusiastically assimilated into English history.[12] For Henry the modern term 'Anglo-Norman' would have had no meaning. As Ralph Davis observed, 'the paradox of the Normans is that . . . in the long run the conquest of England turned them into Englishmen'.[13]

For Henry, what defined a nation, *gens*, was kingdom, *regnum*. He saw the Anglo-Saxon period as the story of the unification of the English monarchy: disorder and war among the first Anglo-Saxon invaders gave way to rule by petty kings, wars between these kings ended in rule by stronger kings over larger kingdoms, and by the year 1000 the kings of Wessex had become the kings of the entire English people. The main theme of *The History of the English People* for the period between 1000 and 1154 is the Norman Conquest of the English kingdom: its causes and origins, its immediate impact, and its long-term consequences.

In the book entitled 'The Coming of the Normans' (below, part II), he tells of the decline of the Old English kingdom after 1000, the victory of the Normans at Hastings, and the establishment of Norman rule, ending with William I's death in 1087. To his translated extracts from the Anglo-Saxon Chronicle, he adds lively details

---

[11] Ibid. 23.

[12] To the evocation of these Norman triumphs, 'Every Englishman answered and the hills and mountains echoed, "Amen! Amen!"' (below, IV. 9).

[13] R. H. C. Davis, *The Normans and their Myth* (London, 1976), 122.

and stories from unknown sources, including the murder of Edmund Ironside (c. 14), Cnut and the waves (c. 17), Earl Siward's reaction to his son's death (c. 22) and his last words (c. 24), the death of Earl Godwine (c. 23), and William FitzOsbern's trick on the eve of the Norman invasion (c. 27).

'The Kingdom of the Normans' (part III) deals with the reigns of William II (1087–1100) and Henry I (1100–35). To his translation of the Anglo-Saxon Chronicle Henry adds a good deal of independent material, which often reflects his contemptuous view of worldly pomp. Into his account of William II's reign he interpolates an abbreviated history of the First Crusade (cc. 5–18). When describing the period when he was close to the royal court, under Henry I, he gives details from first-hand experience and also inserts several poems of his own composition. He is the first writer to attribute Henry I's death to lampreys (c. 43).

The final part of the narrative, 'The Present Time' (part IV), covers the reign of Stephen (1135–54), for which—although less detailed than some other chronicles—it is the only complete contemporary account. Henry was clearly dismayed and disgusted by the conduct of King Stephen and the barons in the civil war, but turned his narrative of death and destruction into memorable literature by interposing well-wrought battle-speeches, battle-scenes, and poems. For some events he was certainly an eyewitness, as for example at Geoffrey de Mandeville's sacrilegious occupation of Ramsey abbey in 1144 (c. 22). The book concludes with a long poem on the accession of Henry II.

An essential element of Henry's interpretation of history is the belief that without God, man is nothing, his pride and glory come to nought. The theme, familiar from the Bible, especially Psalm 58,[14] runs throughout the *History*. In the earliest versions of the text, *c*.1133, all its three elements—prologue, historical narrative, and epilogue—concluded with the same idea, the passing of the world into nothingness. At best, historical record keeps nothingness, oblivion, at bay for a while, and its study distinguishes men from beasts. Individual men, and even entire peoples and kingdoms, may be destroyed without any written record of their existence.[15] They are very

---

[14] Ps. 58: 7, echoed in HH, 137, 237, 531, and below, III. 40, V. 15, VII. 6.

[15] See Henry's comments on the disappearance of the Picts, HH, 25, and on the impossibility of identifying some of the sites of Arthur's battles, ibid. 101.

small when viewed in the context of earthly time: in the epilogue (part VII) Henry looks not only into the distant past, but also into the future, asking to be remembered by those who are to come in the third, fourth and fifth millennia since Christ.

The frailty of humanity is a recurring motif in the *History* and is the main topic of 'On Contempt for the World' (part V). Sudden reversals of fortune, brought about by the judgement of God, strike individuals as well as nations. 'Pride goeth before destruction, and an haughty spirit before a fall' (Prov. 16: 18). In Henry's own lifetime he was particularly moved by the drowning of Henry I's only son in the wreck of the *White Ship*, by the deaths of Ranulf the chancellor, Philip, the son of the French king, Robert Marmion, Geoffrey de Mandeville and his henchmen, and by the arrest and death of the bishop of Salisbury. The most striking example, however, was King Henry I, the 'most powerful of kings', whose life came to an end in the utter humiliation of food-poisoning after he greedily devoured a dish of lampreys.

But Henry of Huntingdon did not see English history solely as a dismal tale of foolishness, sin, and disaster. It was illuminated by the lives of the saints, whose 'saving beams . . . are like the lights of heaven'. He devoted a whole book to 'The Miracles of the English', mostly taken from Bede but containing passages of his own composition about the saints since the time of Bede, including a contemporary, Wulfric of Haselbury, of whom Henry's is the earliest surviving record (part VI).

Sources

As Henry states in the prologue, Bishop Alexander advised him to use, for the period before his own time and observation, Bede's *The Ecclesiastical History of the English People*, which goes down to the year 731. Bede's work had an enormous influence on Henry, and even his title, *Historia Anglorum*, was the abbreviated name normally given in the twelfth century to Bede's work (in full, *Historia Ecclesiastica Gentis Anglorum*).

For the period not covered by Bede, the bishop advised the gathering of data by 'selecting material from other authors and borrowing from chronicles preserved in ancient libraries'. The principal chronicle Henry used down to the year 1133 was a (now lost) version of the Anglo-Saxon Chronicle which was similar to the one kept and continued at Peterborough (the E-version), though from time to time he borrowed additional material from a version akin to that at Abingdon (the C-version) and also had access to a third version which was also used by the chronicler John of Worcester.

Henry's Latin translation of the Anglo-Saxon Chronicle gives a chronological framework to the *History*: he recounts events year by year, like an annalist, even when he is not borrowing from the Anglo-Saxon Chronicle. But unlike an annalist, Henry largely neglects to give dates, instead relying on regnal years, 'the first year of the reign', 'the second year', and so on. Between 1000 and 1154 his text gives only a handful of dates: 1000, 1002, 1003, the first years of the millennium; 1066, the Norman invasion; 1096, the First Crusade; 1100, the beginning of the century; 1120, the wreck of the *White Ship*.

Henry used other written sources, such as a set of brief Norman annals, an abbreviated history of the First Crusade, and saints' lives. But increasingly from the year 1000 he drew on oral tradition and on his own recollections. In an addition to the *ASC* annal for 1010, he describes the massacre at Balsham, Cambridgeshire, and the courage of a single English defender who resisted the Danes from 'the steps of the church tower which still stands there' (II. 6). This was probably a familiar tale in Henry's boyhood. He speaks of the discovery of the body of St Yvo in 1001 as being 'not long before the time that I can remember' (VI. 5). As he was not born until *c*.1088, he must mean that the story was handed down, like that of the massacre of St Brice's Day, 1002, about which he says he had heard very old men talking when he was a boy—presumably the sons or grandsons of eyewitnesses (II. 2).

Many of the stories in the *History* which cannot be traced to a surviving written source contain direct speech. Most of these are found in the section covering the first half of the eleventh century—for example, details of the battle of Ashingdon, the murder of Edmund Ironside, the story of Cnut and the waves, the murder of the ætheling Alfred, stories of Earl Siward, the death of Earl Godwine, and William FitzOsbern's trick on the eve of the Norman invasion. It has been suggested that the stories about Siward may derive from a lost *Siwards Saga* that circulated in the east midlands, and it is likely that some of the other tales were drawn from cycles of English stories or ballads.

As the son of a Norman father, and himself a member of the Norman ruling elite, Henry was fluent in French as well as English and Latin. French vernacular sources, written or oral, seem to lie behind some material in Henry's account of the battle of Hastings: the story of Taillefer, the use of the word 'Standard', and words and allusions in the Conqueror's speech before the battle such as the exploits of Hasting, the name 'Rou' (for Rollo), the expedition to 'Mimande near the Alps', and the death of Ralph the chamberlain. These may well have derived from stories or songs in French that had evolved by the early twelfth century to celebrate the Norman past.

Henry's own knowledge begins to suffuse his narrative in the account of Henry I's reign, providing first-hand information about the king's itinerary and his ministers, to which are added details of events in France and Flanders which were doubtless gleaned from personal informants. The piece entitled 'On Contempt for the World', written in the form of a letter, is entirely drawn from Henry's own experience, and gives character portraits of most of the leading men of Henry I's time. The narrative of Stephen's reign is based totally on Henry's own observation and is particularly well informed on events in the north and east midlands, and at the heart of government, in the royal court. But even a cursory glance at the sections of the *History* that recount the period of Henry's adult career, from his father's death in 1110 to the end in 1154, reveals that they are not 'history' in the sense of objective reporting. They are written in a highly rhetorical style, and are embellished with poetry.

Style

Henry was not a collector of facts for their own sake. The idea of objective study of history would have been quite alien to him and his contemporaries. In his world, history was a literary genre, and the writing of history required imagination and rhetorical skills. He did not seek to be a realistic reporter, but rather to represent selected events in an overarching interpretation and in appropriate style. He was following the ancient dictum that style should match content. Like the best writers among his contemporaries, Henry had developed his literary style from his training in rhetoric.

The invention of speeches was part of basic rhetorical training. Pupils were required, in an exercise known as impersonation, to preserve the character of imaginary persons and situations by choosing appropriate words and style. In the *History*, Henry composed several long exhortatory speeches for war leaders on the point of going into battle: for Julius Caesar, for William the Conqueror before Hastings, and for military leaders in his own day, at the battles of the Standard (1138) and Lincoln (1141). The structure and themes of all the pieces owe much to the Roman historian Sallust. There are recurring elements—appeals to virtue and courage, expositions of the just cause, exclamations that there is no hope in flight, rehearsal of past victories, demands for revenge for injuries. Henry also used the invented speech as a lively method of conveying information: messengers announce dramatic news in direct speech; even a rather lengthy genealogy of the Frankish kings is written in the form of an oration.

Colourful description, especially of set-piece battle-scenes, is another feature of rhetorical writing. Such scenes, often in heightened prose, with alliteration, rhyme, rhythm, metaphor, onomatopoeia, and other rhetorical devices, are found throughout the *History*. Much of the warfare in Henry's own time was civil war. In approaching this subject, Henry had a classical model in Lucan's poem on the war between Caesar and Pompey. Lucan's example explains Henry's exaggerated language emphasizing violence, danger, and calamity in the period of his lifetime, and especially in Stephen's reign. The prose passages, with their vivid images of warfare, their rhythms and cadences, approach poetry.

Poetry was one of the arts of rhetoric. As a young man, Henry had written several books of poetry—epigrams, love poems, and a collection on herbs. His ability as a poet was doubtless known to Bishop Alexander when he commissioned the *History*. Henry continued to write poetry throughout his life. Although only two out of at least twenty-four books of his collected poems survive, this is enough to show that he was a poet of considerable stature.[16] He also intermingled poems with prose in the *History*, more frequently in the narrative books dealing with the period of his adult life (parts III and IV), where the verse amounts in all to 132 lines. Under Henry I's reign there are eight poems, ranging from two to eleven lines each: four epitaphs (on Henry's father, Queen Matilda, Bishop

---

[16] Ibid., pp. cvii–cxv, 805–25.

Robert Bloet, and Henry I), a lament (on the *White Ship*), and three panegyrics (on the battle of Brémule, Queen Adela, and Bishop Alexander). The civil war of the 1130s and 1140s produced three longer poems: a lament of eighteen lines on the evils of civil war, and two poems about Duke Henry. In these last two, Henry uses a rhetorical device favoured by Lucan—personification: in both poems England is revived, brought back to life, by the duke, as in Lucan the Roman *patria* is revived by Pompey. In the first poem, of thirty-one lines, England addresses a tearful appeal to the duke; the second, of twenty lines, which forms the closing passage of the *History*, is a panegyric about the duke's revival of a near-dead England.

The study of rhetoric, which taught oratory, colourful writing, and poetry, also included the arts of letter-writing and preaching, in which Henry was an accomplished practitioner. The fictitious letter was a useful form for exploring themes that it was not intended to make the subject of detailed treatment—rather as today we might write an essay or article. Three such letters were collected in a book (entitled 'On Exalted Matters') that Henry added to the *History* *c*.1140: one addressed to King Henry I, on the subject of rulers of the world since Noah;[17] a second to Warin the Breton, summarizing Geoffrey of Monmouth's *History of the Kings of Britain*;[18] and a third to Walter the archdeacon, 'On Contempt for the World' (below, part V).

Henry certainly also wrote sermons, copies of which survived into the sixteenth century but are now lost. In one sense, however, the *History* is itself a sermon. Henry's aim in writing, as he says in the prologue, was to persuade 'the attentive reader [of] what to imitate and what to reject, and by God's help to become a better person . . . Truly, it is quite common for the path of history to lead us straight back to moral purity'. This programme is not far removed from that of the preacher: according to a long tradition from the time of Gregory the Great, historical examples of vices and virtues were resources to be deployed in the rhetoric of the sermon. Throughout the *History* historical persons and their doings are used as moral examples, sometimes subtly, sometimes rather crudely. In preaching, as one of Henry's contemporaries wrote, 'We tell simple stories and introduce past history into the sermon, and embellish our words like

---

[17] Ibid. 502–57.   [18] Ibid. 558–83.

a painter using many different colours in a picture'.[19] If the colours of Henry's style are sometimes too garish for present-day taste, and the moralizations too obvious, his cautionary words are still not out of place: 'Let no one trust in the continuance of happiness, nor take fortune's constancy for granted, nor strive to remain for long in a set place on the revolving wheel' (IV. 11).

Context

The writers who were at work in the field of English history at the same time as Henry of Huntingdon present a broad spectrum.

In the 1130s, Bishop Alexander of Lincoln, in the same way that he had earlier asked Henry to translate the Anglo-Saxon Chronicle from English into Latin, asked Geoffrey of Monmouth to translate the prophecies of Merlin into Latin from Welsh. Geoffrey incorporated his translation in his legendary and entertaining *History of the Kings of Britain*, a largely fictitious account of the period down to the death of Cædwalla in the late seventh century, that was to inspire subsequent Arthurian literature.[20] To the bishop, and to the great majority of Geoffrey's readers, his book was complementary to Henry's: indeed, this was Geoffrey's claim.[21] When Henry read the *History of the Kings of Britain*, to his 'amazement', in Normandy in 1139,[22] he was so impressed that he wrote a summary to append to his *History*, the 'Letter to Warin'. Evidently he found it reliable and in harmony with his own beliefs on the early history of Britain. On the whole, Geoffrey's work was received seriously, with only a few doubters (notably William of Newburgh) questioning its accuracy.

One of those who readily adopted Geoffrey's material was Geffrei Gaimar, who in the late 1130s wrote the first known romance history in French verse, *L'Estoire des Engleis*, in which he spoke of Geoffrey of Monmouth with approval.[23] Although his title might seem to suggest that he knew of Henry's *History of the English People*, and

[19] Guibert of Nogent; see translation in *Readings in Medieval Rhetoric*, ed. J. M. Miller, M. H. Prosser, and T. W. Benson (Bloomington and London, 1973), 170.

[20] *Geoffrey of Monmouth: The History of the Kings of Britain*, trans. L. Thorpe (Harmondsworth, 1966), 170–1.

[21] Ibid. 284 n.

[22] HH, pp. ci–cii, 559.

[23] *L'Estoire des Engleis by Geffrei Gaimar*, ed. Alexander Bell (Oxford, 1960) (French only; a translation of an inferior edition, with slightly different verse-numbering, is found in *Lestoire des engles solum la translacion Maistre Geffrei Gaimar*, ed. and trans. T. D. Hardy and C. T. Martin (2 vols. (Rolls Series, 1888–9), vol. ii).

some stories are found in both, yet there are no traces of direct borrowing from Henry's work. The *Estoire* gives a French verse translation of the Anglo-Saxon Chronicle, to which are added numerous legends, and the whole is taken down to the death of King William Rufus in 1100.

Others at this time were engaged on projects closer in style to Henry's, bringing history down to their own day. They wrote chiefly to inform, though they also introduced rhetorical passages, poetry, and fables. Two of the most renowned, Orderic Vitalis and William of Malmesbury, were, like Henry, the sons of Norman fathers and English mothers, while a third, John of Worcester, was probably wholly English.[24] Orderic wrote in Normandy, William and John in England. As all three were monks, their opportunities to gather contemporary news were more limited than Henry's, and their narratives are more locally focused, lacking the kind of information that Henry was able to collect from the centre of government. By an odd coincidence, all three finished writing at roughly the same time: Orderic's *Ecclesiastical History* ends in the summer of 1141; John's *Chronicle* ends in mid-1140 and its continuation by an anonymous compiler breaks off in the autumn of 1141; and William wrote the last chapter of his *Contemporary History* early in 1143.

In the early 1140s another writer, perhaps a clerk in the circle of Bishop Robert of Bath (possibly even the bishop himself), took up his pen to chronicle *The Deeds of Stephen, King of England and Duke of Normandy* (*Gesta Stephani*).[25] His account is much more detailed than Henry's, especially for events in the Thames valley and southwest of England, but the manuscript has suffered the loss of some passages in the years 1137–40. In its use of rhetoric, the author's literary style is not dissimilar to Henry's, though it is considerably more artificial, with a vocabulary of affected classicisms.

The earliest historian to use Henry's *History* was also writing towards the end of Henry's life. This was the Norman, Robert of

---

[24] For Orderic, see *The Ecclesiastical History of Orderic Vitalis*, ed. and trans. M. M. Chibnall, 6 vols. (Oxford Medieval Texts, 1969–80), esp. i. 29–39; also M. M. Chibnall, *The World of Orderic Vitalis* (Oxford, 1984). For William of Malmesbury, see Rodney Thomson, *William of Malmesbury* (Woodbridge, 1987), 1–10. For John of Worcester, see *The Chronicle of John of Worcester*, ii, *The Annals from 450 to 1066*, ed. and trans. R. R. Darlington and P. McGurk (Oxford Medieval Texts, 1995), pp. lxvii–lxxiii.

[25] *Gesta Stephani*, ed. and trans. K. R. Potter and R. H. C. Davis (Oxford Medieval Texts, 1976).

Torigni, monk of Bec (and from *c.*1154 abbot of Mont Saint-Michel). He it was who had shown Geoffrey of Monmouth's book to Henry in 1139. When he began to write his own chronicle *c.*1150 he incorporated into it much of the text of Henry's *History* down to 1146, from the copy which Bishop Alexander had presented to the abbey in 1147. He added material from Norman sources and from his own knowledge, and from 1147 his chronicle is an important independent source.[26]

The History *after Henry*

The *History* became a popular work in Henry's own time, as we know from the way in which copies began to circulate as early as *c.*1133. It was known to Geoffrey of Monmouth in the 1130s and to Robert of Torigni in the 1140s. Manuscript copies, copies of copies, and copies of descendants of copies continued to be made during the next 500 years, some even after the first printing by Sir Henry Savile in 1596. There survive at least forty-five manuscripts of the complete text, and an uncounted number of fragments, attesting to innumerable copies that are now lost.

But the work reached a far wider audience than this would suggest. Henry's *History* was swallowed into the works of many later medieval historians. As we have seen, when Robert of Torigni began to write his own history *c.*1150, he copied much of Henry's text verbatim. The same technique was employed by others. In the twelfth century the *History* from 1122 to 1148 was taken over by the author of the *History after Bede*, from which source Roger of Howden took large sections into his chronicle, as also did Walter of Guisborough in the late thirteenth century. An anonymous twelfth-century compiler at Crowland incorporated the complete text of the *History* from 1131 to 1154, and his work was reused in the thirteenth-century chronicle attributed to 'Walter of Coventry'. Among other writers who reproduced sections of the *History* in the twelfth century were William of Newburgh, Gervase of Canterbury, and Ralph de Diceto (dean of St Paul's, London): the last-named used Henry's work not directly but via Robert of Torigni's chronicle. At St Albans in the thirteenth century the *History* down to 1146 was used by Roger of Wendover, both directly and through the medium

---

[26] *Chronicles of the Reigns of Stephen, Henry II and Richard I*, ed. R. Howlett, 4 vols. (Rolls Series, 1884–9), vol. iv (Latin only).

of Robert of Torigni, and Roger's work was reused by his successor at St Albans, Matthew Paris. In the later thirteenth century Henry's text for the period 688–1066 was taken over by Bartholomew Cotton at Norwich. In the early fourteenth century Ranulf Higden, a monk of Chester, copied large extracts of the *History* into his *Polychronicon*, which became the third most popular medieval history (surpassed only by Bede and Geoffrey of Monmouth).

Other medieval historians who used the *History*, but were more selective in their borrowings, include: Ailred of Rievaulx, Alfred of Beverley, the annalist of Waverley, Gerald of Wales, and Henry Knighton of Leicester. Others again, such as the continuators of Matthew Paris's *Chronica* or of Ranulf Higden's *Polychronicon*, necessarily copied the borrowings of Henry's *History* that were contained in their basic texts.

The prevalent habit among medieval chroniclers of appropriating lengthy portions of earlier histories, with or without acknowledgement, made elements of Henry's text widely known, so that they became ingredients of the great mass of diversely sourced material that continued to be transmitted in various forms as 'the history of England' at least until the creation of modern critical historiography in the later years of the nineteenth century.

Notions and stories that originated in the *History of the English People* have survived into our own time. Henry I's death by 'a surfeit of lampreys', a story that began in the pages of the *History*, passed into English cultural tradition. The even more famous legend of Cnut and the waves was borrowed and adapted by successive generations. In Henry's original, Cnut's action was an example of humility, but in the course of transmission it has become instead a classic illustration of arrogance, stupidity, and resistance to change.

To historians and literary scholars today, the value of the *History* is not diminished by our recognition of the rhetorical arts that went into its composition. Henry of Huntingdon's poetry belongs in the mainstream of medieval Latin verse, and as a piece of literature his *History* bears comparison with some of the greatest in the genre. His mastery of Latin shows the effect of the renaissance of scholarship that came to England from France after the Norman Conquest. He gives us a twelfth-century view of the English past, in which local stories which had been passed on orally are preserved alongside evidence from written sources and his own first-hand recollections, skilfully combined to form a compelling narrative with a moral theme.

Medieval authors were taught to conceal their individuality and to write from an elevated, detached point of view. Despite his adoption of this conventional modesty, Henry's shrewd judgement of people gives his writing individuality and immediacy. Some of his thumbnail character-sketches are memorable—one earl is 'a manifest adulterer and distinguished lecher, a faithful follower of Bacchus, though unacquainted with Mars, smelling of wine, unaccustomed to warfare', and there is another 'whose action is only talk, whose gift is mere promise: he talks as if he has acted and promises as if he has given' (IV. 15). His psychological insight is most profound when he considers the private terrors that lay behind King Henry I's majestic appearance (V. 12).

As a narrator of contemporary events Henry is particularly strong on the royal court and courtiers. His views probably represent those of his patron, Bishop Alexander of Lincoln, and thus reflect those of Alexander's uncle, Bishop Roger of Salisbury, who was Henry I's first minister. When Henry describes the king's cruel treatment of his brother, Robert Curthose (V. 12), and speaks of Curthose's son, William Clito, as 'the king's sole heir' (V. 5), we seem to hear the bishops' endorsement of Clito's claim to the throne and their regret at the king's refusal to acknowledge this claim. In the same way, it is probably the bishops' known enmity towards the Beaumont family—Robert of Meulan and his sons Waleran and Robert—that is given expression in Henry's descriptions of the elder Robert's death in 1118 (III. 30, V. 7–8) and of the sons' activities in Stephen's reign (IV. 15, 30–1).

Although the *History* has a carefully crafted unity, it is not without contradictions. Henry admires strong war-leaders, but detests arrogance. He is impressed by the spectacle and ceremony of the court, but disapproves of ostentation. He writes a laudatory and sorrowful elegy on the death of Henry I, but adds a bitterly critical obituary. He delights in battle-scenes and does not flinch from describing the sights and sounds of hand-to-hand fighting, glorying in the clash of weapons, the screams of the wounded and the dying, the blood, the dismembered bodies. But he writes movingly of the pity of war and the suffering of the innocent, applying his sympathetic imagination to conflicts in the past as well as to the civil wars of his own time. Do these contradictions betray something of the author's complex mentality? Or is all the passion in his writing, both the tough and the tender, contrived merely for rhetorical effect? Whichever view we take, most will agree that Henry's *History* is never dull.

NOTE ON THE TEXT AND TRANSLATION

The text printed below consists of all the translated material covering the period between 1000 and 1154 in the first complete edition of the work, *Henry, Archdeacon of Huntingdon: Historia Anglorum: The History of the English People*, ed. and trans. Diana Greenway (Oxford Medieval Texts, 1996) (abbreviated as HH).

The selection is as follows:

The translation is taken from HH, but has been revised as necessary. The numbering of the chapters follows HH, where it was adopted from the Latin edition by Thomas Arnold, *Henrici Archidiaconi Huntendunensis Historia Anglorum* (Rolls Series lxxiv: London, 1879).

Square brackets indicate editorial additions, for example, dates, which were largely omitted by Henry of Huntingdon, and some names of persons and places.

Biblical references to book, chapter, and verse are to the *Revised English Bible*. The variations between the wording of the translations of the biblical quotations below and the text of the *REB* are due to the fact that Henry of Huntingdon used the medieval Latin Vulgate, whereas the *REB* is based on the best Hebrew and Greek texts.

SELECT BIBLIOGRAPHY

General Works

Bartlett, Robert, *England under the Norman and Angevin Kings 1075–1225* (Oxford, 2000).
Chibnall, Marjorie, *The Debate on the Norman Conquest* (Manchester and New York, 1999).
—— *Anglo-Norman England 1066–1166* (Oxford, 1986).
Davis, R. H. C., *The Normans and their Myth* (London, 1976).
Williams, Ann, *The English and the Norman Conquest* (Woodbridge, 1995).

The Church

Barlow, Frank, *The English Church 1000–1066* (2nd edn.: London and New York, 1979).
—— *The English Church 1066–1154* (London and New York, 1979).

England and Normandy before 1087 (for part II of the History)

Barlow, Frank, *Edward the Confessor* (London, 1970; repr. 1979).
Bates, David, *Normandy before 1066* (London and New York, 1982).
—— *William the Conqueror* (London, 1989).
John, Eric, 'The Return of the Vikings' and 'The End of Anglo-Saxon England', in James Campbell (ed.), *The Anglo-Saxons* (Harmondsworth, 1982), chs. 8 and 9.
Lawson, M. K., *Cnut: The Danes in England in the Early Eleventh Century* (London and New York, 1993).
Morillo, Stephen, *The Battle of Hastings: Sources and Interpretations* (Woodbridge, 1996).

England 1087–1135 (for parts III and V of the History)

Barlow, Frank, *William Rufus* (London, 1983; repr. 1990).
Green, Judith A., *The Government of England under Henry I* (Cambridge, 1986).
Hollister, C .W., *Henry I*, ed. A. C. Frost (New Haven and London, 2001).
Phillips, Jonathan (ed.), *The First Crusade: Origins and Impact* (Manchester, 1997).
Southern, R. W., 'The Place of Henry I in English History', in his *Medieval Humanism and Other Studies* (Oxford, 1970), 206–33.

England 1135–1154 (for part IV of the History)

Chibnall, Marjorie, *The Empress Matilda* (Oxford, 1991).

Davis, R. H. C., *King Stephen 1135–1154* (3rd edn.: London and New York, 1990).

Stringer, K. J., *The Reign of Stephen: Kingship, Warfare and Government in Twelfth-Century England* (London and New York, 1993).

Reference Works

Farmer, D. H., *Oxford Dictionary of Saints* (3rd edn.: Oxford, 1992).

Fletcher, R., *Who's Who in Roman Britain and Anglo-Saxon England* (London, 1989).

Hill, David, *An Atlas of Anglo-Saxon England* (Oxford, 1981).

Lapidge, M., Blair, J., Keynes, S., and Scragg, D. (eds.), *The Blackwell Encyclopaedia of Anglo-Saxon England* (Oxford and Malden, Mass., 1999).

Szarmach, P., Tavormina, M. T., and Rosenthal, J. (eds.), *Medieval England: An Encyclopedia* (New York and London, 1998).

Tyerman, C., *Who's Who in Early Medieval England (1066–1272)* (London, 1996).

Sources in Translation

The Anglo-Saxon Chronicle, ed. and trans. D. Whitelock, D. C. Douglas, and S. I. Tucker (London, 1961).

The Chronicle of John of Worcester. Vol. ii, *The Annals from 450 to 1066*, ed. and trans. R. R. Darlington and P. McGurk (Oxford Medieval Texts, 1995). Vol. iii, *The Annals from 1067 to 1140*, ed. and trans. P. McGurk (Oxford Medieval Texts, 1998).

The Ecclesiastical History of Orderic Vitalis, ed. and trans. M. M. Chibnall, 6 vols. (Oxford Medieval Texts, 1969–80).

English Historical Documents 1042–1189, ed. D. C. Douglas and G. W. Greenaway (2nd edn.: London and New York, 1981).

Gesta Stephani, ed. and trans. K. R. Potter and R. H. C. Davis (Oxford Medieval Texts, 1976).

Henry, Archdeacon of Huntingdon, *Historia Anglorum: The History of the English People*, ed. and trans. D. Greenway (Oxford Medieval Texts, 1996).

Lestorie des engles solum la translacion Maistre Geffrei Gaimar, ed. and trans. T. D. Hardy and C. T. Martin (Rolls Series xci, 1888–9), vol. I text, vol. II translation.

William of Malmesbury, *Gesta Regum Anglorum: The History of the English Kings*, i, ed. and trans. R. A. B. Mynors, R. M. Thomson, and M. Winterbottom (Oxford Medieval Texts, 1998).

William of Malmesbury, *Historia Novella: The Contemporary History*, ed. and trans. Edmund King and K. R. Potter (Oxford Medieval Texts, 1998).

Further Reading in Oxford World's Classics

The Anglo-Saxon World, trans. and ed. Kevin Crossley-Holland.

Anselm of Canterbury, *The Major Works*, trans. and ed. Gillian Evans and Brian Davies.

Bede, *The Ecclesiastical History*, trans. Bertram Colgrave, ed. Judith McClure and Roger Collins.

Jocelin of Brakelond, *Chronicle of the Abbey of Bury St Edmunds*, trans. Diana Greenway and Jane Sayers.

A CHRONOLOGY OF HENRY OF HUNTINGDON'S *HISTORY* 1000–1154

1000   King Æthelred II is betrothed to Emma, sister of the duke of Normandy (below, II. 1).

1002   Emma comes to England and marries Æthelred, who orders a massacre of Danes on St Brice's day (II. 2).

1003–13 Incursions by Danes (II. 2–9).

1013   Danish king Swein Forkbeard becomes king of most of England (II. 9).

1014   Swein dies and is succeeded by his son Cnut (II. 10).

1016   Æthelred dies and is succeeded by Edmund Ironside, his son by his first wife, Ælfgifu (II. 11–12). Series of battles between the English under Edmund and the Danes under Cnut (II. 13). Edmund is murdered (II. 14).

1017   King Cnut marries Æthelred's widow, Emma (II. 15).

1035   Cnut dies, and is succeeded by Harold I, his son by his first wife, Ælfgifu of Northampton (II. 17–18).

1040   King Harold dies, and is succeeded by Harthacnut, son of Cnut and Emma (II. 19).

1042   King Harthacnut dies, and is succeeded by Edward (later called the Confessor), son of Æthelred and Emma (II. 20).

1066   King Edward dies childless, and is succeeded by his brother-in-law Harold, against the claim of William, duke of Normandy, grandson of Emma's brother (II. 27). Norman invasion; King Harold II killed at the battle of Hastings; William becomes king (II. 27–30).

1087   King William I, the Conqueror, dies, and is succeeded as duke of Normandy by his eldest son, Robert Curthose, and as king of England by his second son, William Rufus (II. 40).

*c.*1088 Henry of Huntingdon is born, the son of an English mother and a Norman father called Nicholas, who had been appointed archdeacon of Huntingdon by Bishop Remigius of Lincoln (Introduction, p. xiv).

1092   Bishop Remigius dies (III. 2).

1094   Robert Bloet becomes bishop of Lincoln (III. 3).

1096–99 First Crusade, in which Robert Curthose takes a leading part (III. 5–18).

c.1100 or earlier   Henry goes to Lincoln; he lives in the household of Bishop Robert Bloet and is taught at Lincoln by Albinus of Angers (Introduction, p. xv).

1100   King William II, Rufus, dies, and is succeeded by his younger brother, Henry (III. 22).

1106   Robert Curthose is defeated and captured at the battle of Tinchebrai and imprisoned by King Henry I for life. Henry I takes over the duchy of Normandy (III. 25).

1110   Nicholas, archdeacon of Huntingdon, dies, and is succeeded by his son Henry (III. 27).

1119   Henry I defeats the French at the battle of Brémule (III. 31).

1120   Henry I's only legitimate son is drowned in the *White Ship*, leaving as his sole heir his daughter, Matilda, wife of Emperor Henry V (III. 32).

1123   Bishop Robert Bloet dies (III. 34). Alexander 'the Magnificent' becomes bishop of Lincoln (III. 35); between this date and 1130 Alexander asks Henry to write the *History* (I. 4–5).

1127   Henry I requires the barons to swear to uphold the widowed Empress Matilda's succession to the throne of England and the duchy of Normandy.

1128   Matilda marries Geoffrey, count of Anjou (III. 37). William Clito, son of Robert Curthose, is killed in battle in Flanders (III. 39).

1130   Henry composes and dates the epilogue (VII).

c.1133   Henry allows copies to be made of the *History* as completed down to 1129 (III. 40).

1135   King Henry I dies, and the throne is taken by his nephew Stephen of Blois, count of Mortain (III. 43–4, IV. 1). Henry revises the epilogue of the *History* and writes a first draft of 'On Contempt for the World' (V).

1138   Rebellions against King Stephen, and invasion by Scots, who are defeated at the battle of the Standard (IV. 7–9).

1139   Stephen arrests the bishops of Salisbury and Lincoln (IV. 10–11). Matilda arrives in England with her father's illegitimate son Robert, earl of Gloucester, in pursuit of her claim.

1139–47 Sporadic warfare in England.

c.1140   Henry completes a continuation of the *History* down to 1138 (IV. 9); this version also contains 'On Contempt for the World' (V) and 'The Miracles of the English' (VI).

1141   King Stephen is captured at the battle of Lincoln (IV. 13–19) and is exchanged later in the year for Earl Robert of Gloucester, captured at Winchester (IV. 19).

1144   Stephen loses control of Normandy to Geoffrey, count of Anjou.

c.1146   Henry makes final revisions to 'On Contempt for the World' (V).

c.1147   Henry completes a continuation of the *History* down to 1146 (IV. 25).

1148   Bishop Alexander dies, and is succeeded by Robert de Chesney, archdeacon of Leicester (IV. 25–6, 28).

c.1149   Henry completes a continuation of the *History* down to 1149, perhaps for presentation to the new bishop (IV. 28).

1151   Count Geoffrey of Anjou dies, and is succeeded by his and Matilda's son, Henry (IV. 31).

1153   Campaign in England by Henry of Anjou; Stephen's son Eustace dies; treaty of Westminster, arranging for Henry of Anjou's succession on Stephen's death (IV. 33–7). Henry tones down his critical obituary of King Henry I (IV. 1).

1154   King Stephen dies, and is succeeded by Henry of Anjou as King Henry II, whose coronation is the last event in Henry's final continuation of the *History* (IV. 39–40).

c.1155   A copy made of the last version of the *History*.

1156 or a little later   Henry's last appearance in documents (Introduction, p. xviii).

1164 or early 1165   Henry has been succeeded as archdeacon of Huntingdon by Nicholas de Sigillo (Introduction, p. xviii).

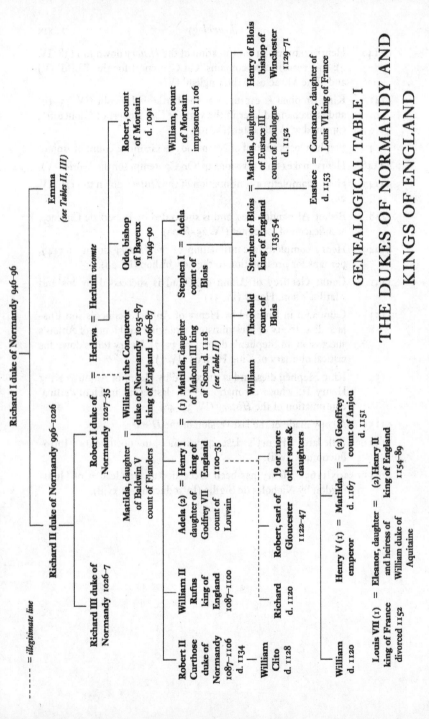

GENEALOGICAL TABLE I

THE DUKES OF NORMANDY AND KINGS OF ENGLAND

- - - - - = *illegitimate line*

Richard I duke of Normandy 946–96

Richard II duke of Normandy 996–1026

Emma (*see Table II, III*)

Robert I duke of Normandy 1027–35

William I the Conqueror duke of Normandy 1035–87 king of England 1066–87 = Herleva = Herluin *vicomte*

Odo, bishop of Bayeux 1049–90

Robert, count of Mortain d. 1091

William, count of Mortain imprisoned 1106

Richard III duke of Normandy 1026–7

Matilda, daughter of Baldwin count of Flanders =

(1) Matilda, daughter of Malcolm III king of Scots, d. 1118 (*see Table II*)

Adela = Stephen I count of Blois

Theobald count of Blois

Stephen of Blois king of England 1135–54 = Matilda, daughter of Eustace III count of Boulogne d. 1152

Henry of Blois bishop of Winchester 1129–71

Robert II Curthose duke of Normandy 1087–1106 d. 1134

William II Rufus king of England 1087–1100

Adela (2) daughter of Godfrey VII count of Louvain = Henry I king of England 1100–35

William

Eustace d. 1153 = Constance, daughter of Louis VI king of France

William Clito d. 1128

Richard d. 1120

Robert, earl of Gloucester 1122–47

19 or more other sons & daughters

Matilda d. 1167 = (2) Geoffrey count of Anjou d. 1151

William d. 1120

Henry V (1) emperor = Matilda = (2) Henry II king of England 1154–89

Louis VII (1) king of France divorced 1152 = Eleanor, daughter and heiress of William duke of Aquitaine

GENEALOGICAL TABLE II

THE KINGS OF ENGLAND AND THE KINGS OF SCOTS

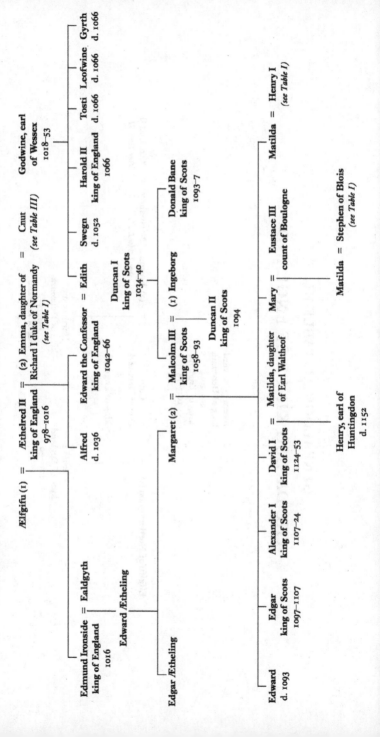

GENEALOGICAL TABLE III

THE DANISH KINGS OF ENGLAND

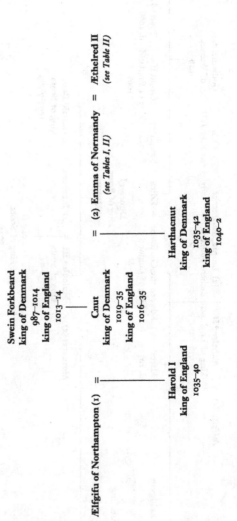

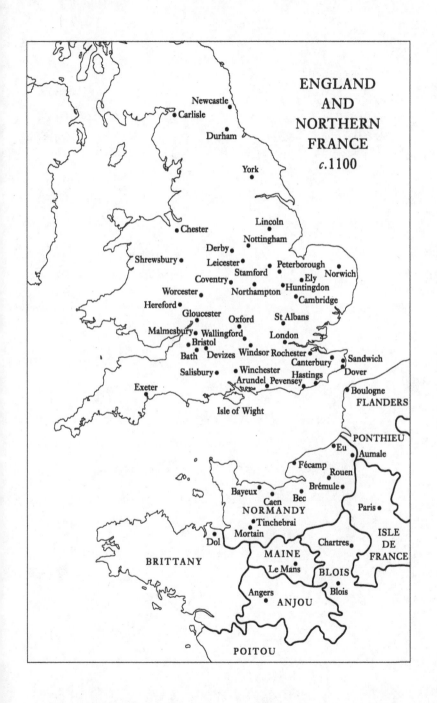

ENGLAND
AND
NORTHERN
FRANCE
c.1100

Newcastle
Carlisle
Durham
York
Lincoln
Chester
Nottingham
Derby
Shrewsbury
Leicester
Peterborough
Norwich
Stamford
Coventry
Ely
Worcester
Northampton
Huntingdon
Hereford
Cambridge
Gloucester
Oxford
St Albans
Malmesbury
Wallingford
London
Bristol
Bath
Devizes
Windsor
Rochester
Sandwich
Canterbury
Salisbury
Winchester
Dover
Arundel
Hastings
Exeter
Pevensey
Boulogne
FLANDERS
Isle of Wight
PONTHIEU
Eu
Aumale
Fécamp
Rouen
Brémule
Bayeux
Bec
Caen
Paris
NORMANDY
Tinchebrai
Dol
Mortain
ISLE
Chartres
DE
FRANCE
MAINE
BRITTANY
Le Mans
BLOIS
Angers
Blois
ANJOU
POITOU

THE HISTORY
OF THE
ENGLISH PEOPLE
1000–1154

PROLOGUE

1. It is my considered opinion that the sweetest relief from suffering and the best comfort in affliction that this world affords are to be found almost entirely in the study of literature,* and so I believe that the splendour of historical writing is to be cherished with the greatest delight and given the pre-eminent and most glorious position. For nothing is more excellent in this life than to investigate and become familiar with the course of worldly events. Where does the grandeur of valiant men shine more brightly, or the wisdom of the prudent, or the discretion of the righteous, or the moderation of the temperate, than in the context of history? Indeed, we have heard what Horace said, in praise of Homeric history, that it 'defines what is noble and what is infamous, what is proper and what is not, more fully and better than Chrysippus and Crantor'. Whereas Crantor and Chrysippus sweated to produce many volumes of moral philosophy, Homer showed, as clearly as in a mirror, the prudence of Ulysses, the fortitude of Agamemnon, the temperance of Nestor, and the justice of Menelaus, and on the other hand, the imprudence of Ajax, the feebleness of Priam, the intemperateness of Achilles, and the injustice of Paris, and in his narrative he discussed what is right and proper more clearly and agreeably than the philosophers.

2. But why do we linger among strangers? See how sacred history* teaches the moral code, giving the attributes of justice to Abraham, fortitude to Moses, temperance to Jacob, and prudence to Joseph, and showing their opposites—injustice in Ahab, feebleness in Oziah, intemperateness in Manasseh, and imprudence in Roboam. Especially, O good God, what a shining example of humility, that holy Moses, having joined with his brother in offering sweet-smelling incense to God, his protector and avenger against all his enemies, flung himself into the midst of terrible danger, and shed tears for the slanderous Miriam, and always laboured in prayer for those who wished him ill! What a beacon of clemency that David, wounded and enraged by Shimei, would not have him slaughtered when he was alone, hard-pressed and weak, and he, David, was strongly armed

and attended by his retinue; and later, when he was restored victorious to his throne, he would not permit vengeance to be taken on Shimei.

3. Yes, indeed, in the recorded deeds of all peoples and nations, which are the very judgements of God, clemency, generosity, honesty, caution, and the like, and their opposites, not only provoke men of the spirit to what is good and deter them from evil, but even encourage worldly men to good deeds and reduce their wickedness. History therefore brings the past into view as though it were present, and allows judgement of the future by representing the past. The knowledge of past events has further virtues, especially in that it distinguishes rational creatures from brutes, for brutes, whether men or beasts, do not know—nor, indeed, do they wish to know—about their origins, their race, and the events and happenings in their native land. Of the two, I consider brutish men to be the more wretched, because what is natural to beasts comes to brutish men from their own mindlessness, and what beasts would not be capable of, even if they wished to be, such men, even if capable, would not desire. But now we must pass over those whose life and death are to be consigned to perpetual silence.*

4. With these considerations in mind, therefore, and at your command, Bishop Alexander,* I have undertaken to narrate the history of this kingdom and the origins of our people, of which you are regarded as the highest and most splendid ornament. On your advice I have followed the Venerable Bede's *Ecclesiastical History* where I could, selecting material also from other authors and borrowing from chronicles preserved in ancient libraries,* and I have described past events down to the time of our own knowledge and observation. In this work the attentive reader will find what to imitate and what to reject, and if, by God's help, he becomes a better person for this emulation and avoidance, that will be for me the reward I most desire. Truly, it is quite common for the path of history to lead us straight back to moral purity.

5. But as we can begin nothing without making an appeal to God, let us commence by calling on Him:*

O Adonai, our creator, shepherd, and defender, source, quickener, and end of all things, we pray Thee to favour this work and guide it to its close: this work which Thou, our Father, hast Thyself brought about among our fathers, raising up and putting down peoples and kingdoms by Thy

judgement, that operates sometimes secretly and sometimes openly, delaying the punishment of some until they finish their crimes, while hurling
punishment at others when their crimes are complete. For whatever kings
or peoples plan to do, if it is accomplished, it is by Thy action, Who
makest peace and createst evil, as the prophet attests,* a unique entity,
remaining as great as Thou hast desired, from Whom and by Whom and
in Whom Alone, all things exist.

And we pray you, Bishop Alexander, father of the fatherland, prince
second to the king, that anything we have written well may be brightened
by your praise, and that you will improve what is less good. Here you see
kings and peoples whom the lottery of fate has raised up and put down,
but judge the future by them. See, great father, what has become of the
powerful: see how the honour, the pleasure, the glory of the world come to
nothing.

1000–1087: THE COMING OF THE NORMANS

1. In the thousandth year after the Lord's incarnation, King
Æthelred planned, for the protection of his kingdom, to take as his
wife the daughter of Richard,* count of the Normans. Now this man
was extremely powerful and was feared throughout the French kingdom, whereas Æthelred recognized his own and his people's weakness, and was greatly fearful of future disaster. It is clear that this
happened at God's command, so that evil would befall the ungodly.
For the Lord Almighty had planned a double affliction for the
English people, which He had decided to exterminate for their compelling crimes, just as the Britons had been humbled when their sins
accused them. This He brought about as if laying a military ambush.
I mean that on one side the persecution by the Danes was raging,
and on the other the connection with the Normans was growing, so
that even if they were to escape the obvious lightning fire of the
Danes, valour would not help them to escape the insidious danger
from the Normans. This became apparent in subsequent events,
since from this union of the English king with the daughter of the
Norman duke, the Normans were justified according to the law of
peoples,* in both claiming and gaining possession of England.

A certain man of God, too, proclaimed to them that because of the
enormity of their crimes—for they were not only at all times bent on
slaughter and treachery, but also continually given over to drunkenness and the neglect of the Lord's house—an unforeseen lordship
would come upon them from France. This would for ever suppress
their pre-eminence and would scatter their honour to the winds,
never to be recovered. He also predicted that not only that people,
but also the Scots, whom they considered to be most vile, would lord
it over them to their well-merited confusion.* In addition, he predicted that a generation must be born so fickle that the changeableness which was hidden in the minds of men and was revealed in their
deeds, would be represented in the manifold diversity of their
apparel and garments.*

And so, fulfilling this prophecy, the English king sent emissaries to the duke of the Normans, and obtaining the grant of his request, at the appointed time English nobles worthy of this great office were sent to Normandy to receive and conduct their lady, whom they brought to England in great pomp, appropriate to royalty.

2. In the year 1002, Emma, the jewel of the Normans, came to England, and received the crown and title of queen. With her arrival, King Æthelred's pride increased and his faithlessness grew: in a treacherous plot, he ordered all the Danes who were living peacefully in England to be put to death on the same day, namely the feast of St Brice [13 November]. Concerning this crime, in my childhood I heard very old men* say that the king had sent secret letters to every city, according to which the English either maimed all the unsuspecting Danes on the same day and hour with their swords, or, suddenly, at the same moment, captured them and destroyed them by fire. In the same year the king exiled Ealdorman Leofsige because he had killed Æfic the king's sheriff.

In the year 1003, the Danes were inflamed with justifiable anger, like a fire which someone had tried to extinguish with fat. So flying down like a swarm of locusts, some of them came to Exeter, and utterly destroyed the whole city, and took off with them all its spoils, leaving only ashes. They were allied in destruction with Hugh the Norman, whom Queen Emma had appointed sheriff. The people of Hampshire and Wiltshire gathered together to fight the army. When they were on the point of engaging in battle, their ealdorman, Ælfric, feigned illness, and forced himself to vomit, and thus betrayed the English people under his command. And since it is true that, as is commonly said, 'When the leader fails, the army becomes worthless', the Danes, seeing the failure of the enemy, pursued them as far as Wilton, which they pillaged and burnt before coming to Salisbury, and then triumphantly returned to their ships with their booty.

3. In the fourth year [1004], Swein [Forkbeard], a very powerful man, for whom God had destined the kingdom of England, came with many ships to Norwich, and plundered and burnt it. When Ulfcetel, the ealdorman of that shire, saw this, he made peace with the army as he was unable to put up a resistance against their unforeseen arrival. But three weeks later, during the truce, the army secretly advanced to Thetford and plundered and burnt it. When Ealdorman Ulfcetel learned of this, he took a small force and ambushed the army at dawn as it returned to the ships. But although

he withstood fiercely and for a long time, he was not strong enough to prevail.

In the fifth year [1005], the Danes returned to their own country. But because England could not be free of plagues meanwhile, a greater desolation of famine invaded Britain than anyone could remember.

In the sixth year [1006], Swein, a very audacious man, returned to Sandwich with a large fleet: with him were always associated his three companions—plunder, burning, and killing—and all England lamented and shook like a reed-bed struck by the quivering west wind.* The king gathered his army and fought against them throughout the autumn, but to no avail. For they played their usual game, moving their fleet to another area. At the beginning of the winter they stayed in the Isle of Wight, and as it is said by the prophet, 'I will turn your festival days into mourning',* at Christmas they went through Hampshire and Berkshire as far as Reading. Thence to Wallingford. Thence to Cholsey. Thence by Ashdown to Cuckamsley.

Wherever they passed they ate joyfully what had been prepared, and when they departed they made payment for their keep by murdering their host and setting fire to their lodging-place. The army of Wessex met up with the Danes on their return to the sea, and fought against them. But being defeated, what did it achieve other than enrich the Danes in spoils? The people of Winchester saw a hostile army, proud and bold, passing by the gates of the city, carrying with them food which they had collected more than fifty miles inland and spoils which they had taken from those they had defeated in battle.

King Æthelred, in sorrow and confusion, stayed at his manor in Shropshire, stung repeatedly by painful news.

4. In the seventh year [1007], the king and the English witan, perplexed about what to do and what not to do, by common consent made a solemn agreement with the Danish army, and gave it £30,000 to keep the peace. In the same year, by God's plan for the destruction of the English, Eadric was made ealdorman over Mercia, a new but outstanding traitor.

In the eighth year [1008], which is the thirtieth year of the said king's reign, he had one ship supplied from every 310 hides throughout all England and a hauberk and helmet from every eight hides. A hide in English means the land that can be cultivated annually by one plough.

5. In the ninth year [1009], the king sent messengers* to Richard, duke of the Normans, to seek his advice and assistance. The fleet mentioned above was gathered at Sandwich and armed with the best men. There never was a greater fleet in Britain in the time of any man. But God made sport of them. The king had banished Wulfnoth Child, a nobleman of Sussex, who began to ravage along the sea-coast with twenty ships. So Brihtric, brother of Ealdorman Eadric, wishing to win praise for himself, took with him eighty vessels of the said fleet, and promised to bring the enemy to the king, alive or dead. But while he was on the journey, a fearful and extraordinary wind drove all his ships ashore and destroyed them. Wulfnoth, falling on them, immediately burnt them. In great alarm at this bad news, the remaining ships returned to London. The army also was divided, and thus all the labour of the English was brought to nothing.

At harvest time a new and enormous Danish army came to Sandwich, and marching thence to Canterbury, would immediately have captured it if the citizens had not begged for peace and given £3,000. So the Danes went into the Isle of Wight, and thence pillaged in Sussex, Hampshire, and Berkshire. King Æthelred collected together all the strength of the English and met the Danes on their return. He would have put an end to the savagery, if Ealdorman Eadric, forever a traitor, had not dissuaded the king from battle by false reports and fictitious alarms.

Afterwards the Danes returned and wintered in the Thames. They frequently attacked London, but were repulsed every time. After Christmas they proceeded over the Chilterns to Oxford. Having burnt it, they returned to Kent via Staines, and in Lent they repaired their ships, which had been brought to meet them.

6. In the tenth year [1010], the Danes came to Ipswich on Ascension Day [18 May]. Their army attacked Ealdorman Ulfcetel, and the East Anglians immediately fled. But the men of Cambridgeshire resisted manfully, for while the English had their kingdom, the county of Cambridge was splendidly renowned. Their squadrons, fighting invincibly, scorned the hazard of death, but Æthelstan, the king's brother-in-law, was killed, and Ealdorman Oswig, and Eadwig brother of Æfic, and Earl Wulfric, and many thegns with him. Then, while there was no thought of flight among the English, Thurcetel

Mireneheued, that is 'ant's head',* was the first to flee, and earned
everlasting disgrace. Within three months the victorious Danes had
either plundered or burnt the land of East Anglia, and also the
marshes described in the previous book,* with their churches. They
also destroyed Thetford, and burnt Cambridge. And withdrawing
from there over some pretty hills to a delightful place which is called
Balsham, they put to death there everyone they found, and took away
children, tossing them on the points of their lances.* But one man,
worthy of widespread renown, climbed the steps of the church tower
which still stands there, and strengthened both by the place and by
his prowess, defended himself, one against the whole army.*

Thence the Danes, crossing through Essex, came to the river
Thames. Without delay they pushed their forces on into Oxfordshire
and into Buckinghamshire, and thus along the Ouse to Bedford and
thus to Tempsford. The river Ouse flows past three strongholds that
are the chief towns of shires, that is Buckingham, Bedford, and
Huntingdon. This Huntingdon, or 'the hill of the hunters', on the
site of Godmanchester, formerly a noble city and now an attractive
town situated on the other side of the river, is far superior to the two
other said strongholds, for the splendour of its site and for its beauty,
as well as for its proximity to the said marshes and for the abundance
of its wild beasts and fish.* At the feast of St Andrew they turned
aside to Northampton. Having burnt it, they crossed the Thames
and burned all Canningsmarsh, and at Christmas they returned to
their fleet.

7. In the eleventh year [1011], the Danes had already plundered
on the north of the Thames: East Anglia, Cambridgeshire, Essex,
Middlesex, Hertfordshire, Oxfordshire, Buckinghamshire, Bedfordshire, the part of Huntingdonshire that is on the south of the river
[Ouse], and much of Northamptonshire. And on the south of the
Thames: Kent, Surrey, Hastings, Sussex, Berkshire, Hampshire, and
much of Wiltshire.

They then laid siege to Canterbury, the chief cathedral city of
England, and took it by treachery. For Ælfmær, whom Archbishop
Ælfheah had saved from death, betrayed it. So they entered and took
captive Archbishop Ælfheah, Bishop Godwine, Abbess Leofrun,
Ælfweard the king's agent, and clergy, whether monks or not, both
men and women. And thus the victors returned to their ships.
You would have seen a terrible sight: the whole of the ancient and

beautiful city reduced to ashes, corpses of the citizens lying packed together in the streets, the ground and the river blackened with blood, the lamenting and wailing of women and children being led away into captivity, and the head of the English faith and the source of Christian doctrine [Archbishop Ælfheah] taken in chains and shamefully dragged away.

8. In the twelfth year [1012], on the Saturday of Easter week [12 April], the Danes were aroused against the archbishop, because he refused to be ransomed. They were also drunk with wine from the south. So they brought the archbishop into the midst of them, and threw the bones and heads of oxen at him. Then as he gave joyful thanks to Almighty God from the depths of his heart, he was struck on the head with an axe. So the man of God fell, sprinkling the earth with his holy blood, and his blessed soul adorned the temples of heaven. In the morning Bishops Eadnoth and Ælfhun took his body and bore it away with due honour, and buried it at St Paul's cathedral [London]. In this place God has shown the merits of the holy martyr. Lyfing succeeded him as archbishop.

Then the king, too late, made peace with the Danish army, giving them £8,000. For peace was never made at a suitable time, but only when the land was weary with crushing defeats. The Danes submitted to the king forty-five ships, promising to protect England, and the king was to find their food and clothing.

9. In the thirteenth year [1013], King Swein of the Danes came via the Humber as far as Gainsborough. And Uhtred, ealdorman of Northumbria,* and all his people, immediately surrendered to him. Also the people of Lindsey, and the people of the Five Boroughs,* and all on the northern side of Watling Street gave hostages to him. The king handed over the hostages and ships into the custody of his son Cnut, and going on to Oxford and Winchester, he accepted the submission of those peoples. Then returning to London, he lost many of his men in the Thames, because they did not trouble to go to the bridge. But the citizens resisted him bravely, since King Æthelred was within. So Swein withdrew from there, and went to Wallingford and then to Bath, and all Wessex was subjected to him. But afterwards, when Swein had returned to his ships, the Londoners submitted to him, because they were afraid he would reduce them to ruin.

Observing this, King Æthelred sent Queen Emma to her brother

Richard in Normandy, and later he sent Edward and Alfred, his sons. Swein was regarded as king by all the people. He ordered food and tribute to be given to his army throughout England. Thorkel ordered the same to be given to the army that was at Greenwich. Then Æthelred went to the Isle of Wight, whence, having stayed over Christmas, he crossed the channel as a fugitive, to go to Richard, duke of Normandy.

10. In the fourteenth year [1014], Swein, now king of the English, succumbed to sudden death at the beginning of his reign. His army chose his son Cnut as king. The English sent messengers to Normandy, to tell King Æthelred that if he would treat them more humanely than previously, they would be happier to accept him as king than any other. He promised them, by his son Edward, who was sent over in advance, everything that was right for king and people, and when he arrived he was received joyfully by all the English people.

But Cnut, with his army, stayed at Gainsborough until Easter, and came to an agreement with the men of Lindsey. When King Æthelred heard of this, he came down with a very great army, burnt that district, and put to death nearly all the inhabitants of the area. Then Cnut, inwardly grieving that this people had been destroyed on account of him, went with ships to Sandwich. There he put ashore the noble hostages who had been given to his father, cutting off their hands and noses. On top of this evil, the king commanded that £21,000 be rendered to the army which was at Greenwich. But to these familiar evils, the Lord added an extraordinary misfortune: the sea rose higher than usual and overwhelmed villages, drowning large numbers of people.

In the fifteenth year [1015], Ealdorman Eadric betrayed the outstanding noblemen, Sigeferth and Morcar: having invited them into his chamber, he had them put to death. Edmund, son of King Æthelred, seized their land and married Sigeferth's wife. Then Cnut returned to Sandwich from Denmark. Moving to Frome in Wessex, he pillaged Dorset, Somerset, and Wiltshire from there. However, King Æthelred lay sick at Cosham [Hants]. Then, when Edmund, the king's son, and Ealdorman Eadric had gathered an army against Cnut, and had met up, the ealdorman sought to betray the ætheling. So they parted, and the battle was abandoned. Consequently Wessex submitted to Cnut, the Danish king.

11. In the sixteenth year [1016], Ealdorman Eadric with forty ships submitted to King Cnut, and he and Cnut, who had 160 ships, gathered in the Thames. Proceeding to Cricklade, they destroyed Warwickshire by fire and sword. But King Æthelred put out an edict that every able-bodied Englishman was to advance with him into battle. However, when a countless host had gathered, the king was told that his men would betray him. Accordingly he dismissed the army and returned to London.

Then Edmund went to Uhtred, ealdorman of Northumbria, and they plundered together in Staffordshire, Shrewsbury, and Leicester. On the other side Cnut went through Buckinghamshire into Bedfordshire and from there into Huntingdonshire, and thence beside the marshes at Stamford, and thus into Lincolnshire, and then into Nottinghamshire, and so into Northumbria, towards York. Hearing of this, Uhtred abandoned his pillaging and returned to Northumbria, and of necessity submitted to Cnut, and all Northumbria with him, and he gave hostages, but nevertheless he was put to death there. Edmund returned to London to his father. But Cnut, appointing Eric as earl over Northumbria in place of Uhtred, returned to his ships before Easter. After Easter he sailed for London with his fleet.

When Æthelred had reigned for thirty-seven years, he passed away in London after his many labours and anxieties, before the enemy fleet arrived.

12. To succeed him, Edmund his son was chosen as king, who was called 'Ironside', because he possessed tremendous strength and remarkable endurance in warfare. King Edmund went into Wessex, and all the people submitted to him. Meanwhile Danish ships came to Greenwich and then to London. And making a large channel on the south bank, they pulled their ships to the western side of the bridge. And digging round the city so that no one could come in or out, they made frequent and heavy assaults on the city, but the citizens withstood them with caution and courage. But concerning the battles of King Edmund, and his courage, are these not written in the histories of the ancients* with high praise?

13. Edmund waged his first battle against the Danish army at Penselwood [Som.] near Gillingham. He gained a clear victory. He waged his second battle against King Cnut at Sherston [Wilts.], where the fighting was very fierce. Ealdorman Eadric and Ælfmær Darling were at the battle, opposing King Edmund. Many fell on either side, and the armies separated of their own accord. Third, he came with a select band of warriors to London. And by forcing the army that had besieged the city to take to their ships, he delivered it with great strength, and entered it in deserved triumph. Two days later, at Brentford [Middx.], he waged his fourth battle against the same army. But many of his men were drowned in the river while crossing over too hastily. However, he obtained the joyous glory of the battle.

And so King Cnut, constrained by great fear, increased his troops by summoning many additional forces. King Cnut and Ealdorman Eadric even planned to conquer by treachery him whom they were unable to conquer by arms. Thus Ealdorman Eadric came to an agreement with Edmund in order to betray him. On Eadric's advice, Edmund went to Wessex to lead a great army against Cnut. Cnut, meanwhile, who was besieging London, assaulted it strongly by land and water, but the citizens resisted him manfully.

The fifth time, King Edmund again crossed the Thames at Brentford, and went into Kent to fight the Danes. But as soon as the standard-bearers who preceded the armies met, the Danes were filled with enormous fear, and turned back in flight. Then Edmund pursued them with great slaughter as far as Aylesford. If he had continued to pursue them that would have been 'the last day of the war and of the Danes'.* But Ealdorman Eadric, giving very evil counsel, got him to stop. Worse advice had never been given in England.

Edmund entered upon the sixth battle with a great host, and Cnut with all the Danish armies gathered in Essex at Ashingdon. And so the fiercest and final battle was fought, and both sides stood their ground unconquerably, despising death. There the valour of young Edmund was made manifest. For when he saw that the Danes were fighting more fiercely than usual, he left his royal position, which was customarily between the dragon and the sign which is called the 'Standard',* and rushed, creating fear, towards the first line. He split the line like lightning, brandishing a sword chosen and worthy for the arm of the young Edmund, and tearing into the line he passed through the centre, and left his followers to overwhelm it. Then he sped towards the royal line. When shouting and shrieking began there, Ealdorman Eadric, realizing that the downfall of the Danes was imminent, shouted to the English nation: 'Flet Engle. Flet

Engle. Ded is Edmund.' In translation this is: 'Flee, Englishmen. Flee, Englishmen. Edmund is dead.'* Shouting these words, he was the first, with his men, to take to flight, and the whole English nation followed. So in that place there followed amazing slaughter of the English army. That was where Bishop Eadnoth was killed, and Ealdorman Ælfric, Ealdorman Godwine, Ulfcetel of East Anglia, Æthelweard son of Ealdorman Æthelwine, and all the flower of the nobility of Britain. King Cnut, strengthened by this great victory, took London and the royal authority.

The seventh time, the armies were gathered in Gloucestershire. But the nobles, fearing on one side the strength of King Edmund and on the other that of King Cnut, said among themselves, 'Why do we so often rush foolishly into mortal danger? Let those who want to reign as individuals fight as individuals.' The idea was acceptable to the kings. For King Cnut was not lacking in prowess. The kings stationed themselves in Alney and began the duel.* When both had shattered spears and lances against the most superior of all armour, they carried on with swords. The crowds on both sides heard and saw with groans and shouts the frightful clang and fiery clashes. At length the incomparable valour of Edmund began to thunder. King Cnut, resisting with great vigour, and yet in fear for himself, said to him, 'O most brave of all young men, why should either of us perish by the sword for the sake of holding kingly power? Let us be brothers by adoption, and share the kingdom, and let us rule, I in your affairs and you in mine. Let Denmark also be governed by your imperial rule.' With these words the generous mind of the young man was softened and the kiss of peace was exchanged. So with the people assenting with tears of joy, Edmund received the kingdom of Wessex. Cnut received the kingdom of Mercia and returned to London.

14. A few days after this, King Edmund was treacherously killed at Oxford. This is how he was killed.* When the king, fearful and most formidable to his enemies, was prospering in his kingdom, he went one night to the lavatory to answer a call of nature. There the son of Ealdorman Eadric, who by his father's plan was concealed in the pit of the privy, struck the king twice with a sharp knife in the private parts, and leaving the weapon in his bowels, fled away. Then Eadric came to King Cnut* and saluted him, saying, 'Hail, sole king!' When he revealed what had happened, the king answered, 'As a reward for

your great service, I shall make you higher than all the English nobles.' Then he ordered him to be beheaded, and his head to be fixed on a stake on London's highest tower.

Thus perished brave King Edmund, when he had reigned for one year, and he was buried at Glastonbury next to Edgar his grandfather.

15. Cnut, king of the English, married Emma, daughter of the duke of Normandy and widow of King Æthelred. Later, the king paid the English a fitting recompense for their villainy. For while he had Wessex in his lordship, Eric had Northumbria, Thorkel had East Anglia, and Eadric had Mercia. But King Cnut put Eadric to death, exiled Thorkel, and forced Eric to flee. In addition, he fell upon the leading nobles: he killed Ealdorman Northman; he did away with Eadwig the ætheling; he cut down Æthelweard; he exiled Eadwig, nicknamed 'king of the peasants'; he took Brihtric's life by the sword. He levied a remarkable tax throughout England, namely £72,000, in addition to £11,000 which the Londoners paid. In this way the just Lord imposed on the English the tax-gatherer they deserved.

In the third year of his reign [1019], Cnut went to Denmark, leading an army of English and Danes against the Wends.* When he had moved close to the enemy in readiness to attack the following day, Godwine, the English earl, led the army in a night attack on the enemy without the king's knowledge. He fell upon them unawares, slaughtered and routed them. But when dawn broke, the king thought that the English had fled or faithlessly gone over to the enemy, so he directed his army, in battle formation, against the enemy, but found only blood, corpses, and spoil in the enemy camp. Because of this, he henceforth esteemed the English as highly as the Danes. When this was done he returned to England. Around this time [1022] Æthelnoth, successor to the deceased Archbishop Lyfing, went to Rome. With him went Leofwine, abbot of Ely, who was restored by order of Pope Benedict [VIII] to the abbey of which he had been unjustly deprived. When the archbishop returned from Rome he transferred the body of St Ælfheah from London to Canterbury.

16. In King Cnut's eighth year [1024], Duke Richard II of the Normans, father of Emma, queen of the English, ended his life. After him his son Richard ruled for nearly a year. And after him his

brother Robert for eight years.* In the following year the king took
an English army to Denmark to oppose Ulf and Eilaf, who brought a
formidable host from the Swedish nation to attack him by land and
sea. A great many Englishmen and Danes on Cnut's side perished
there, and the Swedes were victorious.

In the twelfth year [1028], King Cnut went from England to
Norway with fifty ships, and in a battle he routed Olaf, king of
the Norwegians, and took that kingdom as his own. Then when
Cnut had returned to England, King Olaf went back to Norway
and was killed by the people of his own country. And Cnut retained
that kingdom as long as he lived. Around this time Robert, king
of France, was succeeded by his son, Henry.*

In King Cnut's fifteenth year [1031], Robert, duke of Normandy,
died on pilgrimage to Jerusalem. William, his bastard son, succeeded
him, at a tender age.* King Cnut travelled to Rome in splendour, and
assigned in perpetuity the alms, called 'Rome-scot',* which his predecessors had given to the Roman church. Who may number his
alms, his bountiful gifts, and the mighty deeds that the great king
performed on the pilgrimage? There was no king within the bounds
of the western world who visited the holy places of Rome in so much
splendour and glory. Returning from Rome in the same year [1027],
he proceeded to Scotland, and Malcolm, king of Scotland, submitted
to him, and two other kings, Mælbæth and Iehmarc.

17. When King Cnut had reigned for twenty years, he departed this
life at Shaftesbury and was buried at Winchester in the Old Minster.
A few words must be devoted to the power of this king. Before him
there had never been in England a king of such great authority. He
was lord of all Denmark, of all England, of all Norway, and also of
Scotland. In addition to the many wars in which he was most particularly illustrious, he performed three fine and magnificent deeds.
The first is that he gave his daughter in marriage to the Roman
emperor,* with indescribable riches. The second, that on his journey
to Rome, he had the evil taxes that were levied on the road that goes
through France, called tolls or passage tax, reduced by half at his
own expense. The third, that when he was at the height of his
ascendancy, he ordered his chair to be placed on the sea-shore as the
tide was coming in.* Then he said to the rising tide, 'You are subject
to me, as the land on which I am sitting is mine, and no one has
resisted my overlordship with impunity. I command you, therefore,

not to rise on to my land, nor to presume to wet the clothing or limbs of your master.' But the sea came up as usual, and disrespectfully drenched the king's feet and shins. So jumping back, the king cried, 'Let all the world know that the power of kings is empty and worthless, and there is no king worthy of the name save Him by whose will heaven, earth, and sea obey eternal laws.' Thereafter King Cnut never wore the golden crown, but placed it on the image of the crucified Lord, in eternal praise of God the great king. By whose mercy may the soul of King Cnut enjoy rest.

18. Harold [I], the son of King Cnut and Ælfgifu, daughter of Ealdorman Ælfhelm, was chosen king [1035]. For there was a witan at Oxford, where Earl Leofric and all the leading men north of the Thames, together with the Londoners, chose Harold in order to safeguard the kingdom for his brother Harthacnut who was in Denmark. Earl Godwine, however, father of Harold the later king, with the Wessex nobility, made to oppose this, but to no avail. Therefore they devised a scheme that Queen Emma, with the household of the deceased king, should take care of Wessex from Winchester, on behalf of her son. Earl Godwine would be their leader in military affairs.

King Harold sent Queen Emma, that is, his stepmother, into exile. She went to Baldwin, count of Flanders, from whom she received the castle of Bruges so that henceforth she might live there [1037]. For while William, the lord of the Normans, was still a child, staying with the French king, Normandy's revenues belonged to the French royal treasury.* In the following year [1038], when Æthelnoth, archbishop of Canterbury, died, Eadsige succeeded him.

19. When King Harold had reigned for four years and four months [March 1040], he tasted death at Oxford, and was buried at Westminster. In his days, as in the time of his father, every port had rendered eight marks of silver for sixteen ships.*

Harthacnut, son of King Cnut and Queen Emma, coming from Denmark, was immediately received at Sandwich and chosen king by both the English and the Danes. In his second year [1041], tribute of £21,099 was paid to the Danish army, and afterwards £11,048 was paid for thirty-two ships. In the same year Edward, son of King Æthelred, came from Normandy to Harthacnut his brother. They were both sons of Emma, daughter of Count Richard.

20. When he had reigned for two years [1042], King Harthacnut was

snatched away by death at Lambeth, in the full flower of youth. He had been honourable by nature and had the benevolence of youth towards his men. It is said that so great was his generosity that he ordered royal meals to be served four times a day to all his court, preferring rather that they should be invited and leave scraps of what was set before them, than that they should not be invited and beg for scraps to be given to them, since in our time it is the custom among princes, either from avarice or, as they themselves say, from fastidiousness, to serve food to their men only once a day.* King Harthacnut was buried at Winchester, in the Old Minster, beside Cnut his father. The English nobles, joyful now to be freed from Danish rule, sent messengers for Alfred, the first-born son of Æthelred,* so that he might be raised up to the crown of the kingdom. He, being English on his father's side and Norman on his mother's, brought with him from Normandy into England many of his mother's kinsmen from among those of his own age who were his companions in war.

But Godwine, since he was a mighty earl and a ruthless traitor, planned to give his daughter to be queen for Edward, Alfred's younger and more simple brother. He foresaw that this Alfred, because he possessed high nobility as the first-born, would certainly not consider his daughter a worthy match. So he suggested to the English nobles that Alfred had brought too great a force of Normans with him and had promised them lands belonging to the English, and that it was not safe for the English to establish among them a strong and cunning nation. He said that the Normans ought to pay the penalty, lest in the future others should dare to foist themselves on the English because of kinship with the king. So the Normans were captured and bound, and when they were sitting in ranks at Guildford, nine of every ten were beheaded and only the tenth one survived. But when they had all been killed, except one out of every ten, it seemed to the English that there were too many survivors, and they had the tenth decimated, and so only a very few escaped. They took the captive Alfred to Ely and put out his eyes, and he died.

Then they sent messengers and hostages to Normandy to Edward, the younger, insisting that he should bring with him only a very few Normans, and saying that they would faithfully establish him as king. Edward appeared and came to England with a few men, and was chosen king by all the people and consecrated by Archbishop

Eadsige at Winchester on Easter day. Then Archbishop Eadsige resigned the archbishopric on account of illness, and Siward was consecrated in his place.* At that time, too, Stigand was made bishop of East Anglia.

21. King Edward, for the protection of his kingdom, married the daughter of the mighty Earl Godwine, Edith by name, the sister of the future King Harold [II]. Around this time so great a famine struck England, that a sester of grain, which is a horse's normal load, was being sold for 5s, and even more. Afterwards Stigand, who was bishop in East Anglia, was also made bishop of Winchester. The king sent Earl Swegn, son of the said Earl Godwine, into exile, who went to Baldwin, count of Flanders, and spent the winter at Bruges.

In King Edward's sixth year [1047–8], a battle was fought at Val-ès-Dunes,* between Henry, the French king, and the nobles of Normandy, because they would not accept William as their lord. Duke William took the defeated nobles into captivity, exiling some and mutilating others. At that time, two Danish princes, Lothen and Yrling, landed at Sandwich. They seized countless spoils, and an abundance of gold and silver, and then went round by sea and plundered Essex. Then they took the passage to Flanders, and having sold their plunder, they returned to the place they had come from.

In the following year, Earl Swegn came back to England to seek peace with the king. When Harold his brother and Earl Beorn* opposed this, he came later to his father Godwine at Pevensey. Humbly beseeching him and his brothers, Harold and Tosti, and Earl Beorn, he obtained from them that Earl Beorn would travel with them to Sandwich to seek the king's friendship. Then Beorn, embarking in Earl Swegn's ships to give him aid, was foully murdered by them. His body was thrown out and his friends buried him at Winchester, next to his uncle King Cnut. Swegn returned to Flanders.

In the following year [1049–50], Swegn came to an agreement with the king on the surety of his father Godwine. At that time Pope Leo [IX] held a synod at Vercelli, when Bishop Ulf was present, and he would have been deprived of his bishopric if he had not given a great sum of money. For he did not know his office as a bishop ought. Archbishop Eadsige's life came to an end. His successor Siward* had also died.

22. In the tenth year of his reign [1051–2], King Edward gave the

bishopric of Canterbury to Robert, bishop of London. It was reported to the king that Godwine, his father-in-law, with his sons Swegn and Harold, was about to betray him. They were summoned to answer the charge, and when they refused to come without first receiving hostages, the king exiled them. Godwine and Swegn went to Flanders, while Harold went to Ireland. The king was inflamed to extreme anger, and sending the queen away he took her treasure and her lands from her. He gave the earldom of Devon, Somerset, and Dorset to Odda, and Harold's earldom to Ælfgar, son of Earl Leofric.

In King Edward's eleventh year [1052–3], Emma the Norman, the wife of kings and the mother of kings, submitted to the law of death. But Earl Godwine and Swegn his son* hastened with full sails from Flanders to the Isle of Wight and plundered it. He also plundered Portland. Then Harold, coming from Ireland, plundered at Porlock, and coming thence to his father in the Isle of Wight, continued to Pevensey and thence to Dungeness, Romney, Hythe, Folkestone, Dover, Sandwich, and Sheppey, everywhere taking hostages and ships. Some landed at King's Milton, a royal vill, and set fire to it. But as their fleet was going past 'Northmouth',* on the way to London, it met fifty ships, which included one with the king on board. Through intermediaries, hostages were then given on the advice of Bishop Stigand, and the king and his father-in-law were reconciled. The king restored to Godwine and to his men their lands and everything that they had possessed before, and he took back the queen again. But Archbishop Robert and all the Frenchmen, on whose advice the king had exiled Godwine, were now sent into exile, and Stigand was made archbishop of Canterbury.

Around this time Siward, the mighty earl of Northumbria, almost a giant in stature, very strong mentally and physically, sent his son to conquer Scotland. When they came back and reported to his father that he had been killed in battle, he asked, 'Did he receive his fatal wound in the front or the back of his body?' The messengers said, 'In the front.' Then he said, 'That makes me very happy, for I consider no other death worthy for me or my son.'* Then Siward set out for Scotland, and defeated the king in battle, destroyed the whole realm, and having destroyed it, subjected it to himself.

23. In the twelfth year of his reign [1053–4], when Edward was feasting at Windsor, where he often used to stay, his father-in-law,

the traitor Godwine, was lying next to him, and said, 'It has frequently been falsely reported to you, king, that I have been intent on your betrayal. But if the God of heaven is true and just, may He grant that this little piece of bread shall not pass my throat if I have ever thought of betraying you.' But the true and just God heard the voice of the traitor, and in a short time he was choked by that very bread, and tasted endless death.* Then his son Harold gained possession of his father's earldom, and Ælfgar, earl of Chester, had Harold's earldom.

24. In Edward's thirteenth year [1054–5], the nobles of Normandy fought against the French people at a castle called Mortemer. Ralph the chamberlain,* leader of the French army, was killed, and victory belonged to the Normans. But Henry, the French king, and William, the Norman duke, were not present at the battle. In the following year, Siward, the stalwart earl, being stricken by dysentery, felt that death was near, and said, 'How shameful it is that I, who could not die in so many battles, should have been saved for the ignominious death of a cow! At least clothe me in my impenetrable breastplate, gird me with my sword, place my helmet on my head, my shield in my left hand, my gilded battle-axe in my right, that I, the bravest of soldiers, may die like a soldier.' He spoke, and armed as he had requested, he gave up his spirit with honour.* But since Waltheof his son was still a small boy,* his earldom was given to Tosti, son of Earl Godwine.

In the same year Earl Ælfgar of Chester was sent into exile, because he had been convicted in council of treason against the king. He went to Griffith, king of North Wales, and returning with that king he burnt Hereford and the church of St Æthelberht.

Afterwards Edward, son of Edmund Ironside, came into this land. And immediately he died and was buried in the church of St Paul in London. This man was the father of Margaret, queen of Scots, and of Edgar the ætheling. Margaret was the mother of Matilda, the English queen, and of David, the elegant king of Scots.

Leofric, the noble earl of Chester, also died at this time. His wife, Godgifu, worthy of perpetual renown, was famous for her great goodness, and built the abbey at Coventry, and incomparably endowed it with gold and silver. She also built the church of Stow [Lincs.], below the ridge on which Lincoln stands, and many other churches. Ælfgar, Leofric's son, received the earldom of Chester.

25. In King Edward's twenty-second year [1059–60], when, after the death of King Henry, his son Philip reigned, William, duke of the Normans, subjected Maine to himself.

Now Harold, who was making the crossing to Flanders, was driven by a storm into the province of Ponthieu. He was captured, and the count of Ponthieu handed him over to William, duke of Normandy. Harold swore to William, on many precious relics of the saints, that he would marry his daughter and after Edward's death would preserve England for William's benefit. On his return to England, he who had been received with great honour and many gifts, chose to commit the crime of perjury.*

In the following year [1063], Harold and Tosti went on campaign into Wales. The people of that country were subjugated to them and gave hostages. Afterwards they killed their king, Griffith, and took his head to Harold. Then Harold set up another king there.

It happened in the same year that in the king's presence in the royal hall at Windsor, just as his brother Harold was serving wine to the king, Tosti grabbed Harold by the hair. For Tosti nourished a burning jealousy and hatred because, although he was himself the first-born, his brother was higher in the king's affection. So, driven by a surge of rage, he was unable to check his hand from his brother's flowing locks. The king, however, foretold that their destruction was already approaching, and that the wrath of God would be delayed no longer. Such was the savagery of those brothers that when they saw any village in a flourishing state, they would order the lord and all his family to be murdered in the night, and would take possession of the dead man's property. And these, if you please, were the justices of the realm! So Tosti, departing in anger from the king and from his brother, went to Hereford, where his brother had prepared an enormous royal banquet. There he dismembered all his brother's servants, and put a human leg, head, or arm into each vessel for wine, mead, ale, spiced wine, wine with mulberry juice, and cider. Then he sent to the king, saying that when he came to his farm he would find enough in salted food, and that he should take care to bring the rest with him. For such an immeasurable crime the king commanded him to be outlawed and exiled.*

26. In Edward's twenty-fourth year [1065–6], when the Northumbrians heard of these events, they drove out Tosti, their earl, who had brought much slaughter and ruin upon them. Killing all his

household, both Danes and Englishmen, they took his treasure and
his arms in York. Then they set up Morcar, son of Earl Ælfgar, to be
earl over them. He marched with that people and with the men of
Lincolnshire, Nottinghamshire, and Derbyshire, as far as Northampton, and his brother Edwin, with the men of his earldom and
also many Welsh, came out to meet him. Then Earl Harold came to
them, and they sent him to the king, and messengers with him,
requesting that they might have Morcar as earl over them. The king
granted this, and sent Harold back to them at Northampton, who
confirmed it to them. But meanwhile they did not spare that district,
burning and plundering and killing. When they had gained their
petition, they took away with them many thousands of men, thus
rendering that part of the kingdom poorer for many years to come.
Tosti and his wife went away to Baldwin, count of Flanders, and
wintered there.

27. In the year of grace 1066, the Lord, the ruler, brought to fulfil-
ment what He had long planned for the English people: He delivered
them up to be destroyed by the violent and cunning Norman race.
After the basilica of St Peter's at Westminster had been dedicated on
the day of the Holy Innocents [28 December 1065], and later, on the
eve of the Epiphany [5 January 1066], King Edward had left the
world, and had been buried in the same church (which he himself
had built and had endowed with many possessions), some of the
English wanted to elevate Edgar the ætheling as king. But Harold,
relying on his forces and his birth, usurped the crown of the
kingdom.*

Then William, duke of Normandy, was provoked in his mind and
inwardly incensed, for three reasons: First, because Godwine and his
sons had dishonoured and murdered his kinsman Alfred.* Second,
because Godwine and his sons had, by their cunning, exiled from
England Bishop Robert and Earl Odda and all the Frenchmen.
Third, because Harold, who had fallen into perjury, had wrongfully
usurped the kingdom which by the law of peoples* ought to have
been William's.

William FitzOsbern, the duke's steward, was among those who
came to advise the duke. He told them beforehand that an expedition
to conquer England would be very difficult and the English nation
was very strong, and he argued vehemently against the few who
wished to go to England. Hearing this, the nobles were very glad,

and gave him their word that they would all agree with what he was going to say. Then he went into the duke's presence ahead of them, and said, 'I am prepared to set out on this expedition with all my men.' Therefore all the Norman leaders were obliged to follow his word.*

A very large fleet was prepared at the port called Saint-Valéry. Hearing this, King Harold, who was a fierce warrior, set out to sea with a naval force to oppose Duke William.

Meanwhile Earl Tosti came into the Humber with sixty ships. But Earl Edwin came with an army and put him to flight. Fleeing to Scotland, Tosti met Harold, king of Norway, with 300 ships, and very gladly submitted to him. Then they both came up the Humber as far as York, and Earls Edwin and Morcar fought against them near the city. The site of this battle is still pointed out on the south side of the city.* But King Harold of Norway and Tosti with him took possession of the glorious prize of Mars.* When Harold, the English king, heard this, he met them with a strong force at Stamford Bridge. There began a battle that was to be more intense than any that had gone before. They engaged at dawn, and after fearful assaults on both sides they continued steadfastly until midday, the English superiority in numbers forcing the Norwegians to give way but not to flee. Driven back beyond the river, the living crossing over the dead, they resisted stout-heartedly. A single Norwegian,* worthy of eternal fame, resisted on the bridge, and felling more than forty Englishmen with his trusty axe, he alone held up the entire English army until three o'clock in the afternoon. At length someone came up in a boat and through the openings of the bridge struck him in the private parts with a spear. So the English crossed, and killed King Harold and Tosti, and laid low the whole Norwegian line, either with their arms or by consuming with fire those they intercepted.

28. Harold, king of the English, returned to York on the same day* with great joy, and while he was dining he heard a messenger say to him, 'William has invaded on the south coast, and has built a castle at Hastings.' So the king, hastening down without delay, drew up his lines on the flat land at Hastings.* Then William nobly led out five companies of knights against the enemy, and when they were terrifyingly deployed he delivered a speech* to them, as follows:

29. 'I address you, O Normans, the bravest of peoples, not because I

am uncertain of your prowess, or unsure of victory, which could never, by any chance or impediment, escape you. If, on a single occasion, you had been unable to gain victory, you would perhaps need to be exhorted, so that your prowess might shine forth.

'But what exhortation can your natural and inevitable conduct require? O most valiant of mortals, what could the French king, with that whole nation stretching from Lotharingia as far as Spain, accomplish in wars against our ancestor Hasting?* Hasting took for himself as much as he wanted of France, and as much as he wanted the king to have, that he allowed him. He held it as long as he pleased, and when he was satisfied, he relinquished it, striving for yet greater things. Did not Rou my ancestor,* the first duke and originator of our race, together with your ancestors, defeat the French king in battle at Paris, in the heartland of his realm? And the only hope of safety for the French king was as a humble petitioner, to offer both his daughter and the land you call Normandy. Did not your fathers capture the French king in Rouen, and hold him until he gave up Normandy to the boy Richard, your duke, with the condition that in every conference between the king of France and the duke of Normandy, the duke would be armed with his sword, while the king would not be allowed to carry a sword, nor even a small knife? Your fathers put the great king under compulsion, and established this perpetual decree. Did not the same duke lead your fathers as far as Mimande near the Alps, and waging war at will force the duke of the city to release his son-in-law? And lest it should seem enough to have conquered men, he himself overcame the devil in the flesh, wrestling with him and overthrowing him, and binding his hands behind his back, and as victor of angels* he left him defeated.

'But why do I tell stories of what happened long ago? When, in my time, you fought at Mortemer, did not the French prefer headlong flight to battle, spurs to spears? When Ralph* the high commander of the French was killed, were you not, in taking possession of fame and spoils, maintaining by force of habit the good that is natural to you? Ah! Let any of the Englishmen whom our Danish and Norwegian ancestors have conquered in a hundred battles, come forth and prove that the nation of Rou, from his time until now, have ever been routed in the field, and I will withdraw in defeat. Is it not shameful to you that a people accustomed to defeat, a people devoid of military knowledge, a people that does not even possess arrows, should advance as if in battle order against you, O bravest? Are you not ashamed that King Harold, who has broken the oath he made to me* in your presence, should have presumed to show you his face? It is amazing to me that you have seen with your own eyes those who by execrable treachery beheaded your kin, together with my kinsman Alfred,* and that their impious heads should still stand on their shoulders.

'Raise your standards, men, and let there be no measure or moderation to your righteous anger. Let the lightning of your glory be seen from the east to the west, let the thunder of your charge be heard, and may you be the avengers of most noble blood.'

30. Duke William had not yet concluded his speech when all his men, boiling with unbelievable anger, charged forward in their lines with indescribable force against the enemy, and left the duke alone, speaking to himself. Shortly before the warriors entered the battle, one man, named Taillefer,* played a game of juggling swords in front of the English nation, and while they all gazed at him in astonishment, he killed an English standard-bearer. He repeated this, a second time. The third time, in the act of doing it again, he was himself killed, and the lines fell upon him.

Then began death-bearing clouds of arrows. There followed the thunder of blows. The clash of helmets and swords produced dancing sparks. Harold had placed all his people very closely in a single line, constructing a sort of castle with them, so that they were impregnable to the Normans. So Duke William instructed his people to simulate flight, but as they fled they came to a large ditch, cunningly hidden. A great number of them fell and were trampled. While the English were continuing in pursuit, the principal line of Normans broke through the central company of the English. When those who were pursuing saw this, they were obliged to return over the said ditch, and the greater part of them perished there. Also Duke William instructed the archers not to shoot their arrows directly at the enemy, but rather into the air,* so that the arrows might blind the enemy squadron. This caused great losses among the English. Twenty of the most valiant knights gave their word to one another that they would break through the English line and snatch away the royal banner, which is called the 'Standard'. When they went to do this, several of them were killed. But some of them, making a way with their swords, carried off the Standard.

Meanwhile the whole shower sent by the archers fell around King
Harold, and he himself sank to the ground, struck in the eye.* A
host of knights broke through and killed the wounded king, and
Earl Gyrth and Earl Leofwine, his brothers, with him. And so the
English army was shattered.

Then William, taking possession of this great victory, was
received peacefully by the Londoners, and was crowned at Westminster by Ealdred, archbishop of York. Thus occurred a change in the
right hand of the Most High,* which a huge comet had presaged at
the beginning of the same year. Whence it was said: 'In the year one
thousand, sixty and six, the English lands saw the flames of the
comet.'* The battle took place in the month of September, on the
feast day of St Calixtus.* In that place King William later built a
noble abbey for the souls of the departed, and called it by the fitting
name of Battle [Sussex].

31. In the following year [1067], King William crossed the sea, taking with him hostages and treasure. And he came back in the same
year, and divided the land among his warriors. But Edgar the ætheling-
ling, with many soldiers, went to Scotland and betrothed his sister
Margaret to Malcolm, king of Scots. King William gave the earldom
of Northumbria to Earl Robert, but the inhabitants of the province
killed him and 900 men. Then Edgar the ætheling came to York with
all the people of Northumbria, and the townsmen made peace with
him. Then the king arrived with his army, and sacking the city, he
made great slaughter of the treacherous people, and Edgar returned
to Scotland.

32. In King William's third year [1069], there came into the Humber two sons of Swein, the Danish king, and Osbeorn his brother,
with 300 ships. Earl Waltheof and Edgar the ætheling went to join
them. Danes and English in alliance captured the castle of York.
They killed many Frenchmen, and binding their leaders, they took
them off, with treasure, to their ships, and spent the winter between
the Ouse and the Trent. When the king arrived he drove the Danes
away, and destroyed the English of that province. Then Earl
Waltheof was reconciled with the king.

In the following year [1070], Baldwin, count of Flanders, died,
whose daughter King William had married, and his son Arnulf succeeded, with the support of William, the English king, and Philip,
the French king. But Robert the Frisian, his brother, took up arms,

and killed Count Arnulf and William FitzOsbern, of whom I have previously spoken, and many thousand men of both kings.

33. In King William's fifth year [1071], Earls Morcar and Edwin took to ravaging through fields and woods. But Edwin was killed by his own men. Morcar, Hereward, and Bishop Æthelwine came to Ely. Then the king led an army by land and sea and besieged the island, building a bridge and very skilfully constructing a castle, which still survives today,* and entering the island, he killed the aforesaid men, except for the valiant Hereward, who bravely led his men away. In the following year [1072], the king took an army by land and sea to Scotland. Then Malcolm, the Scots king, became his man and gave him hostages. In the next year [1073], the king led an army of Englishmen and Frenchmen to Maine. The English destroyed that land, burning villages, and cutting down vineyards, and they made it subject to the king. In the next year [1074], the king went into Normandy, and Edgar the ætheling was reconciled with him and stayed for a long while in the king's court.

34. In King William's ninth year [1075], Ralph, to whom the king had given the earldom of East Anglia, laid a plot, together with Earl Waltheof and Roger, son of William FitzOsbern, to drive the king out of the kingdom. Earl Ralph married Roger's sister, and at the wedding they made this treason known. The nobles of the realm strongly opposed him, so Ralph took ship at Norwich and withdrew to Denmark. When the king returned to England, he sent Earl Roger, his kinsman, to prison. But he had Earl Waltheof beheaded at Winchester, and he was buried at Crowland. Of the rest who had been present at the treacherous wedding, he banished many and had many others blinded. Earl Ralph, however, bringing Cnut, son of the Danish king Swein, and Earl Håkon, returned to England with 200 ships. But as they did not dare fight against King William, they crossed over into Flanders. In the same year Queen Edith died, and was buried next to her husband Edward at Westminster.

In the following year [1076] the king crossed over and besieged Dol. But the Bretons defended the castle manfully, until the king of France came and delivered them. Afterwards the English and French kings were reconciled. Malcolm, king of Scots, pillaged in Northumbria as far as the Tyne, and took back with him a great amount of plunder and many men in chains. King William also, fighting against his son Robert in a military uprising at Gerberoi, which is a castle in

France, was thrown from his horse, and William his son was wounded and many of his men killed. The king cursed his son Robert.* In addition, the Northumbrians treacherously killed Walcher, bishop of Durham, at an assembly held peacefully on the Tyne, and a hundred men with him.

35. In his fifteenth year [1081], King William led an army into Wales and subjected it to himself. Later, he put his brother, Bishop Odo, into prison. After these events, Queen Matilda died. At this time the king took 6s from every hide in England. Then Thurstan, abbot of Glastonbury, committed a disgraceful crime: for he had three monks killed who were sheltering under the altar, and eighteen wounded, with the result that their blood ran from the altar over the steps, and from the steps over the floor.

36. In his eighteenth year [1085], the year in which Urban [II] was made pope at Rome,* King William returned from Normandy to England with so great an army of Frenchmen, Normans, and Bretons, that it was a wonder this land was able to feed them. For he had learned from widespread reports that Cnut [IV], king of Denmark, and Robert the Frisian, count of Flanders, wished to place England under their control by martial assaults. But when, by God's will, their preparations came to nothing, the king sent back the greater part of the armies to their native soil. The mighty king thereafter sent his justices through every shire, that is, province, of England, and made them enquire on oath how many hides (that is, land sufficient for one plough per annum) there were in every village and how many animals. He also had them enquire what each city, castle, village, farm, river, marsh, and wood rendered per annum. All these things were written in charters and brought to the king, and kept among the treasures,* preserved until today. In the same year, Maurice was made bishop of London, who began a very great church [St Paul's], which is not yet finished.*

37. In the twentieth year of his reign [1086], when by custom King William the strong had held his court at Christmas at Gloucester, at Easter at Winchester, at Whitsun at London, he clothed Henry his youngest son with the arms of manhood.* Then he accepted the homage of all the landholders of England, to whichever lordship they belonged, and received also their oaths of fealty. Afterwards the king, having acquired great quantities of treasure from whomsoever, on whatever grounds, whether just or unjust, went to Normandy.

38. In King William's twenty-first year [1087], when the Normans had fulfilled the just will of the Lord upon the English people, and there was scarcely a noble of English descent in England, but all had been reduced to servitude and lamentation, and it was even disgraceful to be called English, William, the agent of this vengeance, ended his life. For God had chosen the Normans to wipe out the English nation, because He had seen that they surpassed all other people in their unparalleled savagery. Indeed, their character is such that when they have brought their enemies so low that they can cast them down no further, they bring themselves down, and reduce their own lands to poverty and waste. Always the Norman lords, when they have crushed their enemies, since they cannot avoid acting brutally, crush their own men also in wars. This is increasingly apparent in the best lands that God has made subject to them, that is, in Normandy and England, Apulia, Calabria, Sicily, and Antioch.*

Thus in England they increased in those times unjust tolls and very evil customs. All the leaders had been so blinded by desire for gold and silver that it might truly have been said of them, 'Whence it may be had, no one enquires, but have it they must.'* The more they spoke of right, the greater injustice was done. Those who were called justices were the source of all injustice. Sheriffs and officials whose responsibility was justice and judgement were more frightful than thieves and robbers, and crueller than the most cruel. The king himself, when he had leased out his lands as dearly as he could, would ignore his agreement and would give them to another who offered more, and then to another, always intent on getting more. Nor did he care how great an injury was done to the poor by petty officials. And so in this year God sent plagues of sickness and famine to England, and those who escaped the fevers died of hunger. He also sent tempests and storms, by which He killed many men, and did not spare animals or beasts.

In this year King William had gone to France, and plundered the kingdom of King Philip [I] and put many of his men to death. He also burnt a fine stronghold called Mantes, and all the churches in it, and he delivered many of the common people and two holy hermits to the fire. God was angered because of all this, and when the king returned from there He submitted him to sickness and later to death. The good and evil must be briefly outlined from the life of this most mighty king, so that examples may be taken from the good and caution may be learned from the evil.

39. William was the strongest of the dukes of Normandy. He was the most powerful of the kings of the English. He was more worthy of praise than any of his predecessors. He was wise but cunning, wealthy but avaricious, glorious but hungry for fame. He was humble towards God's servants, but unyielding towards those who opposed him. He placed earls and nobles in prison, deprived bishops and abbots of their possessions, did not spare his own brother, and there was no one who would oppose him. He seized thousands in gold and silver, even from the mightiest. He went beyond everyone else in castle-building. If anyone caught a stag or a boar, he put out his eyes, and no one murmured. He loved the beasts of the chase as if he were their father. On account of this, in the woodlands reserved for hunting, which are called the 'New Forest', he had villages rooted out and people removed, and made it a habitation for wild beasts. When he robbed his men of their property, not for any need, but from his excessive greed, they were embittered and consumed in their innermost hearts. But he scorned their anger. Everyone had to comply with the king's will if they wished to enjoy either his favour or their own money, lands, or life. Alas! how sadly is it to be lamented that any man, since he is ashes and a worm, should be so haughty as to exalt himself alone above all men, forgetful of death.

Normandy had come to the king by inheritance. Maine he had won by arms. Brittany he had made his dependency. Over all England he had been sole ruler, so that there was not one solitary hide there of which he did not know the ownership and value. Scotland also he subjected to himself. Inspiring fear, he took Wales as his own. He had created such complete peace that a young girl, laden with gold, could travel unharmed through the kingdom of England. If anyone had killed any person whatsoever, for whatever reason, he subjected him to the death sentence. If anyone ravished any woman, he would be castrated.

He built the abbey [at Battle], already mentioned, and that at Caen in Normandy, in which he was buried. His wife Matilda built an abbey there for nuns, in which she was buried. Upon whose souls may He have mercy who alone may heal them after death. So you who read and regard the virtues and vices of so great a man, follow the good and turn away from the evil, so as to go by the direct way which leads to the perfect life.

40. In the same year [1087], the pagans preyed upon the Christians in Spain and occupied great parts of the kingdom. Alfonso [VI], the Christian king, receiving aid from Christians all round, fought back, and killed and drove out the pagans, and repaired the losses to the land that had been taken away. It happened also in Denmark that the Danes, who had never before broken faith with their lord, treacherously murdered their king, Cnut [IV], in a monastery.

King William had bequeathed Normandy to Robert, his first-born son. The kingdom of England to William, his second son. A store of treasure to Henry, his third son. When Robert had sold Henry part of Normandy in return for this treasure, he took the land away from him.* This was very displeasing to God, but He deferred vengeance for a time. William, going to Winchester, divided his father's treasure as he wished. In the treasury there was £60,000 in silver, in addition to gold, jewels, vessels, and hangings.* Of this he gave to certain churches ten marks of gold, to others six, and to the church of each village 5s, and he sent to each county £100 to be distributed among the poor. He also freed all those bound in chains on his father's orders. Then the new king held his court at Christmas at London, in which there were present* Archbishop Lanfranc, who had consecrated him king; Thomas, bishop of York; Maurice of London; Walkelin of Winchester; Osbern, bishop of Exeter; Wulfstan, the saintly bishop of Worcester; William of Thetford; Robert of Chester; William of Durham; Odo, bishop of Bayeux, justice and ruler of all England;* and Remigius, bishop of Lincoln,* about whom it is necessary to say a few words.*

41. The king had given the bishopric of Dorchester [Oxon.], which is situated on the Thames, to Remigius, who had been a monk at Fécamp. Now since this bishopric was larger than any other in England, stretching from the Thames up to the Humber, it seemed inconvenient to the bishop that the cathedral of the bishopric was at the extremity. It also displeased him that the city was of middling size, while in the same bishopric the famous city of Lincoln seemed more appropriate for the cathedral. On purchased estates at the very top of the city, near the lofty castle, with its strong towers, he built the church, strong in a strong place, beautiful in a beautiful place, dedicated to the Virgin of virgins, which would be pleasing to God's servants and, as time went on, impregnable to enemies. But the archbishop of York claimed the province of Lindsey,* from ancient times. Remigius, disregarding his petition, proceeded with the task in hand without delay, and when it was finished, he adorned it with clergy who were highly regarded for their learning and way of life. He was short of stature, but great in heart; dark in complexion, but fair in deeds. He had been accused of treason* against the king, but a member of his household purged his lord by the hot iron,* and he was restored to the king's favour, and his pontifical dignity was cleansed of stain. At this time, and for these reasons, the modern church of Lincoln was begun by this founder.

42. But now affairs have been brought down to our own time, and new events demand a new book. If some explanatory recapitulation of the above is required here, these few words will not inconvenience the reader. So here is a summary of the kings in the book just finished:

Æthelred reigned over all the territories of England for thirty-seven years, always with difficulty.

Edmund, the bravest of young men, reigned for one year and was killed by treachery.

Cnut, greater than all his predecessors, reigned gloriously for twenty years.

Harold [I], his son, reigned for four years and sixteen weeks.

Harthacnut, the munificent son of King Cnut, was cut off by death when he had reigned for two years all but ten days.

Edward, the good and peaceable king, reigned in peace for twenty-four years.

Harold [II], the perjured king, for one incomplete year, was destroyed through his own injustice.

William [I], higher than all the preceding, shone gloriously until his twenty-first year. Of whom it was said:* 'If nature denied you, Caesar, a head of hair, the long-haired star, William, gave it to you.'

1087–1135: THE KINGDOM OF THE NORMANS

1. Down to this point the matters discussed have been those that I have either discovered from reading the books of the ancients or learned from common report. Now, however, the matters to be stud- ied are those that I have either seen for myself or heard about from those who did see them.* It has already been made very clear how the Lord deservedly took away from the English race their safety and honour, and commanded that they should no longer exist as a people. From this point it will be shown how He began to afflict the Normans themselves, His own avengers, with various disasters.

All the higher nobility faithlessly raised wars against William [II], the Younger, and adopting his brother Robert for kingship they all raged furiously in their own districts [1088]. Odo, bishop of Bayeux, the chief man and governor of England, raising rebellion in Kent, invaded and burnt villages of the king and the archbishop. Robert, count of Mortain, began the same round Pevensey. Bishop Geoffrey [of Coutances], advancing from Bristol, destroyed the town of Bath, and Berkeley, and the surrounding area. Roger [Bigod], in the castle of Norwich, was not slower to begin the exercise of crime through- out East Anglia. Hugh [de Grandmesnil] behaved no more gently in the district of Leicester and Northampton. William, bishop of Durham, perpetrated similar misdeeds in the borders. The chief men of Herefordshire and Shropshire, plundering together with the Welsh, burnt the shire of Worcester right up to the gates of the city. But when they were preparing their assault on the cathedral and the castle, the saintly Bishop Wulfstan, in his dire need, called on a certain familiar friend, namely the most high God, by whose help, as he lay in prayer before the altar, having sent out only a few soldiers, he either killed or captured 5,000* of the enemy. He miraculously put the rest to flight.

The king assembled the English people, and restored to them their rights of hunting and forests, and promised them desirable laws. Then he marched to the castle of Tonbridge, where Gilbert [Fitz Richard] was in revolt against him. But when the royal army stormed the castle, he was reconciled with the king. Then the king advanced to Pevensey and there besieged Bishop Odo and Count Robert [of Mortain] for six weeks.

Meanwhile Robert, duke of Normandy, in haste to come to England to take possession of it with the assistance of the aforesaid men, sent part of his army ahead to aid them, intending to follow them with huge forces. But the English who were keeping watch over the sea overwhelmed and sank a large number of them. And so those who were at Pevensey and whose food had run out, surrendered the castle to the king.

Bishop Odo swore an oath that he would leave England and surrender the castle of Rochester. But when he came there, with the king's men, to surrender it, Count Eustace [of Boulogne] and other nobles who were in the city seized the bishop and the king's officials by a trick, and threw them into prison. When the king heard this he laid siege to Rochester until the stronghold was yielded up to him, and Bishop Odo crossed the sea, never to return.

The king also sent an army to Durham to besiege it until it was surrendered to him. The bishop and many of the traitors were driven into exile, and the king redistributed to the men who were loyal to him the lands he had confiscated from the disloyal.

In the following year [1089], Archbishop Lanfranc, distinguished teacher of the clergy and kindest father of monks, passed over from transitory affairs. In the same year there was a terrible earthquake.

2. In the third year of his reign [1090], William the Younger prepared to avenge the injuries which his brother had done him, and by giving bribes, he gained for himself the castle of Saint-Valéry and Aumale. Sending his soldiers, he began to plunder and burn his brother's land.

In the next year [1091], the king followed them and made an agreement with his brother. Those castles which his brother had taken from him were to be returned to the king, and the king was to assist him in the conquest of all that his father had held. They also agreed that if either of them should predecease the other without a son, the survivor would become his heir. Twelve magnates swore this agreement on behalf of the king, and twelve on behalf of the duke. Meanwhile, Malcolm [III], king of Scots, came into England to pillage, and caused great distress. So the king, together with Robert his brother, came to England and ordered their forces against

Scotland. Malcolm, therefore, compelled by fear, became the king's man, and subject to him by an oath of fealty. When Duke Robert, who continued to stay with his brother for a while, discovered that his affection for him was more apparent than real, he crossed the sea to his own lands.

In the following year [1092], the king rebuilt the city of Carlisle, and sent settlers there from the south of England. Then, on the day before the church of Lincoln was to be dedicated, Bishop Remigius was struck down by illness and breathed his last.

3. In the sixth year of his reign [1093], William the Younger fell ill at Gloucester in Lent [2 March–16 April]. And he gave the arch-bishopric of Canterbury to Abbot Anselm, a saintly and venerable man. Also he gave the bishopric of Lincoln to Robert, surnamed Bloet, his chancellor, than whom there was no one more handsome in appearance, more serene in mind, or more agreeable in conversation.* The king also promised to amend evil laws and to establish peace in the house of the Lord. But as soon as he recovered he went back on this, and behaved worse than ever. He regretted that he had not sold the bishopric of Lincoln, and so, when the archbishop of York falsely claimed against Bishop Robert that the city of Lincoln and the district of Lindsey ought to be subject to the archbishopric, the case was only concluded after Robert had pledged £5,000 to the king for the liberty of his church. The blame for this act of simony belonged to the king, whereas the bishop behaved correctly.*

In the same year Malcolm, king of Scotland, was ambushed and killed while on a plundering raid into England, along with Edward his son, who if he had lived would have been his heir. When Queen Margaret heard of this, her spirit was stricken to death by the double grief. And making her confession in church and receiving communion, she commended herself with prayers to the Lord and gave up the ghost. Then the Scots chose Donald Bane, Malcolm's brother, as king. But Duncan [II], King Malcolm's son, who was a hostage in King William's court, arrived with help from that king, and drove out his uncle and was received as king. In the following year [1094], by counsel of the same Donald Bane, the Scots ambushed and killed Duncan their king.

4. In the seventh year of his reign [1094], William the Younger, provoked by his brother's failure to keep his oath, crossed to Normandy. When the brothers met about this, the oath-swearers put all

the blame on the king. But disregarding this and going off in a rage, the savage king attacked and took the castle of Bures-en-Bray. The duke, in retaliation, captured the castle of Argentan, and in it the king's count, called Roger the Poitevin, and the 700 soldiers who were with him, and afterwards he took the castle at Houlme. Meanwhile the king had 20,000 English foot-soldiers called up to come to Normandy. But when they arrived at the coast, the king took from each of them the cost of his food, that is, 10s, and sent them home. Then Duke Robert brought with him Philip [I], the French king, and a well-supplied army, to besiege King William at Eu. But through King William's intrigue and cash, the French king was turned back, and thus the whole army disappeared, obscured by dark clouds of money. King William commanded his brother Henry, who was at Domfront, to meet him in England at Christmas. So at Christmas Henry was in London, but the king was at Wissant, from where he made for Dover.

In the following year [1095], he sent his brother Henry to Normandy with a great deal of money, to attack it on his behalf with daily raids. When, however, Robert de Mowbray, earl of Northumberland, puffed up with pride at having laid low the king of Scots, refused to attend the king's court, the king marched an army up to Northumbria. He immediately captured all the earl's leading barons in a stronghold called Newcastle. Thence he took the castle of Tynemouth, and in it the earl's brother. After this he laid siege to the earl at Bamburgh. Since it appeared to be impregnable to attack, he built another castle in front of it, which he named 'Malveisin', and leaving part of the army there, he withdrew. One night the earl left Bamburgh, and was pursued by the royal army as far as Tynemouth. There he unsuccessfully attempted to defend himself, but was wounded and captured, and put into prison at Windsor. So the castle of Bamburgh was surrendered to the king. Then those who had favoured the earl were harshly subdued, for William of Eu had his eyes put out, and Odo, count of Champagne, and several others, were disinherited.

In the same year the energetic king directed his standards against Wales. This was the reason: in the previous year they had killed many Frenchmen, and had stormed the strongholds of the nobles, and had invaded the borders with sword and fire, and in the present year they had destroyed the castle of Montgomery and murdered the inhabitants. So the king crossed the border right into Wales, but as he was unable to pursue them into the wilds of the mountains and woods, he left having accomplished little or nothing. At that time stars were seen to fall from heaven in such quick succession that they could not be counted.

5. In the year 1096, there occurred the crusade* to Jerusalem, on the preaching of Pope Urban [II]. And so Robert, duke of Normandy, setting out thither, mortgaged Normandy with his brother King William. With him went Robert, duke of Flanders, and Eustace, count of Boulogne. In another party there went Duke Godfrey [of Lower Lorraine] and Baldwin, count of Le Bourg, and another Baldwin [of Boulogne], future kings of Jerusalem. In a third party went Raymond, count of Saint-Gilles, and the bishop of Le Puy. But who would omit Hugh the Great, the brother of the French king, and Stephen, count of Blois? Who would not remember Bohemond [of Taranto] and his nephew Tancred? This is the Lord's great miracle, unheard of in all ages, that came about in our own times, that such diverse nations and such courageous noblemen, leaving behind their splendid possessions, wives, and sons, all with one mind sought totally unknown places, spurning death! On account of the magnitude of this event, I beg the reader's indulgence for a digression, for it would be impossible to keep silent about the wonderful and mighty works of God, even if I should wish or be compelled to do so, since they concern the duke of the Normans.

6. When Alexius was emperor at Constantinople, all the nobles mentioned were gathered there with the emperor's consent, which he gave either willingly or by compulsion. Crossing the narrow strait which was formerly called the Hellespont, and now the 'arm of St George', they laid siege to the city of Nicaea, which is the chief town of Rum. Duke Robert of Normandy beset the east gate, and beside him the count of Flanders. At the north gate was Duke Bohemond, and beside him Tancred. At the west gate was Duke Godfrey, and beside him Hugh the Great and Count Stephen. At the south was Count Raymond, and beside him the bishop of Le Puy. An innumerable host was there from England, Normandy, Brittany, Aquitaine, Spain, Provence, France, Flanders, Denmark, Saxony, Germany, Italy, Greece, and many regions. The rays of the sun did not, from its first creation, shine on so great and so illustrious an army, so terrible,

so numerous a crowd, with so many and such warlike leaders. Let Troy stand back, let Thebes stand back, that they may be excused from naming the leaders and princes of their destruction. Here were present the foremost of all ages, shining sons of the west, all signed with the sign of the Cross, all stronger than any left behind in their kingdoms.

And so on the day of the Lord's Ascension [14 May 1097], with clarions sounding all round, the city was attacked. The heavens are filled with shouts. The sky grows dark with arrows. The ground rumbles with the advance. The waters echo with harsh sounds. The wall is reached. The sappers do their work. The pagans' arrows are of no avail, nor spears, nor pieces of wood, nor stones, nor rocks, nor weights, nor water, nor fire, nor skill, nor strength, nor catapulted missiles. When, lo! from the south there appeared a fearful army of Turks, lined up for battle, with banners upright. Count Raymond and the bishop of Le Puy, protected by the divine power and gleaming with earthly weapons, joyfully march out with their army to meet them. So when our men eagerly rush towards them, the Turks are weakened by unexpected fear, and by God's command they are scattered. Indeed, the majority of the fugitives had their heads cut off, which were hurled by catapults into the city, causing great fear to the inhabitants. So, being terrified beyond measure, they surrender the city to our men, who yield it to the emperor [Alexius], as they promised.

7. When they had stayed there for seven weeks and three days, they took the road for Antioch [26 June 1097]. It came about, however, that on the third day the army was divided into two. In one the leaders were Robert, duke of the Normans, Bohemond, Richard of the Principality [of Salerno], Tancred, Everard du Puiset, Achard of Montmerle, and many others. They were surrounded by 360,000 Parthians, who are now called Turks, and Persians, Paulicians, Medes, Cilicians, Saracens, and Agulani, besides innumerable Arabs. Therefore a messenger is sent from the said princes to the other [crusading] army. But meanwhile a fearful battle is waged.* Whereas the Turks, Persians, and Medes inflict death with arrows, the Cilicians and Agulani do so with spears, and the Saracens and Arabs with lances, and the Paulicians with maces of iron and swords. The Christians were put furiously to the slaughter. Their horses, unable to endure the strange shouts, the sound of war trumpets, and the

banging of drums, would not respond to their spurs. Our men, also, overcome by the terrible noise, did not know where they were.

As the Christians were already thinking of flight, or beginning to flee, Robert, duke of Normandy, raced up, crying, 'Where, soldiers, where are you fleeing? Their horses are faster than ours. There is no safety in flight. It is better to die here. Decide with me. Follow me.' He spoke, and thrust at one pagan king with the point of his lance, which split open wood, brass, and flesh alike. And in a moment he laid low a second, and a third. And so Tancred the tireless and Bohemond the warlike, and Richard of the Principality, and Robert of Anzi, a very brave commander and soldier, are not slower in dealing blows. Courage returns to our men.

A very great and fearfully long-drawn-out battle is engaged, when, lo! Hugh the Great and Anselm of Ribemont, with only one hundred soldiers, charging ahead of the other army, being fresh, cut through the weary pagans. Hugh's lance flies like lightning, Anselm's sword like forked flame. Then two of our leaders are slaughtered, while the more Arabs are slain, the more take their places. William, brother of Tancred, in the act of piercing a king with his lance, is himself pierced by that king's lance. Also Godfrey of Monte Scaglioso, as he cuts off an Arab's head, is pierced in the body by a Parthian's arrow, which his hauberk, which has become hot, does not withstand.

The Franks could endure the weight and number of the enemy no longer, when lo! from the opposite direction a forest of standards appeared, belonging to the second army. The battle had gone on until three o'clock in the afternoon, and great numbers of the first army had been slain, and if the other division had not arrived, there would have been not one survivor. At no time afterwards did the pagans fight so unremittingly.

8. Godfrey's line was at the head of the forces that were just arriving. On his right was the line that Baldwin led. On his left, Count Stephen and Isard of Mouzon. Count Raymond, with his men, followed Baldwin's line at a distance; Robert, the very valiant count of Flanders, with his men, followed Stephen's line; and a line of nobles and a countless host followed Godfrey's line. The bishop of Le Puy appeared from another mountain with his invincible army. When the pagans who were fighting saw so many enemy forces coming down unexpectedly, as if the heavens were about to fall upon them, their

courage evaporated, and they gave way to flight with Suliman,* their leader. The Christians, although suffering losses and much looting, gained the victory on the first day of July.

9. Following their plan to march to Antioch, the Franks arrived at Ereghli. Thence to Tarsus, which was taken by the wonder-working Count Baldwin. Then Adana and Mamistra were taken by the brave Tancred. The noble duke of the Normans gave a certain Turkish city to Simeon. The great Count Raymond and Bohemond the war-commander gave another city to Peter of Aulps. Thence the Christians went as far as Göksun, a city which they subjugated to themselves. A certain nobleman, named Peter of Roaix, captured Rusa and several fortresses. The Christians reached Marash, which surrendered to them. Thence they came to the Iron Bridge.

Afterwards, on 21 October, they laid siege to Antioch, which is the chief town of Syria. Bohemond, hearing that the Turks were gathered in a castle called Harim, went with his army to fight them, and by God's will with a few men he overthrew a multitude. And he brought many to be beheaded in front of the city gate, to terrify the citizens. When the Christians had celebrated Christmas in the siege, Bohemond and the count of Flanders marched forth into the land of the Saracens, with 20,000 warriors. Many had been assembled from Jerusalem, Damascus, Aleppo, and other kingdoms, for the relief of Antioch. In a combined attack on them, our men put some to flight and killed others. On their return, the said leaders, with enormous booty, were received by our men in deserved triumph. Meanwhile those trapped inside fiercely renewed the fight against the besiegers. They put to death the standard-bearer of the bishop of Le Puy and many others. In February there gathered an amazing pagan army beyond the Iron Bridge, at the castle of Harim. Leaving all the foot-soldiers at the siege, our leaders led all the knights into battle, and prepared six lines of horsemen. The invincible duke of the Normans led the first. Duke Godfrey of the Germans the second. The illustrious Count Raymond the third. Robert, the pride of Flanders, the fourth. The most noble bishop of Le Puy the fifth. Bohemond, with Tancred, the sixth and largest.

10. With the utmost bravery they clashed with the enemy, and the clamour resounded to the heavens. Showers of spears darkened the day. Every man cut through and was cut through. Then a very great force of Parthians, which had been in the rear, came up and attacked

our men so fiercely that little by little they gave way. But Bohemond, the arbiter of wars and the judge of conflicts, sent his squadron, still unbroken, into the midst of the enemy. Then Robert, son of Gerard, his best knight and standard-bearer, like a lion among gathered flocks, rushed forward between the Turkish lines, and all the while the tongues of his standard fluttered above the heads of the Turks. When the others saw this, they recovered their spirits, and with one mind charged the enemy. With his sword the duke of the Normans split open one man's head, teeth, neck, and shoulders, down to his breast. Then Duke Godfrey cut another man in half, so that one part fell to the ground and his horse bore the other part of its lord among the pagans as they fought, a monstrous sight that so terrified them all that they fled and went away to the wrath of damnation. The heads of many of them were joyfully carried to Antioch. This battle was fought at the beginning of Lent [9 February 1098].

11. Meanwhile, many subjects of the emir of Cairo had come to Antioch. When our men were building a fortress before the gate, where the bridge and the mosque are, and Raymond and Bohemond had gone to the port of St Simeon for provisions, the army of the city marched out boldly to battle. Rushing on our men they put them to flight, and having killed many they drove them as far as their tents.

On the next day they attacked Bohemond and Raymond, and killed 1,000 of their men. The leaders fled and ran towards our men. So the Franks, doubly injured and driven to anger, drew up their fearful battle lines in the field before the city gates. The pagans lost no time in putting their ranks into formation, and attacked our men. But the Christians, proclaiming the battle-cry of the Cross, struck and drove the enemy so fiercely in the first onslaught that they immediately took flight, and coming to the narrow bridge they were either cut down by swords or drowned in the river, for few were able to escape by the bridge. The swollen tide of the river flowed red with blood. Thus twelve of the emir's men were slain. And the Lord gave a most famous victory to His people.*

The next day, when the citizens had buried their dead, our men dug them up, and taking the gold and silver, and the cloths in which they were wrapped, hurled their heads into the city. So by now all the citizens' hope and pride had vanished. For Tancred, who was guarding the fortress in front of the gate, robbed them of all hope of provisions. So Firuz, a certain emir of the Turkish race, who had often been offered friendship by Bohemond, foreseeing that his men would perish, surrendered to Bohemond the three towers that were under his control. Their standards erect above the towers, the Franks broke down the gates and rushed into the city. Some of the Turks were killed while resisting; others fled the city. But some of them held out in the citadel. Yaghi-Siyan, the lord of the city, was captured by the Syrians as he fled, and his head was brought to Bohemond. Thus, on 3 June, Antioch was taken.

12. Kerbogha, commander-in-chief of the army of the sultan of Persia, together with the king of Damascus and the king of Jerusalem, brought Turks, Arabs, Saracens, Azymites, Kurds, Persians, and Agulani to besiege the Franks. But how may I count the sand of the sea?* And so they laid siege to the city. Kerbogha stationed part of his army in the citadel, and they fought our men day and night. Others besieged the city so that no foodstuffs could enter. On the third day, the sons of God went out against the sons of the devil,* whom they thought, having prepared for battle, they would be able to withstand. But so great was the strength and number of the infidels, that many of our men were killed by the enemy's weapons, and others, being forced to re-enter the city, were crushed to death at the entrance to the gate.

13. The next day, four leading men of the army, namely William and Aubrey [of Grandmesnil], Guy [Troussel], and Lambert ['the Poor'], fled secretly to the port of St Simeon. At their persuasion, all the victualling fleet sailed away with them. Then our men, being unable to endure the repeated attacks of those who were guarding the citadel, built a wall between them. As confidence grew among the pagans, so did the hunger among the Christians. For while they were waiting for the promised arrival of the emperor [Alexius], they would buy a hen for 15s, an egg for 2s, or a walnut for 1d. They also cooked and ate the leaves of trees and thistles and the dried skins of horses and asses. Then Count Stephen [of Blois], fleeing like a woman, met the emperor [Alexius], and telling him that the whole army of the Franks was already lost, caused him to turn back weeping.

14. And so there was no hope left for the people of God when, defeated by hunger, they could no longer bear arms. But then fire appeared from heaven, and fell to earth among the Turkish army. The Lord appeared in a vision to His servant. And God said, 'Say

this to the sons of the west: "I have delivered the city of Nicaea to you, and every battle with the foreigners, and the mighty city of Antioch. But when you had taken possession joyfully and safely, you gave yourselves up to women, both Christian and pagan, the stench whereof rises to heaven."' The man of God fell at His feet, saying, 'Lord, give help in our overwhelming need.' And the Lord said, 'I have given help and will do so. Say to my people, "Return to me, and I will return to you, and within five days I will myself come to you as your champion."' Then St Andrew the Apostle appeared to someone, showing forth the lance with which the Saviour was pierced, as he confirmed to the people on oath.

15. After three days of fasting, with solemn processions, masses, and almsgiving, they marched out tearfully to battle, arranged in six lines with God as their commander. Hugh the Great and the count of Flanders led the first line. Duke Godfrey and Baldwin the second. Robert the brave Norman the third. The bishop of Le Puy and William of Montpellier the fourth, with the army of Count Raymond, who stayed to guard the city. Tancred with Prince Richard led the fifth. Bohemond with the count of Roscignolo the sixth. When they had marched out they set up a seventh, in honour of the Holy Spirit, which was led by Rainald. The bishops, priests, clerks, and monks, dressed in holy vestments, chanted hymns to God upon the city walls. And they saw a heavenly army, with white horses and sun-gleaming arms, whose leaders were George, Mercurius, and Demetrius.*

Kerbogha, never happier than at that time, having arranged his countless troops, had a large supply of hay set on fire on the opposite hill to blind our men with smoke. But the Lord of the winds, being present, changed the wind, and the pagans were blinded with the smoke and fell headlong. The Christians pursued them, with great slaughter. Never, in any battle, was there so much plunder. When the emir who guarded the citadel saw this, he surrendered it to the Christians, and became a Christian. The Lord waged this battle on the vigil of Peter and Paul [28 June 1098], and 'His name only was exalted'* on that day.

The Christians joyfully remained in that kingdom until 1 November. Meanwhile, one of the nobles, whose name was Raymond Pilet, gathered an army and captured a castle called Tell-Mannas. Thence he came to a city called Ma'arrat al-Nu'man, which was filled with

Saracens who had come from Aleppo. The barbarians fought against our men, and were at first forced to flee, but in the end they were victorious, and a great slaughter of Franks occurred there.

16. In the month of November, the Christian leaders and the army gathered together to take the road to Jerusalem. On the fourth day before the end of November [28 November], they came to Ma'arrat al-Nu'man and assaulted it, and stormed it by means of a wooden tower moving on four wheels, and other engines, on 11 December. Staying in that city until Christmas, they remained there for one month and four days, because the journey to Jerusalem was interrupted through a dispute between Bohemond and Raymond over the possession of Antioch.

Such a great famine hit the Christians there that they cooked and ate pieces of the corpses of pagans. But on 14 January they went forth and captured two castles that were stocked with all kinds of provisions. Afterwards a city which is called Rafaniyah. Thence a very rich castle in the valley of Sem.

Then from the middle of February they besieged the castle of 'Arqah, for almost three months. Easter was celebrated there [10 April]. But Anselm of Ribemont, a very brave knight, died there, struck by a stone, and William of Picardy, and many others. Then the king of the city of Homs made peace with the army. Meanwhile, part of the army took the town of Tortosa and the city of Maraclea. The emir of Jabala made peace with them. Afterwards, in front of the city of Tripoli, they killed a host of citizens, so that all the waters of the city and even the cisterns turned red. So then the king of Tripoli released 300 captive pilgrims, and gave 15,000 Byzantine gold coins and fifteen costly horses to the Frankish leaders, so that they would leave Tripoli and the castle of 'Arqah which belonged to him.

17. And so the Franks, passing by the castle of al-Batrun, arrived on Ascension Day [19 May] at a city next to the sea which is called Beirut. Thence to Sidon. Thence to Tyre. Thence to Acre. Thence to Haifa. Thence to Caesarea at Whitsun. Thence to the village of St George [Ramla]. Thence to Jerusalem, and they laid siege to it on 7 June. On the north the most excellent duke of the Normans. On the east Count Robert. On the west Duke Godfrey and Tancred. On the south, that is on Mount Sion, Count Raymond. Then, frequently attacking the city, they erected a very high wooden castle. But when the pagans built stone towers against it, our men demolished the

wooden tower and erected it in another part of the city that was not fortified. Then, oppressing the city and climbing the walls with ladders, they took the city,* and killed many who were holding out in the Lord's temple, and the sons of God cleansed the holy city from the impure nations.

18. Then they offered the kingdom of Jerusalem to the duke of the Normans. Because he refused it,* on account of the labour involved, God was offended against him, and nothing favourable happened to him thereafter. Thus he and the count of Flanders and Count Raymond returned to their own lands. Then Duke Godfrey reigned in Jerusalem. And after him Baldwin the valiant. And afterwards Baldwin II, and afterwards Fulk of Anjou, and, after him, his son Baldwin [III], waging many very grievous wars. They subdued to Christ the furthest provinces and towns, except Ascalon, which still persisted in its sin.

19. In the tenth year of his reign [1097], William the Younger, having arranged affairs according to his pleasure in Normandy, which he had accepted in pledge from his brother Robert when he set out for Jerusalem,* returned to England on the eve of Easter and landed at Arundel. After he had joyously worn his crown at Windsor at Whitsun [24 May], he marched into Wales with a large army and defeated numerous bands of Welshmen, but also lost many of his own men in the narrow defiles of those regions. So, seeing that they could not be conquered, more because of the nature of the terrain than from their valour and arms, he had castles built on the borders of Wales and returned to England. Then Archbishop Anselm left England because the evil king would permit nothing right to be done in his kingdom. He harassed the shires through taxes which never ceased: for the building of the wall round the Tower of London, for the building of the royal hall at Westminster, and to satisfy the rapacious and aggressive habits of his household wherever he went. At Martinmas [*c.*11 November] the king returned over the sea to Normandy, and sent Edgar the ætheling, with an army, into Scotland, who drove out King Donald Bane in a great battle. And he set up as king his kinsman Edgar, son of King Malcolm. In the same year a comet appeared.

20. In the eleventh year of his reign [1098], William the Younger was in Normandy, constantly occupied with incursions and revolts and the troubles of warfare, meanwhile not shaving but skinning the

English peoples with taxation and the worst exactions. In summer blood was seen to bubble up from a certain pool at Finchampstead in Berkshire. After this the sky appeared to burn nearly all night. In the same year, Walkelin, bishop of Winchester, died. And Hugh, earl of Shrewsbury, was killed by the Irish, and was succeeded by his brother, Robert of Bellême.

21. In the twelfth year of his reign [1099], William the Younger, on his return to England, for the first time held his court in the new hall at Westminster. When he first entered, to view it, some said that it was a good size, and others said that it was too large. The king said that it was only half large enough.* This saying was that of a great king, but it was little to his credit. When he was hunting in the New Forest, a messenger suddenly arrived from Le Mans, to tell him that his troops were being besieged there. He instantly went down to the sea in haste and embarked in the ships. The sailors asked him, 'Why, O greatest of kings, do you challenge the height of an impossibly stormy sea: have you no fear as you stand in danger of death?' The king to them, 'I have never heard tell of a king who drowned in the waves.'* Then he crossed the sea and did nothing in his lifetime that brought him so much fame and glorious honour. Going to Le Mans he put Count Elias to flight, and commanded it as his own, and returned to England. In that year the king gave the bishopric of Durham to Ranulf [Flambard], of all England the judge, but the perverter of justice, and the tax-collector, but despoiler. In this year also Osmund, bishop of Salisbury, died.

22. In the year 1100, in the thirteenth year of his reign, King William ended his cruel life in a wretched death. For when he had gloriously, and with historic pomp, held his court at Gloucester at Christmas, at Winchester at Easter [1 April], and in London at Whitsun [20 May], he went to hunt in the New Forest on 2 August. There Walter Tirel, aiming at a stag, accidentally hit the king with an arrow. The king was struck in the heart, and fell without uttering a word. A little earlier blood had been seen to bubble up from the ground in Berkshire. William was rightly cut off in the midst of his injustice. For in himself, and because of the counsels of wicked men, whom he invariably chose, he was more evil to his people than any man, and most evil to himself; he harassed his neighbours with wars, and his own men with frequent armies and continual gelds. England was miserably stifled and could not breathe. Since, however, the

king's friends robbed and subverted everything, even going unpunished when they committed rape, whatever evil had been planted earlier was brought to fruition, and whatever evil had not appeared previously put up its shoots in those times. For the hated king, most evil to God and to the people, either sold bishoprics and abbeys or held on to them and took rent for short leases. He intended to be the inheritor of everything. On the day of his death he had in his own hands the archbishopric of Canterbury, the bishoprics of Winchester and Salisbury, and eleven abbeys let out for rent.* Finally, whatever was displeasing to God and to those who loved God was pleasing to this king and those who loved him. Nor did they exercise their unspeakable debauchery* in secret, but unashamedly in the light of day. He was buried at Winchester on the day after his perdition.

Then Henry was chosen king there, and he gave the bishopric of Winchester to William Giffard. Going to London, he was consecrated there by Maurice, bishop of London, having promised a wished-for amendment of laws and customs.* When he heard this, Archbishop Anselm returned to England and conducted the marriage of Matilda, daughter of King Malcolm and Queen Margaret of Scotland, to Henry the new king. When the city of Jerusalem had been taken, as has been described, and a huge battle had been victoriously concluded against the army of the emir of Egypt, Duke Robert returned to Normandy in the month of August, and was joyfully received by all the people. Thomas, archbishop of York, who was a man of abundant genius and an accomplished poet, vanished from the sight of men.

23. When King Henry had held his court at Westminster at Christmas, and at Winchester at Easter [21 April 1101], the leading men of England were roused up against the king in support of his brother Robert, who was approaching with an army. The king sent a fleet to fight a sea battle to prevent his brother's landing, but some of them submitted to Robert when he came. When he arrived at Portsmouth, before 1 August, and the king marched against him with very great forces, the nobles, preferring not to take sides in a war between brothers, arranged a peace treaty between them, with the stipulation that Robert was to have 3,000 marks of silver from England each year, and that whoever lived the longer would be the other's heir if he should die without a son. Twelve of the higher nobility swore this

on either side. So Robert remained peacefully in his brother's kingdom until Michaelmas [29 September], and returned to his own
lands. But Ranulf [Flambard], the perverse bishop of Durham,
whom King Henry had put in chains on the advice of the English
people, secretly escaped from prison and went to Normandy,
influencing Robert against his brother by his counsel and advice.

24. King Henry stood up to that most evil and treacherous count,
Robert of Bellême,* and justly exiled him. First he laid siege to the
castle of Arundel. Since taking it was going to be extremely difficult,
he built castles in front of it, and went to besiege Bridgnorth until
that castle was surrendered to him, and the mournful Robert of
Bellême departed to Normandy. In the same year [1102] Archbishop
Anselm held a council in London at Michaelmas [29 September], in
which he forbade English priests to have wives,* which had not been
prohibited before. This seemed to some to be the greatest purity, but
to others there seemed a danger that if they sought a purity beyond
their capacity, they might fall into horrible uncleanness, to the utter
disgrace of the Christian name. In that council many abbots, who
had acquired their abbeys against God's will, lost them according to
God's will.

   In the following year [1103], Robert, duke of the Normans, came
to England. He was persuaded for various reasons, and because he
was wary of the king's cunning, to pardon him the 3,000 marks
which the king owed him each year. In the same year, blood was seen
to bubble up from the ground at Finchampstead.

   In the course of the next year [1104], the king and his brother
were at odds over several matters. So the king sent soldiers into
Normandy, who were received by those who were plotting against
the duke, and they caused considerable damage to the duke's property by plundering and burning. Then William, count of Mortain,
disinherited by the king in England because of treachery, went to
Normandy. A most upright man, righteous in spirit and impetuous
in action, he declared and conducted a civil war that brought many
disasters to the royal forces. In this year, four white circles appeared
round the sun at midday.

25. In the fifth year of his reign [1105], Henry crossed to Normandy
to make war on his brother. He took Caen by means of money, and
Bayeux by arms, with the aid of the count of Anjou. He also captured many other castles, and almost all the chief men of Normandy

submitted to the king. When this was done, he went back to England in the month of August.

In the following year [1106], the duke of the Normans came to the king his brother at Northampton, amicably seeking from him the free restoration of what had been taken away from his paternal inheritance. But God would not approve their concord, and so the duke went off in anger to Normandy, and the king followed him before August. Then the king laid siege to the castle of Tinchebrai,* and the duke of the Normans came with Robert of Bellême, [William,] the count of Mortain, and all their allies. But the king was not without support, and had with him all the nobility of Normandy and the flower of England, Anjou, and Brittany.

When 'the bugles had sounded their harsh calls',* the duke of Normandy, with his few, boldly attacked the many. Experienced in the Jerusalem wars, he repulsed the royal line with awesome strength. William, count of Mortain, also pressed the English line by harassing it at different points. When the Breton cavalry (for both the king and the duke and the other lines were on foot, in order to fight with more stability) suddenly rushed on the duke's line from the other side, and split it open, the duke's host, overwhelmed by such massive strength, was scattered and defeated. As soon as Robert of Bellême saw this, he saved himself by flight.

So the brave duke of the Normans was captured, and the count of Mortain. The Lord repaid Duke Robert, because when He had allowed him to be glorious in the exploits at Jerusalem, he had refused the kingdom of Jerusalem when it was offered to him. He had chosen rather to devote himself to quietness and inactivity in Normandy than to toil for the Lord of kings in the holy city. So God condemned him to everlasting inactivity and perpetual imprisonment.* A sign of this, a comet, had appeared in the same year. There were seen also, on Maundy Thursday [22 March], two full moons, one in the east and the other in the west.

26. In the seventh year of his reign [1107], King Henry returned to England, having arranged affairs in Normandy as he pleased now that his enemies were either destroyed or reduced to submission. He threw his brother the noble duke, and the count of Mortain, into the darkness of incarceration. Thus victorious, and strong for the first time, the king held his court at Windsor at Easter [14 April]. The nobles of both England and Normandy attended it with fear and

trembling. Earlier, when he was a young man, and after he had become king, he was held in the greatest contempt. But God, who judges far differently from the sons of men, who 'exalts the humble and puts down the mighty',* removed the illustrious Robert from everyone's favour, and caused the fame of the despised Henry to shine throughout all the world. The Almighty Lord freely gave him three gifts: wisdom, victory, and wealth.* With these he prospered in everything, surpassing all his predecessors. In this year died Bishop Maurice, who began the church of London, and Edgar, king of Scotland, to whom his brother Alexander succeeded with the consent of King Henry.

27. In the eighth year of his reign [1108], after the death of Philip [I], the French king, Henry crossed to Normandy to wage extensive war against the new king of France, Louis [VI], son of Philip. Later in the same year Thomas succeeded the deceased Gerard, archbishop of York. During the course of the next year [1109], envoys remarkable for their massive physique and magnificent apparel were sent by Henry [V], the Roman emperor, to ask for the king's daughter [Matilda] in marriage* with their lord. So, holding his court in London, which was more splendid than any he had held, he received from the emperor's legates at Whitsun [24 May] the oaths he required concerning his daughter's marriage. Archbishop Anselm, the philosopher of Christ, had died in Lent.

In the following year [1110], the king's daughter [Matilda] was given to the emperor in a manner that was—to be concise—fitting.* The king accordingly took 3s from every hide in England. In the same year, when the king had held his court at Whitsun [29 May] at New Windsor, which he had built himself, he disinherited those who had caused him injury—that is, Philip de Briouze, William Malet, and William Bainard. Elias, count of Maine, who held it under King Henry, was released from this life. But the count of Anjou, who had received Maine with Elias's daughter, held it against King Henry. In this year, a comet appeared in an unusual way: for rising in the east it climbed into the sky and was then seen to go backwards. In the same year, Nicholas, the father of the man who has written this *History*, yielded to the law of death, and was buried at Lincoln. Of him I have said this:*

The star of the clergy falls, the light of Nicholas fades: may the clergy's falling star shine in God's citadel.

The writer has inserted this in his work in order to gain from his readers the reward for his labour that they might consider it fitting to say, in a spirit of piety, 'May his soul rest in peace, Amen.'*

28. In the eleventh year of his reign [1111], Henry went to Normandy and waged war resolutely, with fire and sword, against the count of Anjou, who held Maine against his will. Then Robert, count of Flanders, died, who had been illustrious in the Jerusalem campaign: for this reason his memory shall not fade for all eternity. After him his son Baldwin was made count, a young man who was extremely valiant in arms. In the next year [1112] the king exiled the count of Evreux and William Crispin from Normandy, and captured Robert of Bellême, the wicked man of whom I spoke earlier. Returning to England in the following year [1113], he put him into perpetual imprisonment at Wareham. In the succeeding year [1114], the king gave the archbishopric of Canterbury to Ralph, bishop of Rochester. Then Thomas, archbishop of York, also died, and Thurstan succeeded. But a great dispute arose between Archbishops Ralph and Thurstan,* since York refused to submit to Canterbury according to custom. The case has been heard frequently, both before the king and before the pope, but has not yet been settled. In this year, the king led an army into Wales. Then the Welsh submitted to all that the majesty of his pleasure desired. A huge comet appeared at the end of May. Then the king crossed to Normandy. And in the following year [1115], he made all the nobility of the land swear to William his son* the fealty they owed their lord. And he returned to England.

29. In his sixteenth year, at Christmas [25 December 1115], King Henry was present at the dedication of the church of St Albans,* which Robert, the venerable bishop of Lincoln, dedicated for Richard, the famous abbot of that place. When the king crossed over to Normandy, at Easter [2 April 1116], there was a great quarrel between him and the French king. The cause was this. Theobald, count of Blois, the nephew of King Henry, had taken up arms against his lord, the French king. To aid him, the English king sent his commanders and a military force, and caused considerable damage to King Louis.

Then in the course of the following year [1117], very serious trouble arose for King Henry, because the French king, the count of Flanders, and the count of Anjou took an oath that they would wrest Normandy from him and give it to William [Clito], son of Robert, the duke of the Normans. Many of the king's nobles also left him, which was a great loss to him. But the king was not without support, having the said Theobald and the count of the Bretons to assist him. So the French king and the count of Flanders came with an army into Normandy. When they had been there for one night, they went back to their own lands without a fight, fearing the arrival of King Henry and his Englishmen, Normans, and Bretons. In this year, due to the king's pressing needs, England was squeezed by repeated gelds and various exactions. Then there were storms, with thunder and hail, on 1 December, and in the same month the sky appeared red, as if on fire. At the same time, a great earthquake in Lombardy toppled and destroyed churches, towers, houses, and men.

30. In the course of the next year [1118], continuous warring by the said princes grievously harassed the king, until Baldwin, the most valiant count of Flanders, was mortally wounded at Eu in Normandy, in the armed tumult, and returned to his own land. Afterwards, Robert, count of Meulan, in secular business the wisest man of all living between here and Jerusalem, and King Henry's counsellor, was revealed at his death to be a fool. For he would not be persuaded by priests either to restore the lands he had stolen or make a confession as he ought, and so, by his own choice, he died* in great poverty of soul. Well was it said, 'The wisdom of this world is foolishness with God.'* Then also Queen Matilda was cut off from the light of day. Of her refinement and the superiority of her way of life I have said this:*

Successes did not make her happy, nor did troubles make her sad: troubles brought a smile to her, successes fear. Beauty did not produce weakness in her, nor power pride: she alone was both powerful and humble, both beautiful and chaste. The first day of May, at night-time as we reckon it on earth, took her away, to enter into endless day.

31. In the fifty-second year after the Normans obtained England, and in the nineteenth year of his reign [1119], King Henry fought gloriously against the French king.* The line that the king of the French placed at the front was under the command of William

[Clito], son of Robert, King Henry's brother. The king himself was in the next line, with very great forces. On the other side, King Henry posted his nobles in his first line. He sat on horseback in the second, with his household. In the third he had gathered his sons with a great force of foot-soldiers. The French front-line immediately unhorsed and scattered the troop of Norman nobles. But then, clashing with the line where King Henry was, it was itself dispersed. The royal lines struck out at one another, and there was fierce fighting. Every spear is broken. They carry on with swords. Meanwhile, William Crispin struck King Henry's head twice with his sword. His hauberk could not be pierced, yet the strength of the blows forced the hauberk itself a little way into the king's head, so that blood gushed out. Then the king hit back at his attacker so strongly with his sword that, although his helmet was impenetrable, yet the massive blow overturned knight and horse, and he was immediately captured at the king's feet. Then the infantry line in which Henry's sons were stationed, not yet on the attack, but soon to be so, rushed in from the opposite direction with levelled lances. Seeing this, the French were dissolved by sudden fear, and turned their backs. King Henry, however, stayed in the field of victory until the enemy nobles were captured and brought to his feet. He then returned to Rouen, amid the sounds of battle-cries and the chanting of the clergy, and glorified God who is the Lord of hosts. I have written in hexameters* of the magnificence of this victory, as follows:

Henry, king and ornament of kings, has robbed the French of their proud spirits, for a greater king has overcome the great King Louis in the field of Noyon.* Gauls ran headlong, preferring flight to fight, spurs to spears. Laurels and eternal praise crown the Normans, as they gained mastery of fame and spoils. Thus this flower of commanders humbled their swollen hearts, and forced the proud mouths of the French to bleat.

In the same year, Pope Gelasius [II] died, and was buried at Cluny. Then Guy, archbishop of Vienne, was elected pope, with the name Calixtus [II], and he held a council at Reims. Then he went to Gisors to meet King Henry and they conferred together, the great priest and the great king. Also Baldwin, count of Flanders, died from the wound he had received in Normandy, and was succeeded by Charles his kinsman, son of St Cnut [IV], the king of the Danes.

32. In the year of grace 1120, when all were subdued and pacified in

Gaul, Henry joyfully returned to England. But in the same sea-crossing, two of the king's sons, William and Richard, and the king's daughter and his niece, as well as many of the king's nobles, stewards, chamberlains, and butlers, and Earl Richard of Chester, were shipwrecked.* All of them, or nearly all, were said to be tainted with sodomy and they were snared and caught. Behold the glittering vengeance of God! They perished and almost all of them had no burial. And so death suddenly devoured those who had deserved it, although the sea was very calm and there was no wind. This is how I have written of it:*

As the famous Normans, having overcome the Gauls, sought the English kingdoms, God Himself obstructed them. For as they sailed over the wild sea in a frail boat, He brought down dense cloud on the swelling sea. While the wandering sailors were snatched away on unseen paths, hidden rocks smashed the bottoms of the boats. Thus the victorious sea crept through the last plank and drowned the king's offspring, and the honour of the world perished.

33. At Christmas [1120], King Henry was at Brampton with Theobald, count of Blois, and after this, at Windsor, he married Adela, daughter of the duke of Louvain, because of her beauty. After the king had been at Berkeley at Easter [10 April 1121], he wore his crown in London at Whitsun [29 May], with his new queen. Then in the summer, as he went with his army to Wales, the Welsh humbly came to meet him, and agreed to everything that the majesty of his pleasure desired. But on Christmas Eve, an extraordinary wind demolished not only houses but also stone towers. I have spoken in elegiacs* of the beauty of the said queen:

O queen of the English, Adela, the very muse who prepares to call to mind your graces is frozen in wonder. What to you, most beautiful one, is a crown? What to you are jewels? A jewel grows pale on you, and a crown does not shine. Put adornment aside, for nature provides your adornment, and a fortunate beauty cannot be improved. Beware ornaments, for you take no light from them; they shine brightly only through your light. I was not ashamed to give my modest praise to great qualities, so be not ashamed, I pray, to be my lady.

34. In the following year, King Henry was at Norwich at Christmas [25 December 1121], Northampton at Easter [26 March 1122], and Windsor at Whitsun [14 May]. Thence to London and Kent. And

later he went on to Durham* in Northumberland. In the same year Ralph, archbishop of Canterbury, died. And John, bishop of Bath. In the year after this, the king was at Dunstable at Christmas [25 December 1122] and went on from there to Berkhamsted. There God showed forth a just event. For there was a certain chancellor of the king, Ranulf, who had been consumed by illness for twenty years, though all the time he remained in the court. More ready than a youth for any crime, oppressing the innocent, stealing many lands for himself. He boasted that while he was weak in body, he was strong in spirit. Now as he was conducting the king on the way to giving him hospitality, and had reached the very top of the hill from which his castle could be seen, in his exaltation of mind he fell from his horse, and a monk rode over him. He was so badly injured by this that after a few days his life ended.* See how wretchedly perished such great pride when God willed! Thence the king went to Woodstock [1123], a remarkable place which he had made a dwelling-place for men and beasts.* And there Robert, bishop of Lincoln, closed his last day. This is his epitaph:*

Robert, the glory of pontiffs, has died, but shall not die, for his surviving fame will allow him to live for ever. He was humble in riches (a wonderful thing!); merciful in power; compassionate in revenge; meek in suffering. He did not wish to lord it over his men, but strove to be their father, always in adversity a wall and armour to his men. On the tenth of January he departed the dreams of the deceitful world, and waking sees truth eternally.

35. Later, at the feast of the Purification [2 February 1123], the king gave the archbishopric of Canterbury to William of Corbeil, who had been prior at St Osyth. Then at Easter [15 April], at Winchester, he gave the bishopric of Lincoln to Alexander, the reverend man who is the nephew of Roger, bishop of Salisbury. Roger, indeed, is justice of all England and second to the king.* The king also gave the bishopric of Bath to Godfrey, the queen's chancellor. Then around Whitsun [3 June] he crossed the sea. And [Waleran,] count of Meulan, deserted him, in open hostility. But the king besieged and took his castle, which is called Pont Audemer.

In the following year [1124], the king was blessed by good fortune. For William de Tancarville, the king's chamberlain, fighting a pitched battle, captured the said count and Hugh de Montfort, his

brother-in-law, and Hugh son of Gervase. And he handed them over
to the king. Then the king put them in prison. In the same year died
Theulf, bishop of Worcester, and Ernulf, bishop of Rochester.

For the whole of the following year [1125], the king was in Normandy. And there he gave the bishopric of Worcester to Simon, the
queen's clerk. Also to Seffrid, abbot of Glastonbury, he gave the
bishopric of Chichester. Afterwards, Archbishop William gave
the bishopric of Rochester to John, his archdeacon.

36. At Easter [29 March], John of Crema, a Roman cardinal, arrived
in England. He travelled round the bishoprics and abbeys, receiving
large gifts, and at the nativity of St Mary [8 September] he held a
solemn council in London.* But as Moses, God's scribe,* wrote in
the sacred history of the vices, as well as the virtues, even of his own
ancestors, that is to say the incest of Lot, Reuben's sin, the treachery
of Simeon and Levi, the inhumanity of Joseph's brothers, it is right
that we also follow a true law of history* concerning good and evil
deeds. If this should displease any Roman or any church leader, let
him keep silence, lest he should seem to want to follow the example
of John of Crema. For in the council he dealt most severely with the
matter of priests' wives, saying that it was the greatest sin to rise
from the side of a whore and go to make the body of Christ. Yet,
although on the very same day he had made the body of Christ, he
was discovered after vespers with a whore.* This affair was very well
known and could not be denied. The high honour which he had
enjoyed everywhere was transformed into utter disgrace. So he
retreated to his own land, confounded and discredited by the
judgement of God.

In the same year died Henry [V], the emperor, King Henry's
son-in-law. It is rewarding to hear how severe the king was towards
wicked men. For he had almost all the moneyers throughout
England castrated and their right hands cut off for secretly de-
basing the coinage. This year was the most expensive of all in our
time, when a horse's load of corn was sold for 6s. In this year, too,
William, archbishop of Canterbury, Thurstan, archbishop of York,
and Alexander, bishop of Lincoln, journeyed to Rome. Of the laud-
able generosity and unquenchable fame of the last of these, I have
said in hexameters:*

Alexander's brilliance is bright not so much with honour as honour is bright through him, for he is the flower of men. Reckoning to possess by giving, he collects honour's treasures, and hastening to give freely, lest his gifts should be requested, what he has not yet given, he regards as no longer his to have. O grace, O pattern of life, at whose coming steadfast faith, cheerful clemency, prudent power, light yoke, pleasing teaching, sweet correction,* and fitting liberty have also come, along with courteous modesty. O people of Lincoln, previously great, now forever greatest, may such a man as this long be the protector of your honour.

37. In the twenty-sixth year of his reign, the king tarried in Normandy at Christmas [25 December 1125], Easter [11 April 1126], and Whitsun [30 May]. And when agreements with the princes of France had been confirmed in a manner that satisfied the victorious king, he returned to England around Michaelmas [29 September]. He brought with him his daughter [Matilda], the empress, who, as I have explained above, had been widowed of her great husband. Robert, bishop of Chester, died.

In the following year, the king held his court at Windsor at Christmas [25 December 1126], moving on from there to London. In Lent [16 February–2 April 1127] and Easter [3 April 1127] he was at Woodstock,* when a messenger said to him: 'Charles, count of Flanders, who was very dear to you, has been murdered by his nobles in the cathedral at Bruges,* by abominable treachery. The French king has given Flanders to William, your nephew and enemy,* who, now greatly strengthened, has punished with various torments all those who betrayed Charles.' So the king, worried by these events, held a council in London* at Rogationtide [8 May]. And Archbishop William similarly held a council in the same town, at Westminster. When the king was at Winchester* at Whitsun [22 May], he sent his daughter [Matilda], who was betrothed to [Geoffrey], son of the count of Anjou, to Normandy, and followed her himself in August. Richard, bishop of London, died, whose bishopric he gave to Gilbert the Universal, a most learned man. Richard, bishop of Hereford, also passed away.

38. The most wise King Henry, spending the whole of the following year in Normandy [1128], marched in arms into France because the French king was supporting his nephew and enemy [William Clito]. Staying at Epernon for eight days,* as safely as if he were in his own kingdom, he forced King Louis not to give aid to the count of Flanders. Here, when King Henry enquired the origin and early

history of the Frankish kingdom,* someone who was not uneducated replied: 'O most powerful of kings, like most nations in Europe, the Franks took their origin from the Trojans. For Antenor, with his followers, fled from the fall of Troy to the boundaries of Pannonia and built a city called Siccambria. But after Antenor's death, they set up as dukes over them Torgot and Francio, from whom the Franks were named. When they had died they chose Marcomirus as duke. Now Marcomirus fathered Faramund, the first king of the Franks. King Faramund fathered Clovis the long-haired, from whom the Frankish kings are called long-haired. After the death of Clovis, Meroveus his kinsman reigned, from whom the Franks were called the Merovingians. Meroveus fathered Childeric. Childeric fathered Clovis, whom St Remigius baptized. Clovis fathered Clothair. Clothair fathered Chilperic. Chilperic fathered Clothair II. Clothair fathered Dagobert, a most famous and most sweet-natured king. Dagobert fathered Clovis. Clovis fathered three sons by Bathilda his saintly queen—Clothair, Childeric, and Theodoric. King Theodoric fathered Childebert. Childebert fathered Dagobert. Dagobert fathered Theodoric. Theodoric fathered Clothair. He was the last king of the line. After him Hilderic reigned, who was tonsured and removed to a monastery when Pippin was made king. In another line of blood, from the daughter of King Clothair, Ansbert fathered Arnold. Arnold fathered St Arnulf, the later bishop of Metz. St Arnulf fathered Anchises. Anchises fathered Pippin, the mayor of the palace. Pippin fathered Charles Martel. Charles fathered King Pippin. King Pippin fathered the Emperor Charles the Great, who shone forth like a star over his predecessors and successors. Charles fathered the Emperor Louis. Louis fathered the Emperor Charles the Bald. Charles fathered King Louis, the father of Charles the Simple. Charles the Simple fathered Louis. Louis fathered Lothar. Lothar fathered Louis, the last king of this line. So when Louis had died, the Frankish nobles set up Duke Hugh as king over them, who was the son of Duke Hugh the Great. Then King Hugh fathered King Robert the Pious. Then Robert fathered three sons—Duke Hugh the most sweet, King Henry the most loving, and Robert, duke of Burgundy. King Henry fathered King Philip, who became a monk at the end,* and Hugh the Great, who went, with many other European leaders, to conquer Jerusalem from the pagans in the great crusade in the year of the Lord's incarnation 1096. King Philip fathered Louis, who reigns at the present time.* If he retained a trace of the prowess of his ancestors, you would not rest so safely in his kingdom.'

39. When these things had been said and done, King Henry went back to Normandy. There arrived from Germany a certain Duke Thierry, who had some Flemish nobles with him and who laid claim to Flanders, with the encouragement of King Henry. But William [Clito], count of Flanders, came out to meet him in a pitched battle.* The fighting was fierce. Count William made up for the small size of his forces by his inextinguishable prowess. All his armour stained with enemy blood, he hacked into the enemy's squadrons with his lightning sword. The enemy could not withstand the awesome weight of his youthful arm, and took flight in terror. But while the victorious count was besieging an enemy castle, which would have surrendered the following day, and his enemies were almost annihilated, by God's will he was injured by a small wound in the hand, and died.* In his short life this most noble of youths earned eternal fame. Galo the versifier says this of him:

Mars has died on earth, the gods lament an equal god.*

In this year also, Hugh of Payns, master of the knights of the Temple at Jerusalem, came to England and took many with him to Jerusalem. Among these went forth Fulk, count of Anjou, the future king of Jerusalem. Ranulf Flambard, bishop of Durham, and William Giffard, bishop of Winchester, died.

40. In the following year [1129], Louis [VI], the French king, had his son Philip elevated as king.* Then King Henry, when everything was at peace in France, Flanders, Normandy, Brittany, Maine, and Anjou, returned joyfully to England. He held a great council on 1 August in London, concerning the prohibition of priests' wives. There were present at this council:* William, archbishop of Canterbury; Thurstan, archbishop of York; Alexander, bishop of Lincoln; Roger of Salisbury; Gilbert of London; John of Rochester; Seffrid of Sussex [i.e. Chichester]; Godfrey of Bath; Simon of Worcester; Everard of Norwich; Bernard of St Davids; and Hervey, first bishop of Ely. For Winchester, Durham, Chester, and Hereford had died. These were the pillars of the kingdom and the sunbeams of holiness at this time. But the king deceived them through Archbishop William's simplicity. For they granted the king jurisdiction on the

matter of priests' wives, and showed a lack of foresight. This became obvious later, when the affair came to a most disgraceful conclusion. For the king took vast sums of money from the priests, and released them.* Then in vain did the bishops repent of their concession, when it became clear before the eyes of the whole world how the church leaders had been duped and the lower clergy humiliated.

In the same year, evil befell those whom Hugh of Payns, who has been mentioned above, took with him to Jerusalem. The settlers in the Holy Land had given grave offence to God by their debauchery, depredations, and other crimes, as it is written in the books of Moses and Kings, wickedness in those places shall not long go unpunished.* For on the eve of St Nicholas [i.e. 5 December 1129], many Christians were overwhelmed by a few pagans, when previously it had usually been the other way about. At the siege of Damascus,* when many of the Christians were on their way to get food, the pagans were astonished that although both numerous and well-armed, the Christians were running away like women. Pursuing them, they killed very many of them. Those who fled, seeking safety in the mountains, were pursued by God that night, in a storm of snow and cold, so that scarcely any of them escaped.

It happened also that the son of the French king, who, as has been said before, had been crowned with the crown of the kingdom, was galloping his steed in sport, when he encountered a boar, which the feet of his horse struck as he galloped, and the new king fell and died of a broken neck.* What an unusual event, most deserving of wonder! How quickly, how easily, such great eminence was brought to nothing!*

41. In the thirtieth year of his reign, King Henry was at Worcester at Christmas [25 December 1129], and at Woodstock at Easter [30 March 1130]. There Geoffrey de Clinton was accused and defamed on a wrongful charge of treason* against the king. At Rogationtide [4 May] he was at Canterbury for the dedication of the new church. At Michaelmas [29 September] he crossed to Normandy. In the same year Pope Honorius [II] died.

In the next year [1131] the king received Pope Innocent [II] at Chartres, refusing to acknowledge Anacletus. For the Romans were divided into two parties and had elected them both. Innocent had been forcibly expelled from the city by Anacletus, who was previously called Pierleoni, and with King Henry's aid had been received throughout all Gaul. After this, in the summer, Henry returned to England, bringing his daughter [Matilda] with him. There was a great assembly at Northampton at the nativity of St Mary [8 September]. All the leading men of England gathered there, and it was decided that his daughter should be restored to her husband, [Geoffrey] the count of Anjou, who was asking for her. After this, the king's daughter was sent to her husband, and was received with the pomp that befitted such a great heroine. After Easter, Reginald died, who had been the abbot of Ramsey and the builder of the new church. At the beginning of winter, Hervey, the first bishop of Ely, died.

42. In the following year, King Henry was at Dunstable at Christmas [25 December 1131]. At Woodstock* at Easter [10 April 1132]. After Easter, there was a great assembly at London.* Here, the most important of several matters to be dealt with was the dispute between the bishop of St Davids and the bishop of Glamorgan [i.e. Llandaff], concerning the boundaries of their dioceses. Baldwin [II], king of Jerusalem, died, and Fulk succeeded. In the thirty-third year, King Henry was ill at Windsor* at Christmas [25 December 1132]. At the beginning of Lent [8 February 1133], there was a council at London* over the bishops of St Davids and Llandaff, and over the dispute between the archbishop of Canterbury and the bishop of Lincoln. At Easter [26 March], the king was at Oxford, in the new hall, and at Rogation [30 April—4 May], there was another council at Winchester* over the matters mentioned above. After Whitsun [14 May], the king gave the bishopric of Ely to Nigel, and the bishopric of Durham to Geoffrey the chancellor. The king also created the new bishopric at Carlisle, and crossed the sea.

43. In the following year, King Henry stayed in Normandy to rejoice in his grandsons, the count of Anjou's children by the king's daughter. Gilbert, bishop of London, died, and the bishop of Llandaff on the way to Rome on the business of his case, which had been proceeding for so long. In this year, Archbishop William [of Canterbury] and Alexander, bishop of Lincoln, went overseas to the king because of their dispute over certain customs of their dioceses.

In the thirty-fifth year [1134–5], King Henry stayed on in Normandy. Several times he planned to return to England, but did not do so, being detained by his daughter on account of various disputes, which arose on a number of issues, between the king and the count of Anjou, due to the machinations of none other than the king's daughter. The king was provoked by these irritations to anger and bitter ill-feeling, which were said by some to have been the origin of the chill in his bowels and later the cause of his death. He had been hunting, and when he came back to Saint-Denis in the forest of Lyons,* he ate the flesh of lampreys,* which always made him ill, though he always loved them. When a doctor forbade him to eat the dish, the king did not take this salutary advice. As it is said, 'We always strive for what is forbidden and long for what is refused.'* So this meal brought on a most destructive humour, and violently stimulated similar symptoms, producing a deadly chill in his aged body,* and a sudden and extreme convulsion. Against this, nature reacted by stirring up an acute fever to dissolve the inflammation with very heavy sweating. But when all power of resistance failed, the great king departed on the first day of December [1135], when he had reigned for thirty-five years and three months.

44. And now at the end of so great a king, I shall announce the end of this book. But I implore the muse to grant him a memorial, if he has deserved it:*

King Henry is dead, once the pride, now the sorrow of the world. The divine powers lament the passing of his divinity. They sigh—Mercury less eloquent than he, Apollo less strong in mind, Jupiter less commanding, and Mars less vigorous, Janus less cautious, Hercules less valiant, Pallas less in combat, Minerva less in art—they sigh. England, which shone on high with the cradle and the sceptre of this divine being, is now cast down in darkness. She along with her king, Normandy along with her duke. The former nourished the boy, the latter has lost the man.

1135-1154: THE PRESENT TIME

1. As usually happens when a man dies, the frank opinions of the people came out after the death of Henry, the great king. Some said that in him there shone three brilliant qualities.* Supreme wisdom, for he was regarded as most profound in counsel, distinguished for his foresight, and renowned for his eloquence. Then military victory, since, among many outstanding feats, he had conquered the French king by the law of warfare. And wealth, in which he had far and away surpassed all his predecessors.

[Version A]*
Others, however, of another school of thought, blackened him for three vices. Excessive greed, in that, like all his kin, although rich, he yearned for tribute and taxes and trapped the poor with snares laid by informers. Then cruelty, in that he put out the eyes of his kinsman, the count of Mortain,* while he was his captive: this fearful villainy was not known until death revealed the king's secrets, and other examples, no less appalling, came to light, which I shall pass over in silence. And debauchery, since he was at all times subject to the power of women, after the manner of King Solomon.* The common people embroidered such tales at will.

[Version B]*
Others, however, of another school of thought, whose intention was to injure him with base venom, maintained that he was filled with enormous greed, in that he yearned for tribute and taxes and trapped the people with snares laid by informers. But those who asserted this did not pay due attention to the fact that through his supreme prowess, he was held in awe by all his neighbours, the very abundance of his vast treasure increasing still more his enemies' fear of him, and that he ruled his lands, although divided by sea, in peace and prosperity, as if their every little dwelling was a castle. Thus different people expressed different views.

But in the dreadful time that followed, which was set on fire by the mad treacheries* of the Normans, what Henry had done—whether in the manner of a tyrant or of a king—seemed, by comparison with worse, to be the summit of excellence. For without delay came Stephen, the younger brother of Count Theobald of Blois,* a man of great valour and boldness, and trusting to his vigour and effrontery, although he had sworn the English realm's oath of fealty to the daughter of King Henry,* he tried God's patience* by seizing the crown of the kingdom. William, archbishop of Canterbury, who had been the first to take the oath, blessed him—alas!—as king. Wherefore God determined the same judgement on him as he had on the one who had struck the great priest Jeremiah, that he would not live beyond a year.* Roger, the great bishop of Salisbury,* who had been the second to take the oath, and had urged everyone else to do so, brought the royal crown to Stephen, as well as the strength of his support. For this reason, by the just judgement of God, he was later arrested and tormented by the very man he had made king, and pitiful ruin became his lot. In short, all those who had sworn the oath—whether bishops, earls, or magnates—gave their approval to Stephen and paid homage to him. It was a bad sign that all England was subjected to him so speedily, without hindrance or difficulty, as 'in the twinkling of an eye'.* After his coronation he held his court at Christmas in London.

2. Meanwhile, the body of King Henry was still unburied in Normandy. He had died on the first day of December [1135]. His body was brought to Rouen, and there his entrails, brain, and eyes were buried together. The remainder of the corpse was cut all round with knives, sprinkled with a great deal of salt, and wrapped in oxhides, to stop the strong, pervasive stench,* which was already causing the deaths of those who watched over it. It even killed the man who had been hired for a great sum of money to cut off the head with an axe and extract the stinking brain, although he had wrapped himself in linen cloths around his head: so he got no benefit from his fee. He was the last of many whom King Henry put to death.

They took the royal corpse to Caen, and it lay there for a time in the church in which his father had been buried. Although it had been filled with much salt and wrapped in many hides, a fearful black fluid ran down continuously, leaking through the hides, and was collected in vessels beneath the bier and cast away by attendants who grew faint with dread. See, then, whoever you are reading this, how the corpse of a most mighty king, whose crowned head had sparkled with gold and the finest jewels, like the splendour of God, whose hands had shone with sceptres, while the rest of his body had been dressed in gorgeous cloth of gold, and his mouth had always fed on the most delicious and choice foods, for whom everyone would rise to their feet, whom everyone feared, with whom everyone rejoiced, and whom everyone admired: see what that body became, how fearfully it melted away, how wretchedly cast down it was! See, I say, the outcome of events, upon which final judgement always depends. And learn to hold in contempt whatever comes to such an end, whatever is reduced to nothing in this way.

At last the remains of the royal corpse were brought to England, and buried within the twelve days of Christmas at the abbey of Reading, which King Henry had founded and endowed with many possessions. King Stephen came there from his court, which he had held in London at Christmas itself, to meet his uncle's body, together with William, archbishop of Canterbury, and many bishops and nobles, and they buried King Henry* with the respect due to so great a man.

3. From there King Stephen went on to Oxford, where he recorded and confirmed the covenants which he had granted to the people and the holy Church on the day of his coronation. They are these:*

First, he vowed never to keep churches in his own hand after bishops had died, but giving speedy consent to canonical election,* to confer them on bishops.

Second, he vowed not to keep in his own hand the woodlands of any clergyman or layman, as King Henry had done, who year after year had prosecuted them if they took game in their own woodlands or uprooted or diminished them for their own requirements. This kind of evil lawsuit was so detestable that if the king's agents saw from afar a thicket that belonged to anyone they thought to have money, they immediately reported it as waste, whether it was or not, so that they might sell it back to the innocent party.*

Third, he vowed that Danegeld—that is, the two shillings per hide which his predecessors used to collect every year—he would remit for all time.*

These were his chief vows to God, and there were others, but he did not keep any of them.

4. King Stephen, in the first year of his reign, went to Oxford at the

close of Christmas [c.5 January 1136], where he heard a messenger say to him, 'The king of Scots, pretending to come to you in peace as a guest, has entered Carlisle and Newcastle and captured them both by trickery.' King Stephen told him, 'What he has taken by trickery I shall take back in victory.' So the energetic king advanced against David, king of Scots, with an army that was greater than any in living memory in England. King David hastened to meet him near Durham and came to an agreement whereby he restored Newcastle to him, but kept Carlisle, by grant of King Stephen. King David, however, did not become the man of King Stephen, because he had been the first of the laymen to swear the oath to the king's daughter, his niece, that England was to be kept for her after King Henry's death. King David's son Henry, however, was made King Stephen's man, and King Stephen gave him in addition the borough which is called Huntingdon.

The king returned in Lent, and during the Easter festival [22 March] in London he held his court, which was more splendid for its throng and size, for gold, silver, jewels, robes, and every kind of sumptuousness, than any that had ever been held in England.

At Rogationtide [26 April], it was reported that the king was dead. Hearing this, Hugh Bigod entered Norwich castle* by stealth and refused to surrender it except to the king himself when he arrived, and even then with great reluctance. So already the madness of the Normans, referred to above, was beginning to spread, in faithlessness and treachery.

The king then took the castle of Bampton [Devon], whose lord, a certain traitor Robert, had gone into revolt against him. Then he laid siege to the city of Exeter, which Baldwin de Redvers was holding against him, and there he spent much time in the construction of many siege-engines and used up much of his treasure. At long last the castle was surrendered to him, and taking the very worst advice, he did not execute punishment on those who had betrayed him. For if he had done so at that time, there would not have been so many castles held against him later. The king then advanced to the Isle of Wight and took it away from Baldwin de Redvers, of whom I have just spoken, and banished him from England.

Buoyed up by his success in these doings, the king came to hunt at Brampton, which is a mile from Huntingdon,* and there he prosecuted his nobles for infringements of the forest laws, that is, of woodlands and hunting, and so he broke his vow and covenant with God and the people.

5. King Stephen in the second year was at Dunstable at Christmas [25 December 1136].* But in Lent [24 February–10 April 1137], he crossed over to Normandy. Alexander, bishop of Lincoln, and many nobles went over with him.* Everything that the king, who was habituated to martial conflicts, began there, he carried out with great success. He thwarted the plots of his enemies, he destroyed enemy castles, he shone brilliantly among commanders. He made an agreement with the French king, and Eustace his son* was made the French king's man for Normandy, which belongs to French overlordship.

When [Geoffrey], count of Anjou, who was his chief enemy, saw this, he accepted a truce with King Stephen. He had, of course, married King Henry's daughter [Matilda], who had been the empress of Germany and had received the oath concerning the kingdom of England, whence husband and wife were laying claim to England. But he realized that for the present he was unable to break through the royal forces, both because of the great number of the king's warriors and because of the large amount of money which was still left from the late king's abundant treasure.

So when everything had gone well, the illustrious king returned to England just before Christmas. These two years, then, were very prosperous for King Stephen. But the third, about which I am going to speak, was mediocre and things were beginning to fall apart. And the two last* were pernicious, with everything torn to pieces.

6. The energetic King Stephen, in the third year of his entry into England, rushed out to Bedford, and besieged it on Christmas Eve [24 December 1137] and for the whole of Christmas. Many considered this displeasing to God, since he was treating the most solemn of festivals as of little or no importance. Bedford surrendered to him, and he advanced his army to Scotland.

The king of Scots, under cover of piety, on account of the oath he had sworn to King Henry's daughter, commanded his men in barbarous deeds. For they ripped open pregnant women and tore out the unborn foetuses. They tossed children on the points of their lances. They dismembered priests on their altars. They put on to the bodies of the slain the heads cut off crucifixes, and changing them round, they put back on the crucifixes the heads of the dead.

Everywhere that the Scots attacked would be filled with horror and barbarity, accompanied by the cries of women, the wailing of the aged, the groans of the dying, the despair of the living. So King Stephen invaded, burned, and laid waste the southern areas of King David's kingdom, but David himself did not dare come to fight him.

7. Then after Easter [3 April 1138], the abominable madness of the traitors flared up. A certain traitor, Talbot by name, held the castle of Hereford in Wales against the king. But the king besieged it and took it back into his own possession. Earl Robert, the bastard son of King Henry, held against him the very strong castle which is called Bristol, and another which is called Leeds [Kent]. Ralph Lovel held the castle at [Castle] Cary [Som.]. Ralph Paynel the castle at [Dudley (Staffs.)]. William de Mohun the castle at Dunster [Som.]. Robert of Lincoln the castle at Wareham [Dorset]. Eustace Fitz John the castle at Malton [Yorks.]. William Fitz Alan the castle at Shrewsbury, which the king took by force of arms, and he hanged several of the men who were captured. Hearing this, Walkelin, who was holding the castle at Dover, surrendered it to the queen* who was besieging it.

Then, while the king was occupied in the south of England, David, king of Scots, marched an immense army into England. He was courageously opposed by the nobility of the north of England, on the summons and command of Thurstan, archbishop of York, and the Standard, that is, the royal banner, was set up at Northallerton. Since the archbishop was prevented by illness from being present at the battle, he sent in his place Ralph, bishop of the Orkneys, who, standing in a high place in the middle of the line, urged them on as follows:*

8. 'Noblemen of England, renowned sons of Normandy, before you go into battle you should call to mind your reputation and origin: consider well who you are and against whom and where you are fighting this battle. For no one has resisted you with impunity. Bold France, when she had put you to the test, melted away. Fruitful England fell to your conquest. Wealthy Apulia, gaining you, renewed herself. Jerusalem, the celebrated, and famous Antioch both submitted to you. Now, however, Scotland, which is rightly subjected to you, attempts to thrust you back, preferring unarmed rashness, more fitting for brawl than battle. There is among them no knowledge of military matters, experience in battle, or regard for discipline. There

is no place, then, for fear, but rather for shame, that those whom we have always sought out and conquered in their own country have overturned this custom by drunkenly and crazily flocking into ours.

'As bishop, deputizing for your archbishop, I declare to you that this has come about by God's providence, so that those who have violated the temples of God in this country, have spilt blood on altars, have murdered priests, have spared neither children nor pregnant women, shall in this same country undergo deserved punishment for their villainy. Through your hands today, God will carry out His just decision according to His plan.

'So lift up your spirits, gentlemen, and rise up against the evil enemy, trusting to the bravery of your country and, still more, to the presence of God. Do not let their rashness move you, because the many banners of our force do not frighten them. They do not know how to arm themselves in war, while you exercise your arms even in peacetime, so that in war you may feel no doubt of its outcome. Your head is covered by a helmet, your breast by a hauberk, your shins by leggings, your whole body by a shield. When the enemy looks carefully and discovers that you are enclosed in steel, he cannot find where to strike. What is there to doubt as we march forward against the unarmed and naked? Their numbers? But it is not so much numerical superiority as the courage of the few that wins a war. For a host that is unaccustomed to discipline is a hindrance to itself—both to victory when things go well, and to flight when things go badly. Besides, very small numbers of you have often defeated greater. Of what avail, then, are ancestral glory, regular training, and military discipline, if, when you are few, you do not conquer the many?

'But the enemy impels me to finish speaking, as it is already rushing forward in disorder and—this greatly rejoices my heart—running together in scattered groups. So you who in today's battle are going to avenge the house of the Lord, the priests of the Lord, the humble flock of the Lord, if any of you fall in combat, as your archbishop's deputy we absolve you from all penalty for sin, in the name of the Father, whose creatures they have foully and horribly destroyed, and the Son, whose altars they have polluted, and the Holy Ghost, whose exalted ones they have slaughtered in their madness.'

9. Every Englishman answered and the hills and mountains echoed, 'Amen! Amen!' At the same moment, the Scots army called out their

ancient rallying-cry, and the shout went up to heaven, 'Albani!
Albani!'* But the cry was drowned by the fearful crash of innumerable blows. The beginning of the battle.* When the line of the men
of Lothian, who had snatched from the reluctant king of Scots the
honour of striking the first blow, hurled their javelins and attacked
the hauberked line of our mounted knights with long lances, they
found their opponents unyielding, like a wall of iron. The archers,
mingling with the knights, and letting off clouds of arrows, struck
into them, for of course they were without armour. The whole
Norman and English host stood its ground unmoved, in one dense
formation round the Standard.

Then the chief commander of the men of Lothian was struck by
an arrow and fell to the ground, and all his clan turned back in flight.
For the high God was displeased with them, and all their strength
was torn down like a spider's web. Seeing this, the largest troop of
Scots, which was fighting fiercely on the other wing, was drained in
spirit and gave way to flight. As soon as the royal line, which King
David had drawn up from several clans, saw this, they began—first
in ones, then in groups—to run away, the king being almost the only
one to remain. When the king's friends saw this, they compelled him
to grab a horse and escape.

While the rest fled, the king's valiant son [Henry], disregarding
what his followers were doing, and longing only for glory and honour, leapt upon the enemy line and struck with amazing violence.
For his was the only line that was mounted, and was composed of
English and Normans who lived in his father's household. But his
mounted knights could by no means continue long against knights in
armour who fought on foot, close together in an immoveable formation. Their lances broken and their horses wounded, they were
forced to retreat, though their action had been glorious.

The story goes that 11,000 Scots* were killed, apart from those
who were hunted down in the hedgerows and woodlands and sum-
marily dispatched. Our men were triumphant, suffering very little
bloodshed. The leaders in this battle were: William, count of
Aumale, William Peverel of Nottingham, Walter Espec, and Ilbert de
Lacy, whose brother was the only one of all the knights to lose his
life. When the outcome of this battle was announced to King
Stephen, he and all who were with him gave high thanks to God.
This battle was fought in the month of August [22 August 1138].

In Advent [4–24 December], Alberic, legate of the Roman church and bishop of Ostia, held a council in London. And there, with the approval of King Stephen, Theobald, abbot of Bec [in Normandy], was made archbishop of Canterbury.*

10. King Stephen took the castle of Leeds [Kent] by siege after Christmas [1138].* After that [1139] he marched to Scotland, where he waged war with Mars and Vulcan* as his commanders, so that the king of Scotland was forced to make peace with him. Taking Henry, the Scottish king's son, with him into England, he laid siege to Ludlow, where this Henry was pulled off his horse by an iron hook, and nearly taken captive, but the king himself bravely rescued him from the enemy.*

Leaving the siege unfinished, he went to Oxford. There an extraordinarily scandalous and quite unprecedented affair took place. For when the king had peacefully received Roger, bishop of Salisbury, and Alexander of Lincoln, Roger's nephew, he violently arrested them in his court, though they—far from refusing to stand trial—earnestly begged a fair hearing. Then, putting Bishop Alexander into prison there, he took the bishop of Salisbury with him to a castle of his called Devizes [Wilts.],* than which there was none more splendid in the whole of Europe. Oppressing him by torturing him with starvation and putting a rope round the neck of his son, who had been the royal chancellor, as if to hang him, he wrested the castle from him in this way, ignoring of the good service which he, before all others, had rendered him on his entry into his kingdom. Such was the recompense he gave him for his devotion. In the same way he seized Sherborne [Dorset], which was almost equal to Devizes in splendour. Taking possession of the bishop's treasure, he used it to acquire Constance, sister of Louis [VII], the French king, for the benefit of his son Eustace.*

11. The king returned from thence and went to Newark, taking with him Bishop Alexander, whom he had released from his captivity at Oxford. At Newark [Lincs.], in a very pleasant site on the river Trent, the bishop had built a most beautiful castle in a florid style. When he arrived there, the king imposed on the bishop an unlawful fast, swearing on oath that he would be deprived of all food until the castle was surrendered to him. With tears and entreaties, the bishop only just succeeded in prevailing upon his men to allow his castle to pass out of his authority and into the custody of strangers. In the

same way, his other castle was surrendered, which is called Sleaford [Lincs.], not inferior in style or position to the one mentioned above.

Not long afterwards, when Henry [of Blois], bishop of Winchester, the king's brother, at this time legate of the Roman church, held a council at Winchester,* he and Theobald, archbishop of Canterbury, and all the bishops present, fell at the royal feet, begging in most eager supplication, that to gain their free forgiveness of all his offences against the said bishops, he should restore their possessions to them. But the king, on the advice of evil men, scorned the awesome abasement of so many great ones, and granted them nothing.

Because of this, the house of King Stephen was exposed to eventual ruin. For King Henry's daughter [Matilda], who had been the empress of Germany and to whom England had been assigned by an oath, immediately came to England. The king besieged her at Arundel, but either because he trusted treacherous advice, or because he thought the castle impregnable, he allowed her to go to Bristol.

In the same year the said Bishop Roger wasted away, worn out by sorrow as well as old age. May all who read this pause to marvel at so great and sudden a reversal of fortune. For so many blessings had come to that man from his earliest youth, and had accumulated without interruption, that anyone would have said that with regard to him fortune's changeableness had been forgotten. During the whole of his life he was unaffected by any adversity, until at the last he was smothered by a great landslide of troubles simultaneously heaped upon him. Therefore let no one trust in the continuance of happiness, nor take fortune's constancy for granted, nor strive to remain for long in a set place on the revolving wheel.

12. In the fifth year, after Christmas [1139], King Stephen drove Nigel, bishop of Ely, out of his bishopric, because he was the nephew of the above-mentioned bishop of Salisbury: the king was now extending to Roger's kin the feeling of hatred he had against him.

But to say where he was at Christmas, or at Easter, is of no importance. At this time, to be sure, the ceremonies of the court and the custom of royal crown-wearings,* handed down from the ancient line, had completely died out; the huge store of treasure had by now disappeared; there was no peace in the realm, but through murder, burning, and pillage everything was being destroyed, everywhere the sound of war, with lamentation and terror. I have composed elegiac verses* on this subject:

Who is to give me a fountain of tears (what better?), that I may weep for my country's impious deeds? Stygian gloom has come, released from the underworld, and thickly veils the face of the realm. See how rage, uproar, arson, robbery, pillage, murder, lack of faith, rush headlong to ruin. Already they are stealing riches, and—O novel robberies!—they bear down upon wealthy lords, even as they slumber in their castles. To break oaths, to make false promises, is a noble accomplishment; to betray even lords is the proper way for men to act. A gang of robbers breaks into graves and churches, and now—lamentable deed!—drags priests away. They torment the anointed of the Lord; and are keen to torture women too—O for shame!—to gain ransom. Their flesh consumed, hunger fills those who mourn; skin and bones breathe out their wandering souls. Who is to bury these great crowds of dying? Behold! Here is a glimpse of the Styx, and its spreading corruption.

13. In the sixth year, during Christmas [24 December 1140–5 January 1141], King Stephen laid siege to the city of Lincoln, the defences of which Ranulf, earl of Chester, had taken by deceit.* The king remained encamped there until the Purification of St Mary [2 February 1141]. Then the said Ranulf brought his father-in-law, Robert [earl of Gloucester], who was a son of King Henry, and other powerful nobles, intending to disperse the king's siege. With difficulty and great daring the earl traversed an almost impassable marsh, and on the very same day disposed his troops and attacked the king in battle.* He had made up the first line from his own men; in the second were those whom King Stephen had disinherited; in the third, Robert [of Gloucester], the great commander, with his men. On the wing was a band of Welshmen, who possessed more daring than military skill. Then the earl of Chester, a warlike man, who gleamed with glorious arms, addressed Earl Robert and the other nobles in this fashion:

14. 'To you, invincible leader, and to you, my noble comrades in arms, I render many thanks, from the bottom of my heart, for you have generously demonstrated that you will risk your own lives for love for me. So since I am the cause of your peril, it is right that I should put myself into danger first, and should be the first to strike out at the line of this treacherous king, who has broken the peace after a truce had been allowed. Indeed, being confident, both of the

king's wrongfulness and of my own courage, I shall now split open the royal squadron and prepare my way* through the midst of the enemy with my sword. It is for you brave men to follow the one who goes before, and imitate him as he strikes through and through. Already in my mind I seem to see the royal lines fleeing across the field, the nobles being trampled under foot, the king himself being pierced through with a sword.' He finished speaking.

Then Earl Robert replied thus to the young man,* and standing on raised ground he delivered the following speech:

15. 'It is quite right that you should demand the honour of striking the first blow, both on account of your noble blood and also because of your exceptional valour. But if you claim it on the grounds of noble birth, I, the son of a most noble king and grandson of a high king, am not surpassed. If on the grounds of valour, there are many very excellent men here, whose prowess cannot be outstripped by any man living.

'However, I am inspired by a far different motive. For the king has cruelly usurped the realm, contrary to the oaths which he swore to my sister; by throwing everything into disorder he is the direct cause of the deaths of many thousands; and by his example in distributing lands to those who have no legal right, he has plundered those who are in rightful possession. So, with the assistance of God, the just Judge, who will provide the punishment, he must be attacked first by those who have been wretchedly disinherited. The One who judges the peoples with equity* from His high dwelling in the heavens will look down* and in this great hour of need will by no means abandon those who are earnestly seeking to right a wrong.

'But there is one thing, all you mighty nobles and knights, that I want to put firmly in your minds: for those seeking to escape there can be no retreat through the marshes which you crossed with such difficulty. Here you must either conquer or die. There is no hope in flight.* The only course left is to use your swords to make a way into the city. If I am right that there is no escape for you, today with God's aid you will be granted the victory. Truly, he for whom there can be no other refuge must of necessity resort to his prowess. As you gain your victory, you will see the citizens of Lincoln, who are stationed very close to their city, their resolution melting away at the pressure of the onslaught, turn tail back to their homes.

'Now, consider who are your opponents* in this battle. Alan, duke of the Bretons,* appears in arms against you—indeed, against God—an abominable man, stained with every kind of crime, not acknowledging an equal in evil, whose impulses are unfailingly harmful, who regards it as the one supreme disgrace not to be incomparable in cruelty. There also appears against you [Waleran,] the count of Meulan,* an expert in deceit, a master of trickery, who was born with wickedness in his blood, falsehood in his mouth, sloth in his deeds, a braggart by nature, stout-hearted in talk, faint-hearted in deed, the last to muster, the first to decamp, slow to attack, quick to retreat. There also appears against you Earl Hugh [Bigod], for whom it seemed insufficient to break his oath towards the empress without the added crime of openly perjuring himself by affirm-ing that King Henry granted the kingdom to Stephen and set aside his daughter;* he doubtless believes falsehood to be a virtue and considers perjury to be a fine thing. The count of Aumale [William le Gros] appears, a man who is remarkably consistent in wrong-doing, swift to enlarge it, intransigent over giving it up, because of whose intolerable filthiness his wife left him and became a fugitive. That earl* appears who stole the said count's wife, a manifest adulterer and distinguished lecher, a faithful follower of Bacchus, though unacquainted with Mars, smelling of wine, unaccustomed to war-fare. Simon [of Senlis], earl of Northampton, appears, whose action is only talk, whose gift is mere promise: he talks as if he has acted and promises as if he has given. But up to now I have had to be silent on the subject of the fugitive William of Ypres.* For words have not yet been invented which can properly describe the extent and ramifica-tions of his treacheries, the filth and horror of his obscenities. There also appear nobles of the same character as their king, practised in robbery, defiled with pillage, grown fat on murder, and lastly, every one of them tainted with perjury.

'And so, you mighty men, whom the great King Henry raised up and this man has thrown down, whom he favoured and this one has ruined, lift up your spirits, relying on your courage, or rather on God's justice, take up God's offer of vengeance on those vicious men and fix your eyes on unfading glory for yourselves and your descend-ants. And now, if you share a determination to carry out this judge-ment of God, vow to advance and swear not to take flight, together raising your right hands to heaven.'

16. He had scarcely finished, when they all renounced flight with a

blood-curdling cry, their hands raised to heaven, and buckling themselves into their armour, made their splendid advance towards the
enemy.

King Stephen, meanwhile, seething in a great sea of troubles,*
had heard Mass with all ceremony. But when, following custom,
he offered a candle fit for a king and was putting it into Bishop
Alexander's hands, it broke in pieces.* This was a warning to the
king that he would be crushed. In the bishop's presence, too, the pyx
above the altar, which contained the Lord's Body, fell,* its chain
having snapped off. This was a sign of the king's downfall.

Then the energetic king went out and with great composure drew
up his lines for the battle. He was himself on foot, and he stationed
round him a densely packed host of knights whose horses had been
led away. He placed the earls, with their men, in two lines to fight on
horseback. But these divisions of cavalry were very small, for the
false and factious earls had brought few forces with them. The royal
line was the largest, although it was marked out by only one banner,
namely, that belonging to the king himself. Then, since King
Stephen did not have a good speaking voice, a speech of exhortation
to the whole company was enjoined upon Baldwin,* a man of great
nobility and a very powerful knight. Standing in a high place, with
the eyes of all raised towards him, he attracted their attention by
pausing in modest silence, and began as follows:

17. 'Everyone about to engage on the battlefield should consider
three things. First, the justice of the cause; then, a plentiful supply
of troops; and lastly, the prowess of the participants. The justice of
the cause, lest the soul should be put at risk. A plentiful supply of
troops, lest the weight of the enemy's numbers should be overwhelming. The prowess of the participants, lest confidence in numbers leads to overthrow through reliance on the weak. On all these
points we observe that the enterprise which we have undertaken is
well prepared. For the justice of our cause is that we stand by the
king, risking our lives to keep what we vowed before God against
those of his men who are false to him. The number of our knights
is no less than theirs, and our infantry is more densely packed. But
who may give a fair description of the prowess of so many earls and
nobles, as well as knights, long practised in warfare? The king's own
boundless valour will stand fast, equal to thousands of you. Since,
therefore, your lord is in your midst, who is the Lord's anointed

and to whom you have pledged your faith, discharge your vow to God, and receive from Him a reward that will be all the greater the more faithful and constant you are to your king—the faithful against the faithless, those who remain true against those who are false.

'In total assurance and filled with high confidence, consider against whom you are fighting this battle. The power of Earl Robert is well known. He, indeed, usually threatens much and does little, with the mouth of a lion and the heart of a rabbit, famous for his eloquence, notorious for his idleness. The earl of Chester has nothing for which he is to be feared, for he is a man of reckless daring, ready for conspiracy, unreliable in performance, impetuous in battle, careless of danger, with designs beyond his powers, panting for the impossible, having few steady followers, collecting together a ragged troop of outcasts. For every time he begins something manfully, he abandons it impotently. Indeed, throughout his career he has been unsuccessful in war, for either he has run away when overcome by his opponents, or, on the rare occasions when he has been victorious, he has sustained losses greater than those of the vanquished. Let the Welshmen he brings with him be no more than objects of scorn to you, for they prefer unarmed boldness to battle and lacking both skill and experience in warfare, they charge like cattle towards the hunting-spears. The others, both noblemen and knights, are deserters and vagabonds: if only more were coming, for the more there are, the worse the result for them!

'So, earls and men of consular rank, rightly bearing in mind your valour and your nobility, raise your abundant prowess today to its full flowering, and imitating your fathers, leave undying glory for your sons. May the permanence of victorious fame be your motive for combat. The permanence of failure will be their motive for flight. They are already sorry they have come—I make no mistake—and are already thinking about flight, if only the difficult terrain would allow it. Therefore, since they can go neither into combat nor into retreat, what have they done, by God's will, other than offer themselves to you, with their baggage? You see their horses, their arms, and their very bodies subjected to your power. So, warriors, stretch out your courage and your invincible right hands, and leaping high, seize what God himself has offered you.' But even before he brought the course of his speech to an end, the enemy's din was upon them, the blare of trumpets,* the snorting of horses, the thundering of the ground.

18. The beginning of the battle. The line of the disinherited, which was in front, struck the royal line, containing Count Alan, the man from Meulan, Earl Hugh of East Anglia, Earl Simon, and the man from Warenne, with such force that immediately, as 'in the twinkling of an eye',* it was routed, and divided into three: for some were killed, some were captured, and some fled. The line commanded by the count of Aumale and William of Ypres attacked the Welsh, who were advancing on the wing, and put them to flight. But the earl of Chester's line overturned the said count's troop and it was routed in a moment, just like the first line. So they fled—all the king's knights and William of Ypres, born in Flanders, a man who had been of consular rank and possessed great prowess. As he was a great expert in warfare, he saw the impossibility of assisting the king and reserved his aid for better times.

So King Stephen, with his force of men on foot, was left in the midst of the enemy who completely surrounded the royal company, and attacked it on every side, as if they were storming a castle. At that moment you would have seen the dread sight of war all round the royal force, sparks leaping up from the clash of helmets and swords; the fearful hissing* and the terrifying shouts re-echoed from the hills and from the city walls. Attacking the royal squadron with a cavalry charge, they killed some, threw others to the ground, and carried off others as captives. No pause or respite was given them, except in the area where the mighty king was standing, his enemies trembling at the incomparable ferocity of the blows he struck. When the earl of Chester saw this, he envied the king's glory, and rushed at him with the whole weight of his knights. Whereupon the king's lightning strength showed itself, as, wielding his great battle-axe, he slew some and scattered others. Now a new clamour arose—all against him, he against all.* Eventually, the royal battle-axe was shattered by incessant blows. He drew out his sword, worthy of a king, and performed wonders with his right hand, until the sword, too, was shattered. Seeing this, William of Cahagnes,* a most puissant knight, rushed upon the king, and seizing his helmet, cried out in a loud voice, 'Here, everyone, here! I have the king!' Everyone flew up, and the king was captured.

Baldwin, who had delivered the speech of exhortation, was also captured, pierced by many wounds and bruised by many blows as he put up a splendid resistance, which earned him everlasting honour. Richard Fitz Urse* was also captured, who gained fame and glory in both dealing and receiving blows. After the king's capture the royal force, unable to escape through the encirclement, continued fighting until they were all either captured or slain. Then the city was sacked according to the law that governs hostilities, and the king was brought into it in misery.

19. God's judgement on the king having been carried out, he was taken to the empress, and put into Bristol castle as a prisoner. The empress was received as Lady* by all the English nation except for the men of Kent, where the queen and William of Ypres opposed her with all their might. She was received first by [Henry of Blois,] the Roman legate and bishop of Winchester, and soon afterwards by the Londoners. But she was lifted up to an insufferable arrogance, because the hazard of war had favoured her supporters, and she alienated the hearts of almost everyone. So either at the instigation of crafty men or by God's will—indeed, whatever men may have done was by God's will—she was driven out of London. Provoked by this into a womanly rage, she ordered the king, the Lord's anointed, to be put in irons.

After some days she came with her uncle, the king of Scots, and her brother Robert, and besieged the bishop of Winchester's castle with concentrated strength. But the bishop sent for the queen and William of Ypres, and for almost all the nobles of England. So there was a large army on both sides. Conflicts took place every day, not in pitched battles but in the excursions of knightly manoeuvres. Valiant exploits were not unrecognizably confused as in the darkness of war, but the prowess and glory earned by individuals appeared in the open, so that for all the participants, exalted in the splendours of illustrious deeds, this interlude was a source of gratification.

Eventually, the London army came and with augmented numbers they fought against the empress, forcing her to flee. In the rout, many were captured. One of the captives was Robert, the empress's brother, in whose castle the king was imprisoned, and by whose capture alone the king could get out, so both were freed. Thus the king, taken captive in misery by God's justice, was miraculously freed by God's mercy, and was received by the English nobility with great rejoicing.

20. In the seventh year [1142], King Stephen built a castle at Wilton [Wilts.]. Then an unexpectedly large enemy host suddenly attacked, and the royal knights who attempted to break through were encircled and overwhelmed, so the king was forced to retreat. Very many of his men were taken prisoner. Among them William Martel, the king's steward, was captured, for whose ransom the king gave the famous castle of Sherborne. In the same year, the king besieged the empress at Oxford, from after Michaelmas until Advent. During the latter season, not long before Christmas, the empress fled across the frozen Thames, clothed in white garments, which reflected and resembled the snow,* deceiving the eyes of the besiegers. She fled to the castle at Wallingford [Berks.], and thus at last Oxford was surrendered to the king.

21. In the eighth year, King Stephen was present at a council in London in mid-Lent [*c.*14 March 1143]. The bishop of Winchester, the legate of the city of Rome, held this council at London because of the clergy's urgent needs: for plunderers were paying no respect either to the clergy or to God's church, and clergy were being taken captive and ransomed just like laymen. At this council it was decreed that any one who laid violent hands on a clergyman could be absolved only by the pope, and that in person. Thanks to this, the clergy enjoyed a bare measure of tranquillity.

In the same year, in his court at St Albans, the king arrested Geoffrey de Mandeville, more in retribution for the earl's wickedness than in accordance with the law of peoples,* more from force of circumstances than because it was right. For if he had not done this, he would have been deprived of his kingdom through the earl's treachery. To gain his release by the king, Geoffrey surrendered to him the Tower of London, and the castle of Walden, and that of Pleshey [both in Essex]. Then, stripped of his possessions, the earl invaded the abbey of Ramsey [Hunts.], and expelling the monks, he sent in plunderers, and turned the church of God into 'a den of thieves'.* Although a man of great prowess, he was extremely stubborn towards God—very diligent in worldly matters, but very negligent of God.

In that very year, before Christmas, the bishop of Winchester journeyed to Rome, and the archbishop of Canterbury followed, both seeking to be appointed legate as Pope Innocent [II] was now dead.* Celestine [II] succeeded him.

22. In the ninth year [1144], King Stephen besieged Lincoln, where, as he was building an earthwork against the castle which [Ranulf] the earl of Chester was holding by force, nearly eighty of his workmen were buried alive by the enemy. So the king withdrew in confusion, leaving the business unfinished.*

In this year, Earl Geoffrey de Mandeville harassed the king exceedingly, and in everything he did he basked in vainglory. But in the month of August the splendour of God showed forth a miracle worthy of His justice. For He inflicted similar punishments on two men who had committed similar sins by forcibly removing monks and turning God's churches into castles. Robert Marmion, a warlike and evil man, had carried this out in the church of Coventry, and Geoffrey, as I have already said, had perpetrated the same crime in the church of Ramsey. Robert Marmion, attacking his enemies in front of the monastery itself, was the only man to be killed, although he was in the midst of his own huge squadrons, and as an excommunicate he is being devoured by eternal death. In the same way, Earl Geoffrey, among the serried ranks of his own men, was the only one to fall, struck by an arrow from a lowly foot-soldier. He scoffed at the wound, but after a few days he died* of this injury, excommunicate.

See how the vengeance of God, of Him who is worthy to be praised, is made known throughout all ages, and is executed in the same way for the same crime! While the church of Ramsey was being held as a castle, blood bubbled out of the walls of the church and the adjacent cloister, clearly demonstrating the divine wrath and prophesying the destruction of the wrongdoers. Many witnessed this, and I myself saw it with my own eyes. So although impious men said that God was asleep, He was aroused* both in this sign and in what it signified.

Indeed, in the same year, Ernulf, the earl's son, who continued to hold the fortified church after his father's death, was captured and sent into exile on account of it, and the commander of the earl's knights fell from his horse at his lodging, and died with his brains pouring out. When the commander of his foot-soldiers, called Reimer, whose job it had been to break into churches or burn them, was crossing the sea with his wife, the ship—as many relate—became totally becalmed. The sailors, horrified at this strange happening, cast lots to find the cause, and the lot fell to Reimer. He disputed this with all his might, and the lot was cast a second time, and a third, and still it came to him. So he and his wife, and the money he had so wickedly acquired, were put in a small boat, and immediately the ship sailed over the open sea, moving as speedily as it had done earlier. But the boat with the evil ones aboard was sucked round by a sudden whirlpool and swallowed up for evermore.*

In the same year, on the death of Pope Celestine, Lucius [II] replaced him.

23. In the tenth year [1145], King Stephen was engaged first in having to deal with the activities of Hugh Bigod. Then in the summer Earl Robert and the whole confederacy of the royal enemies built a castle at Faringdon [Berks.]. The king was quick to assemble forces, and sped there at the head of a formidable and numerous army of Londoners. While Earl Robert and his supporters waited for more troops not far away, the king's army made daily assaults on the castle, and by their herculean efforts they took it with considerable bloodshed. Now at last the king's fortunes began to change for the better and took an upward turn.

In the same year the bishop of Lincoln, Alexander, again went to Rome, behaving as before with the utmost generosity. He was therefore honourably received by the new pope, Eugenius [III], a man worthy of the supreme office. The bishop was always kind-hearted, fair-minded, and discriminating, his countenance not only cheerful but even merry. On his return in the following year, in high favour with the pope himself and all the Curia, he was given a most respectful and joyful welcome by his own people. He restored his church,* which had been gutted by fire, with such delicate craftsmanship that it seemed more beautiful than when it was newly built, and its construction was not surpassed by any building in all England.

24. In the eleventh year [1146], King Stephen gathered a great army and built an impregnable castle positioned against Wallingford, where Ranulf, earl of Chester, now united in a pact with the king, was present with large forces. But when the earl came from thence to the king's court at Northampton, peacefully and not suspecting anything of the kind, the king arrested him and put him in prison until he surrendered to him the famous castle of Lincoln, which he had taken from him by trickery, and any other castles that had been in his power. Then the earl was released from prison and restored to liberty.

25. In the twelfth year, at Christmas [25 December 1146], King

Stephen showed himself in the kingly regalia in the city of Lincoln, where no other king—deterred by superstitious persons—had dared to do so.* This shows that King Stephen possessed great boldness and a spirit that was not fearful of danger.* After the king left, the earl of Chester came to Lincoln with plentiful troops, intending to carry out an assault on it. His commander, a brave and indomitable man, was killed at the entrance to the north gate, and the earl himself, having lost many of his men, was forced to take flight. So the victorious citizens, filled with great joy, ceremoniously rendered their praises and thanks to their protectress, the Virgin of virgins.*

At Whitsun [8 June 1147], King Louis [VII] of France, Count Thierry of Flanders, the count of Saint-Gilles, and an immense army from all over the French kingdom, as well as many Englishmen, took the Cross* and began the journey to Jerusalem to fight against the heathens who had captured the city of Edessa. Emperor Conrad [III] of Germany led an even greater army, and both forces passed through the territories of [Manuel,] the emperor of Constantinople, who later betrayed them.

In the month of August, Alexander, bishop of Lincoln, went to Auxerre, to Pope Eugenius, who was spending time there after a stay in Paris. The bishop was honourably received by the pope, but he returned to England having contracted a sickness brought on by an unseasonal heatwave. Before long he succumbed to illness, then to paralysis, and finally to death.

26. So, in the thirteenth year of King Stephen, Bishop Alexander died, and was buried at Lincoln at the beginning of Lent [25 February 1148]. The truth should be told about this man's character, according to the custom of Moses.* Brought up in the height of luxury by his uncle Roger, bishop of Salisbury, he acquired a pride beyond his means. Wishing to surpass other great men in the bounty of his gifts and in the splendour of his patronage, and finding his own income insufficient for the purpose, he would deliberately coax out of his friends the means to make up the difference between his present need and his earlier abundance. But he was not able to make it up, for he continually squandered more and more. He was, however, a wise man, and so generous, that by the Roman Curia he was called 'the Magnificent'.

27. In the same year the armies of the emperor of Germany and the French king, which marched out with great pride under illustrious

commanders, came to nothing, because 'God despised them'.* For their debauchery, which they practised openly, rose up in the sight of God. They also greatly displeased God by their adulteries, and by robberies, and by all kinds of crimes. So they were laid low, first by the treachery of the emperor of Constantinople, and later by the swords of the enemy. The king of France and the emperor of Germany, with a few followers, fled ignominiously, first to Antioch and later to Jerusalem. Then the king of France, as if about to do something to repair his damaged reputation, took Damascus with the assistance of the knights of the Temple of Jerusalem and with forces gathered from all quarters, but lacking God's grace he succeeded in nothing, and returned to Gaul.

Meanwhile a naval force that was made up of ordinary, rather than powerful, men, and was not supported by any great leader, except Almighty God, prospered a great deal better, because they set out in humility. For although few, they had God's help in their battles, and thus captured from the many a city in Spain which is called Lisbon, and another called Almería, and neighbouring territories. Truly, 'God resists the proud, but gives grace to the humble'.* For the armies of the French king and the emperor had been more splendid and larger than the company which earlier had conquered Jerusalem, and yet they were crushed by very much smaller forces and were destroyed like a spider's web. But no host had been able to withstand the poor men of whom I spoke above, and the large forces who attacked them were reduced to weakness. The greater part of them had come from England.*

28. In the same year, just before Christmas, Robert, whose surname is 'de Chesney', archdeacon of Leicester, a young man worthy of all praise, was elected bishop of Lincoln. He was universally considered worthy of so great an honour, and with the very joyful approval of king, clergy, and people, he was consecrated by the archbishop of Canterbury. With great jubilation he was eagerly awaited at Lincoln, and still more eagerly welcomed, being devotedly received by clergy and people at the Lord's Epiphany [6 January 1149]. May God favour him in evil times, and nourish his young days with the dew of wisdom, and gladden his countenance with spiritual cheer.*

29. In the fourteenth year [1149], David, king of Scots, bestowed the arms of manhood upon his nephew Henry.* But when the king of Scots, with his forces, and his nephew, accompanied by the

nobility of the west of England, were gathered at this ceremony, King Stephen, fearing that they might invade York, came to the city with a great army, and stayed there throughout the month of August. Eustace, the king's son, who had also received the arms of manhood in the same year, fell upon the lands of the noblemen who were with Henry, the son of the empress. There was no one to oppose him, and so, with Mars and Vulcan as his companions, he inflicted much damage. The king of the English and the king of the Scots, of whom the former was at York and the latter at Carlisle, each being wary and afraid of meeting up with the other, kept away from one another and turned back home to their kingdoms.

30. In the fifteenth year [1150], King Stephen assembled his battalions and attacked the beautiful city of Worcester, and having taken it, he ravaged it by fire, but he was unable to capture the castle that was in the city. For that city belonged to Waleran, count of Meulan, to whom King Stephen had given it, to his own disadvantage. Enriched with valuable spoils from the plundered city, the royal troops returned home through their enemies' lands, from which, as there was no one to withstand them, they took away immense booty.

31. In the sixteenth year, Theobald, archbishop of Canterbury and legate of the apostolic see, held a general council in London* in the middle of Lent [18 March 1151], at which King Stephen, his son Eustace, and the nobility of England were present, and the whole of that council was anguished with new appeals.* Now appeals were not in use in England until Henry, bishop of Winchester, while he was legate, brutally introduced them, to his own disadvantage. For in the same council he was appealed three times to the hearing of the pope in Rome.

In the same year King Stephen again invaded Worcester, and since he had not been able to take the castle the previous year, he laboured for its capture with all his might. But when those trapped inside resisted stoutly, he built two earthworks with which to subdue it. Leaving some of his leading men there, he returned to his own possessions. But since it was the king's habit to begin many things energetically but follow them up them slothfully, the king's besieging castles were demolished by the craft of [Robert,] earl of Leicester, and the siege was raised by cunning. This was because the said earl was the brother of the count of Meulan. So the king's endeavours and efforts were wasted and came to nought.

In the same year [Geoffrey,] the count of Anjou, a great and famous man, King Henry's son-in-law and son of the king of Jerusalem, yielded to the laws of death.* Consequently he left Anjou and Normandy to Henry,* his first-born son, and passed to him the hereditary right in England, of which he was in the process of gaining possession, though as yet he did not have it. It happened, however, that Louis, the French king, was separated from his wife [Eleanor], the daughter of the count of Poitou, on grounds of consanguinity. So Henry, the new duke of Normandy, married her,* and through her was enriched by possession of the county of Poitou with all its great honours. But this marriage brought about great enmity and discord between the French king and the duke.

So Eustace, son of King Stephen, rose up, and he and the French king assailed Normandy with heavy attacks. The duke strongly resisted them both and all the French army. However, the king, collecting all his forces, attacked a castle, called Neufmarché, and although it was almost impregnable, he captured it with great strength and took possession of it, and handed it over to Eustace, the son of the king of England, who had married his sister.

32. In the seventeenth year [1152], Stephen proposed to honour his son Eustace with a royal crown.* But when he demanded of the said archbishop and the other bishops whom he had summoned there,* that they anoint Eustace king and confirm him with their blessing, he was refused. Indeed, the pope in a letter had forbidden the archbishop to elevate the king's son as king. It was understood that this was because Stephen had seized the kingdom contrary to the oath. Boiling with rage at this crushing humiliation, father and son ordered them all to be shut up in a particular building, and subjecting them to powerful intimidation, urged them to do what they demanded. They were filled with the greatest dread, for King Stephen had certainly never loved the clergy and some time before had put two bishops into prison. But they maintained their resistance, even though in fear of their lives. They came away unscathed, though robbed of their possessions, which they received back later from the penitent king.

In the same year the king besieged and attacked the castle of Newbury [Berks.], which is not far from Winchester, and eventually took it by assault.* Then he besieged the castle of Wallingford, and at the entrance to the bridge he built a castle to impose a blockade, which prevented those trapped inside from having food taken in and from free passage. They now began to be gravely pressed, and sought from their lord the duke of Normandy that he would either send them aid or permit them to surrender the castle into the king's hands.

33. So in the eighteenth year of King Stephen [1153], the duke of Normandy, compelled by this great emergency, unexpectedly has- tened into England. At that moment, wretched England, long since destroyed, but now, through his coming, about to recover life, broke down in tears, with these words:*

Duke Henry, greatest descendant of great Henry, I am falling into ruin— I, noble England, am falling, though not yet in complete ruin. I can scarcely say 'I had been', for 'I am' has departed. If even the hope that remains for the wretched remained for me, I would cry, 'Have mercy, come, help, stop! Rightfully I belong to you, so you have the power—raise me from my fall.' But now my speech freezes, my voice, my life are going. Yet what is this shouting? 'He comes', they say again, 'he comes'. Who? 'He who is the commander of commanders, a boy in years, an elder in mind.' Hail, jewel of manhood, my hope—while I have hope—greeting! You come too late: I have passed away. But you cry, 'England, arise! Or rather, rise again! Dead one, I give you back your life.' Revived at the sound of your voice, I shall rise again after death. So coming back to life, I tremble at what I see. Do you see the great battles that Stephen is stirring up? 'I want him to start them, for surely there would be no glory if he stirred up no battles.' How many have you led against Stephen's numer- ous forces? 'Few.' Why few? 'The glory is greater when the few conquer the many than when the many do so.' Do the French king, counts, nobles—every one of them—rise up together against you? 'The damage is light: absent I fight back against them, while present I fight for you.' Why both at the same time? 'I shall tell you. If the battle is not twofold, neither shall my glory be twofold. It is much more brilliant to conquer kings than to conquer one king.' Who is your standard-bearer? 'The grace of Christ Himself, which my action, and equally the king's, win for me. For peace alone is pleasing to me, and discord to the king. I sow the seeds of peace, though belatedly; through the bloodshed I seek peace for you, my sweet foster-daughter, for whom I have taken on such great dangers. May I gain possession of you only if, through me, you gain peace. If not, may I die, rather than see you dying.'

34. So when the glorious duke, driven onwards by a storm, had landed on England's shores, the country, blasted by fast-moving rumours, rattled like a reed-bed struck by the quivering west wind.* The news flew, and as usual scattered its seeds—overthrow to some, joy and happiness to others, fear and grief to others. While his men rejoiced greatly at his coming, yet they were somewhat disturbed that he had brought only a few supporters with him. On the other hand, the small numbers of his force went some way towards alleviating the enemy's anxiety. Both sides marvelled at it. That he should have embarked on a stormy sea in the very middle of winter his supporters considered to be heroic, while others thought it rash. But the valiant young man, hating to delay, gathered his men, both those he had found there and those he had brought with him, and laid siege to the castle of Malmesbury [Wilts.]. Since the chivalrous achievements of such a great man are many and great, they must be outlined only briefly, as a fuller description of his deeds might lead to verbosity. He immediately assaulted the fortress that was under siege, for he would never suffer delay in his undertakings, and soon captured it. But when the town had been stormed, the very high keep, of which Jordan had custody by royal authority, remained reducible only by starvation; whence Jordan came out at great speed to take the news to King Stephen.*

Distressed by these evil tidings, the king's face changed from grandeur to wrinkled grief, but he lost no time in gathering all his forces and pitching his tents not far from Malmesbury. On the day after his arrival, he drew up his battle lines in handsome style, filling them with elite horsemen and disposing them according to military precepts. It was indeed a huge army, densely packed with numerous nobles and gleaming with golden banners, and it was both very terrible and beautiful, but God, in whom alone is perfect safety, had retired far away from them.* Opening heaven's floodgates, He sent such squalls into their faces, submitting them to such rigours of harsh cold and such a battering by tempestuous gales,* that God Himself seemed to be fighting on the duke's side. Nevertheless, though buffeted by fearful calamities, they marched in battle order, as if contending against the power of God.

The young man's army was stationed nearby, trusting more in its courage than in its numbers. However, they were given especial strength by God's grace, which He had mercifully brought them because of the justice of the cause for which they stood. They were drawn up not far from the walls of the said town, beside the flowing waters of the river [Avon], which torrential rain and snow had rendered so fast-moving and swollen, that it was terrifying to attempt to ford and impossible to get out of. The illustrious young man marched at the head of his men, distinguished by arms worthy of so great a leader, his bodily appearance reflecting the beauty of his character. He was so dignified in his bearing that one may say that it was not so much that his arms were befitting to him as that his grace gave splendour to his arms. Whereas he and his men had the storm on their backs, it was in the faces of the king and his men, with the result that they could neither hold up their weapons nor handle their spears, which were dripping with water. God had provided that He would deliver the land to His child without bloodshed, and so, when neither of them could cross the river and the king could no longer endure the great floods, he returned to London, frustrated in his exertions and worn out by troubles.

The consequent surrender of the keep which the duke had besieged gave him encouragement to hasten to carry out the purpose of his visit, namely, the relief of the castle of Wallingford, which was now on the verge of starvation. So he gathered a force of knights to bring aid by conveying provisions to Wallingford castle, and God favoured his undertaking, allowing them to achieve this in peace.

Although there were in the area numerous castles packed with royal soldiery, by God's will these were unable to hinder their coming and going. After a short respite, the valiant duke called up all the troops who supported him, and laid siege to the castle of Crowmarsh [Oxon.]. Beginning this arduous and uncertain business laudably, he surrounded the king's castle and his own army with a great rampart, so that his own forces had egress only by way of the castle of Wallingford, while the besieged had no way of escape at all.

When the king heard this, he gathered all the forces from the lands in his power, and came down to overawe the duke. But the duke, quite unmoved by fear, even though he was outnumbered by the royal army, ordered the immediate destruction of the rampart which had served to protect his army, and abandoning the siege he drew up his lines and marched in splendour against the king. When the royal army saw the enemy battle lines unexpectedly rising up against them, they were struck by sudden panic. But the king, not put off by any alarm, commanded that squadrons from his castles should come forth in fearful array.

Then the nobles, or rather the traitors, of England set themselves up, making peace among themselves, for although they loved discord more than anything, they were unwilling to go to war, since they did not care to raise up either Stephen or Henry, lest if one of them were defeated, the other should be free to lord it over them, but rather that if one were in continual fear of the other, neither would be able to exercise royal power over them. So when the king and the duke each discovered their followers' treachery, they were reluctantly compelled to arrange a truce between themselves. God, however, bestowed His customary favour on the young man who was His own. For the royal castle [Crowmarsh] which the duke had besieged was demolished according to the terms of the agreement. Later, the king and the duke, both alone, on either side of a stream, had talks about arranging a lasting peace between them, each of them anxiously complaining of the treachery of his nobles. This was a foretaste of the peace treaty, but it was postponed to another time.

35. So when they had returned to their own affairs, with the quarrel still unresolved, the dawn of perfect happiness broke for the great duke. His fiercest and most powerful enemies—namely, the king's son, Eustace, and Simon, earl of Northampton—who were in fear of nothing of the kind, were destroyed at the same time by the providence of God. As a result of this unexpected turn of events, the courage and hopes of all those opposing him vanished. Both young men* died of the same disease and in the same week. Earl Simon was buried at Northampton, sated with every kind of lawlessness and with every kind of indecency. The king's son was buried in the abbey which his mother had founded at Faversham [Kent]; he was a man proven in military skill, but obdurate against the things of God, very harsh towards the incumbents of churches, very loyal towards those who persecute the Church. Thus, having removed the strongest enemies of His beloved Henry, God Himself was already in His great kindness preparing the tranquillity of His realm.

36. Henry undertook his third siege around the castle of Stamford [Lincs.]. The town was quickly taken, and the men in the keep, who were holding out against the duke, sent messengers to the king, begging for aid for those who were inside. The king, however, had

besieged the castle of Ipswich [Suff.], which Hugh Bigod was holding against him, and since he was unwilling either to give up that
siege or to send help to those trapped inside Stamford castle, it
was surrendered to Henry, the great prince. But the castle that
the king was besieging was surrendered to the king. The duke of the
Normans left Stamford for Nottingham, and quickly captured the
town. But the men in the castle set fire to the town, and the duke,
moved by compassion and grief at the burning of the town, took his
army elsewhere.

37. Meanwhile, Archbishop Theobald was deeply concerned in dis-
cussions with the king on the subject of making a peace treaty with
the duke. He had frequent conversations with the king in person,
and with the duke through intermediaries. He had as his helper
Henry, bishop of Winchester, who earlier had thrown the realm into
grievous disorder, delivering the crown of the kingdom to his brother
Stephen, but now, seeing everything destroyed by robbery, fire, and
slaughter, he was moved to repentance, and worked towards the
ending of such evils through concord between the princes. Now
especially the determination of God, 'creator alike of peace and
woe',* which brought to an end England's well-deserved scourging,
granted them success in their undertaking. By His will the serenity
of peace shone forth when the concord was strengthened by oaths. O
what boundless joy! what a blessed day! when the illustrious young
man was gloriously received in the city of Winchester, led by the
king, with a glittering procession of bishops and famous men, and
applauded by a countless multitude of the people. The king adopted
him as his son, and made him heir to the kingdom.* Then the king
took the duke to London, and there he was received with no less joy
by an innumerable assembly of the common people, with splendid
processions, as was fitting for such a great man. Thus the mercy of
God brought to the broken realm of England a dawn of peace at the
end of a night of misery.

38. When these things had been done, King Stephen and his new
son went their ways in great joy and love, soon to meet again. This
peace was ratified before Christmas [25 December 1153]. On the
octave of Epiphany [13 January 1154], they reconvened at Oxford,*
when the duke had already spent almost a year in the conquest—or
rather the resuscitation—of England. There, at the king's command, the English magnates paid to the duke the homage and fealty

due to their lord, but they were to maintain the honour and faith due to the king while he lived. Delighting in the new peace, they went away joyfully from this magnificent assembly to their own territories.

After a short while they met again at Dunstable.* But there the brilliant day became somewhat clouded over. For the duke was displeased that the castles which had been built for evil purposes all over the land since King Henry's death were not being demolished, as had been settled between them and confirmed in their permanent treaty of peace. Many of the castles had, indeed, been pulled down. But the forbearance or cunning with which the king spared certain of the castles that belonged to his men seemed to impair the mutual observation of the bargain. When the duke complained of this to the king, he suffered a rebuff. But complying with his new father, he regretfully let the matter pass, in order not to appear to be snuffing out the lamp of reconciliation. So they each went their own way in peace. And not long afterwards, having received the king's permission, the victorious duke returned to Normandy.

39. These are the deeds of Henry, the most energetic of young men, on his second visit to England.* Let no one be angry with me because I set down in writing only a few of the many splendid deeds that he performed. From so many great kings and events spread over such a long period of time, I could have compiled a comprehensive history which would need to be in many books, but instead I have undertaken an abbreviated history in a single volume, so that past events may not be unknown to future generations. Now let us return to the subject in hand.

The glorious duke returned to Gaul and was received with appropriate rejoicing and honour by his mother and brothers, and by all the people of Normandy, Anjou, Maine, and Poitou. King Stephen, moreover, ruling in peace, now for the first time had the power, thanks to his adopted son, to gain possession of what was rightfully due to the royal dignity. O detestable madness of mortal men! O abominable corruption! Certain 'sons of men, whose teeth were weapons and arrows, and their tongue a sharp sword',* made it their greatest concern to sow the seeds of discord between the king who was on the spot and the duke who was absent. The king was scarcely able to withstand their persuasive arguments, and it was thought by some that as time passed he was beginning to yield. Not unwilling, yet pretending to be so, he listened too freely to the counsels of the wicked. But the sons of men thought one thing and God thought another: bringing what He had begun to its proper conclusion, He reduced to nothing the counsels and the perverse machinations of the wicked. For after the king had besieged and eventually taken a castle called Drax, near York, and had triumphantly destroyed many other castles, he marched to Dover to have talks with the count of Flanders. While he was talking with him he was struck by illness and then by death, on the eighth day before the feast of All Saints [i.e. 25 October 1154], and he was buried in the abbey of Faversham beside his wife and son, after a troubled and unfortunate reign of nearly nineteen years.

40. Accordingly, Archbishop Theobald and very many of the nobility of England sent messengers to hasten to their lord the duke of Normandy, that he might come without delay to take up the kingship. He was, however, detained by winds and a rough sea and a host of other obstacles, and arrived at the New Forest a few days before Christmas, with his wife and brothers, and with many leading men and large forces. Although England was therefore without a king for six weeks, by God's protecting grace she did not lack peace, through either love or fear of the king who was on his way. After he had arrived, as described, he went directly to London, where, as befitted a man so great and so blessed by God, he was hallowed as king with the utmost jubilation and with tears of joy, and in the greatest splendour he was placed on the throne of the kingdom. I have written in hexameters* of the happiness of that time:

The king has died, but England, although without a king, is not without peace. You, Henry, foremost on earth, work this miracle. Not yet king, not yet present, you achieve what the king could not when he was present, you who are most worthy to wield the sceptre. How well will you bear the sceptre, who already hold the reins of the kingdom! Not yet do you bear the sceptre, delayed beyond the high seas, but through you, though still without you, England enjoys peace. Phoebus, this dawn has outshone thy splendours! Lo! you come in radiance: your beams as you approach us are steadfast faith, cheerful clemency, prudent power, light yoke, fitting punishment, sweet correction,* chaste love, steady honour, restrained desire. So with these beams, while you lend beauty to the beauteous sceptre, you adorn the crown more than the crown adorns you.

England, long numbed by mortal chill, now you grow warm, revived by the heat of a new sun. You raise the country's bowed head, and with tears of sorrow wiped away, you weep for joy. With tears you utter these words to your foster child: 'You are spirit, I am flesh: now as you enter I am restored to life.'

And now a new book* must be devoted to a new king.

V

ON CONTEMPT FOR THE WORLD,
DRAWN FROM MY OWN EXPERIENCE

PREFACE

Walter,* once the flower of youth and the darling of your age, now, alas! you are being wasted by a lingering illness and consumed by grievous pain. In the joyful prime of our lives, I wrote for you a book of epigrammatic verse, and I also composed a poem on love,* which was worthy of your acceptance. As a young man, I dedicated to you, also young, the writings of my youth; as an old one, I send you, now also old, the work of my old age. So I have written for you and for myself some thoughts on contempt for the world, which may occupy your attention in your illness, and to the most important passages of which I shall myself often return.

I shall not debate by means of rhetoric, or consider in the manner of philosophy, what is thundered forth in every page of holy scripture and exercises the great minds of all the philosophers. Rather I shall speak with utter simplicity, so that it may be clear to the many (I mean to the less educated), and I shall speak of events that you and I have witnessed. Would that we old men, taking note of this, might learn to hold in contempt what is contemptible! Accordingly I shall consider nothing from history books and nothing that has been narrated above, but rather what I know from having seen it for myself, since the law admits only such testimony. If the names of people in our time seem strange to future generations, or if this treatise seems rough, irrelevant, and tedious because so many names are introduced, at least it will, I am sure, be of use to you and me.

1. The first chapter, then, will cover events in our church. From boyhood almost all the vices—except lust—put forth their shoots. The hardiest one, that rears itself up the highest and dominates the rest, is excessive love of this world. Even when the natural improvement of maturity clears away the many evils of boyhood, such as ignorance, levity, changeableness, and so on, this one evil, which is more pleasing than the rest and is flavoured with poisoned sweetness,

remains and develops. But with advancing age, what was once sooth-
ing becomes abrasive, what tasted sweet becomes bitter. Minds
almost inextricably caught up in bad habits, as if trapped by a hook,
are held fast by riches and fleeting delights. This I have learned from
my own experience.

For when, throughout my boyhood, adolescence, and young manhood, I saw the glory of Robert [Bloet], our bishop*—I mean his
handsome knights, noble young men, his horses of great price, his
golden and gilded vessels, the number of courses at dinner, the
splendour of those who waited upon him, the purple garments and
satins—I thought that without doubt nothing could be more blessed.
When everyone, and even those who in the schools taught of contempt for the world, bowed down to him, and he himself, who was
looked upon as everyone's father and god, cherished the world with a
strong affection—if anyone had said to me then that those beautiful
things that we all admired ought to be despised, with what kind of
expression or humour would I have received it? I would have judged
him madder than Orestes,* more churlish than Thersites.* I thought
nothing could damage so great a man's so great happiness. But when
I had become a man, I heard an account of the utterly vile insults
directed at him, which if they had been said before such an audience
to me, who have nothing, I should have reckoned myself half-dead.
So I began to put a lower value on that inestimable happiness.

2. Because it usually happens that worldly men meet bitter misfortunes before death, I will relate what happened to him before he
died. Towards the end of his life, he who was justice of all England
and greatly feared by everyone, was twice sued by the king before a
low-born judge, and twice suffered heavy damages and disgrace. He
was so anguished and bewildered, that once, when I was his archdeacon and was sitting next to him at dinner, I saw that he was
shedding tears. Asked the reason, he said, 'In the old days those who
waited on me were dressed in costly apparel. Now, because of the
fines imposed by the king, whose pleasure I have always been most
diligent to serve, they have to be clothed in woollens.' He felt such
despair about the king's friendship that when he was told that the
king, in his absence, had spoken high praise of him, he sighed and
said, 'The king only praises one of his men when he has decided to
destroy him utterly.' For King Henry, if I may say so, was a man of
the utmost animosity, whose purpose was inscrutable.

A few days after this, at a hunting party at Woodstock, while the bishop was in conversation with the king and [Roger,] bishop of Salisbury (these were the highest men in the realm), he was paralysed by a stroke. Still alive, but speechless, he was carried into his lodgings and shortly afterwards, while the king was with him, he died.* The great king whom he had always served, whom he had greatly loved and feared, whom he had regarded so highly, and in whom he had placed such confidence, could give no more help to the poor man in his greatest need. Therefore reflect profitably on the saying, 'Cursed is he who trusts in man, and who makes flesh his arm.'* So when the boy, adolescent, or young man gazes on the fortunate, let him consider how uncertain their deaths may be, and that even in this world they may begin to be worn down by misfortunes. Bishop Robert was meek and humble, building up many and pulling down no one, 'the father of the fatherless',* the delight of his men, and yet this was the end that he had to endure.

3. An account ought to have been given of his predecessor, Remigius,* who came to England with King William and was present at the battle [of Hastings]; who later received the bishopric of Dorchester from the said bountiful king, and then transferred the seat of his bishopric from Dorchester to Lincoln; who founded our church, endowed the foundation with many possessions, and enhanced the endowment with most virtuous dignitaries. But I am not speaking of what I have not heard or seen, and I did not know him. But I did see all the reverend clergy to whom he gave the first appointments in the church. I will recall some of them with a few words.*

As dean he established Ralph, a revered priest. As treasurer he appointed Reiner, whose place his nephew Geoffrey still occupies. Reiner was so pious that he often chanted psalms at the tomb that he had prepared for his death, and accustoming himself to his eternal home, he spent a long time praying that when he came to lie there unable to pray, he might be visited by God's loving-kindness. Happy the example of this distinguished man. The priest Hugh should not be omitted, a memorable man, the origin and, as it were, the foundation-stone of the church. He was succeeded by Osbert, an extremely affable and endearing man. In their place there is now William, a young man of great natural talent. Guerno was made precentor. At the present time his successor Ralph is still precentor. I should not pass over Albinus of Angers, my own master. His virtuous brothers, my friends, who were renowned for their triple attainments—most profound learning, purest chastity, and supreme innocence—were nevertheless, by God's secret judgement, struck down by leprosy, but now they have been cleansed by the purification of death.

4. Remigius appointed seven archdeacons to the seven shires over which he presided. He appointed Richard as archdeacon over Lincoln. He was succeeded by Albert the Lombard. And William of Bayeux followed him. Now Robert the younger, the richest of all the archdeacons of England.*

He appointed Nicholas* over Cambridge, Huntingdon, and Hertford. None was physically more handsome, and his looks did not belie his character. Around the time of his passing, when the county of Cambridge was taken out of our diocese to receive the new bishopric [of Ely], I myself succeeded as archdeacon of the two remaining counties.

Remigius placed Nigel over Northampton as archdeacon. Robert succeeded him, and now in their place is William, the distinguished nephew of Alexander our bishop.

Remigius appointed Ralph for Leicester. Godfrey followed him. Then Walter,* an entirely praiseworthy man. Now, however, Robert de Chesney, a man rightly famous.

Remigius set Alfred over Oxford. To him succeeded Walter, the supreme rhetorician.

Remigius appointed Alfred the Small over Buckingham, to whom succeeded Gilbert, a man most polished in verse and prose, as well as in appearance. To them succeeded Roger, now become bishop of Chester. Afterwards Richard. Now, however, David, brother of the reverend bishop, Alexander, and the fifth from the beginning.

As the seventh archdeacon, Remigius appointed Osbert over Bedford. To him succeeded Ralph, lamentably murdered. To them succeeded Hugh. Now, however, Nicholas, the fourth from the beginning. The other virtuous clergy* must be omitted, lest I should be accused of verbosity.

Consider, then, how these same revered dignitaries have been deprived of life and will soon be swallowed by everlasting oblivion. Turn over in your mind all those whom we saw in the old days on the right of the choir, and on the left. Not one of them now survives. They loved what we love, desired what we desire, hoped what we hope, and death has consigned them all to oblivion. Let us consider then that the same death and oblivion await us. So let us make every effort to seek what will endure, what will be unshakeable, what will be distinct from dreams—indeed, what will be truly valuable—for these present things are nothing.

5. The second chapter in contempt of the world is about men nurtured in the lap of luxury whom we have seen brought down at the last to the greatest misery. I am writing to you in chapters so that this treatise may be more clear and lucid than having the names and deeds of various people scattered and mingled throughout.

We saw William, the king's son, dressed in silken garments stitched with gold, surrounded by a crowd of household attendants and guards, and gleaming in an almost heavenly glory. He was the only son of the king and queen, and had no doubt that he would be raised to the crown. Indeed, it may be that his certain hope of reigning in the future was greater than his father's actual possession of the kingdom: for the father had already reigned for a long time, while the son's reign was all in the future. The father, too, already reflected with anxiety of mind about losing the kingdom, while the son eagerly and joyfully longed with all his heart to possess it. I did not like the excessive reverence that encircled him, nor his immoderate arrogance, which in my opinion foreshadowed future disaster, and I said to myself, 'This pampering in his upbringing will make him fuel for the fire.'* All the time, swollen with extreme pride, he thought of his future kingdom. But God said, 'Not so the wicked, not so.'* Accordingly it came about that instead of wearing a crown of gold, his head was broken open by the rocks of the sea; instead of being dressed in gilded apparel, he was tossed about naked in the waves; instead of gaining the loftiness of kingly rule, he was buried in the bellies of fishes* at the bottom of the ocean.* This was the change in the right hand of the Most High!*

Richard, earl of Chester, too, the only son of Earl Hugh, who had been brought up in the greatest splendour in the full expectation of being his father's distinguished heir, still a beardless youth, perished in the same ship and had the same burial-place.

Richard, also, the king's bastard son, who had been agreeably brought up by Robert, our bishop, and had been shown considerable honour by me and others in the very household where I lived, whose talents we admired and of whom we expected great deeds, was in the same ship. Although there was no wind on the sea, the ship was dashed against the rocks, and Richard was carried away by sudden death and swallowed by the sea.

In the same way, when William [Clito], the king's nephew, namely, the son of Robert, duke of the Normans, now the king's sole heir* and judged worthy in the expectation of all, had gained possession of the county of Flanders by his indescribable prowess, and had conquered Thierry in pitched battle with irresistible force, he perished* from an injury caused by a small blow on the hand. All those who were serenely expecting him to become king and were passing judgement in advance on whomsoever they would, were made a laughing-stock.

6. If I were to pursue individual examples, this letter would turn into a great volume. But here I will not omit our dean, Simon, who was the son of Robert our bishop, whom he had fathered while he was chancellor to the great King William.* Being brought up, appropriately enough, in the royal household, and appointed our dean while still a boy, he soon advanced in the king's close friendship and in offices at court. He was quick-witted, a good speaker, physically handsome, radiant with charm, possessing mature discretion despite his youth, but tainted with the sin of pride. From pride there grew envy, from envy hatred, from hatred slanders, strife, accusations. He made an accurate prediction about himself when he said, 'I pass among the courtiers like salt among live eels.' For as salt tortures eels, so with his accusations he tormented all those who attended the king. But just as salt is ruined by the eels' moisture, so he was destroyed by the whispering of all. He knew the first part of the prophecy, but he did not foresee the second part. He unwittingly spoke the truth of himself. So having been elevated to the top position at court and in the kingdom, after a short time he fell headlong into the king's deepest loathing, and was put into prison, from which he is said to have escaped by way of the sewer, and still a young man he went into exile and misery. The truth of this saying was well demonstrated in him: 'Those who are brought up in beds of roses are surrounded by manure.' So we should not set a great value on noble boys or young men whose appearance, riches, and favours are dazzling to our eyes, since many of them may in time be reduced to the greatest misfortune. Then all the hopes of the foolish are dissolved, and what was brought out of nothing is returned to nothing.

7. The third section on scorn for this fleeting life (O that it were despised by me as much as my spirit desires and its merit demands!) will be on the wisdom of this world, that is to say, on the most important thing in the world. It is, indeed, 'more precious than all the wealth' of the earth 'and nothing that is desired' in the world 'is worthy to be compared with it'.* But it is written, 'The wisdom of this world is foolishness with God.'* I shall pursue this theme from the Apostle with first-hand examples.

Robert, count of Meulan,* was the wisest in secular matters of all living between here and Jerusalem. He was celebrated for his knowledge, persuasive in speech, shrewd and astute, sagaciously far-sighted, cunningly intelligent, unfailingly prudent, profound in his counsel, great in wisdom. Accordingly, by means of these qualities, he had acquired great and varied possessions, which are commonly called 'honours'—towns and castles, villages and farms, rivers and woods. His honours were not only in England, but also in Normandy and in France.* At his will French and English kings would at one time be peacefully allied and at another violently embattled. Anyone he attacked would be humbled and broken. Anyone upon whom he wished to confer benefit would be gloriously elevated. Thus his store of treasure—gold and silver, jewels and hangings—was unbelievably abundant.

8. But when he was at the height of his fame, it happened that another count stole his wife, by intrigue and violent treachery. Because of this, in his old age his mind was troubled, and, darkened by anguish, he passed into the shadows of grief, and never again experienced happiness or cheerfulness. After days given over to sorrow he fell into an illness that heralded his death, and was asked by the archbishop and priests, when they were performing the cleansing office of confession, to restore in penitence the lands which—either by force or by guile—he had stolen from many people, and to wash away his sin with tears. In answer to them he said, 'If I divide up the lands which I have brought together, what—miserable man that I am—shall I leave to my sons?' The Lord's ministers replied, 'Your original inheritance and the lands which you have justly acquired will be sufficient for your sons. Give back the rest. Otherwise you have cursed your soul to hell.' But the count replied, 'I shall leave everything to my sons; let them act mercifully for the salvation of the dead.' But after his death* his sons* took more care to increase by

injustice what had been unjustly built up, than to distribute anything for their father's salvation. So it is clear that at the end, when praise is sung, man's highest wisdom has turned not only into the height of folly, but even into blind insanity.

9. What is my recollection of Gilbert, surnamed the Universal, the bishop of London?* No one was his equal for knowledge, from here to Rome. He was most learned in the arts, unparalleled and unique in speculative thought. He enjoyed matchless and brilliant fame. On this account, while he was master of the schools at Nevers in Gaul, he was summoned to the bishopric of London, and was prevailed upon to accept. Received in high expectation, he set about devoting himself to the sin of avarice, acquiring much, giving little. Even when he died he gave nothing away, but King Henry found an infinite quantity of treasure among his hidden possessions, including his long boots, stuffed with gold and silver, which were brought into the royal treasury. So a man of supreme learning was regarded by all the people as an utter fool.

What shall I say about Ranulf, the king's chancellor? Although he was a most shrewd, astute, and skilful man, he turned the whole force of his wisdom to disinheriting the simple-minded and removing their money. But in the midst of his activities he fell into an incurable illness. Even then, as if resisting God and conquering nature, he did not cease to heap up his misdeeds, preying on those he could. His cupidity increased with his torment, his impiety with his weakness, his deceit with his pain, until he was thrown from his horse and a monk rode over him, and so death destroyed him in strange circumstances.* Out of an infinite abundance of examples, enough have been related to demonstrate the utter foolishness of this world's wisdom.

10. The fourth section deals with the prosperity of men with great names. The Lord spoke of this when He declared to David, His king, in these words: 'I have made thee a great name, like unto the name of the great ones that are on the earth.'* Whereas he possessed his prosperity with happiness, our contemporaries possess it with unhappiness, for in these times no one achieves a great name except by the greatest of crimes.

Thomas,* the great prince who ruled around Laon in Gaul, had a great name because he was supreme in wrongdoing. He was an enemy to the churches of the area and extracted money from them all for his revenues. Anyone held in his custody, by force or trickery, could have said without falsehood, 'The sorrows of hell encompassed me.'* Human slaughter was his passion and his glory. Contrary to convention, he put a countess in prison. Cruel and foul at once, he submitted her to shackles and tortures by day to extract money, and dishonoured her by night to make mock of her. She was carried from prison to the cruel Thomas's bed each night, and taken back from the bed to prison each day. Speaking words of peace, he would smilingly plunge his sword into the heart of his closest friend. For this reason he would wear his sword under his cloak, more often naked than sheathed. So everyone feared him, respected him, held him in awe. His reputation was known throughout all France. As time went on his property increased, his treasury increased, his authority increased. Do you want to hear how this wicked man met his end? He was mortally wounded by a sword, and refusing to repent, he died twisting his neck away from the sacrament of the Lord's body, so that it may rightly be said of him, that 'Your death was appropriate to your life.'*

11. You saw Robert of Bellême,* the Norman prince who was put into prison. He was a Pluto, a Megaera, a Cerberus,* or something even more fearful to describe. He would not trouble to ransom prisoners, but killed them. He tore out the eyes of his little son when he hid under his cloak, as if playing with his thumbs. He drove stakes through people of both sexes, from anus to mouth. Dreadful killings pleased and fed his mind. So he was spoken about by everyone, and sayings were told of the marvels of Robert of Bellême. At last I come to something desirable—his end. This wicked man, who had vexed others in prison, was placed in perpetual imprisonment by King Henry and perished after lengthy torments. While he lived in prison—he whom fame had so greatly cherished—it was not known whether he was alive or dead. Silence and ignorance surrounded the day of his death.*

I have written about these two among many. I have no more to say of such people, who must be feared by the demons themselves.

12. The fifth part will deal with men at the top, who in human affairs are subject to circumstances like everyone else. Kings of peoples are like God to their subjects, who all pledge themselves to them by an oath: even the stars of heaven seem to obey them. So great is the majesty of the world's highest, that others never weary

of looking at them and even those who live in their company are regarded as above mankind. No wonder that crowds of women and youths, and grown men of the shallow kind, rush to gaze at them. Even the wise and serious-minded are driven by a kind of pleasurable deference to look at those they have seen many times before.

So what is it like? What could be more agreeable? What more blessed? I wish one of them would speak to you and reveal his heart's inmost secrets. You would judge far differently. For while others consider them blessed, they are themselves twisted by pain, consumed by fear, no one in their kingdom their equal in misfortunes, no one their equal in crimes. Hence the saying, 'Royal business is wickedness.'

King Henry placed Robert, his brother and lord, in everlasting imprisonment, and kept him there until he died.* He had his nieces' eyes put out, captured many by treachery, killed many by deception, did much contrary to his oaths. He was at all times dedicated to cupidity and avarice. What terrors did he suffer when his brother Robert led his armies from Normandy to England against him? Terrified, he reached an agreement with him, but he made his leading nobles commit perjury when he broke the peace and captured his brother. What terrors did he feel when the count of Anjou destroyed his castles and he dared not march against him? What terrors when Baldwin, the count of Flanders, inflamed Normandy in front of him, and he dared not march against him? How crushed was he in spirit when his sons and daughters and nobles were swallowed up by the ocean? What cares struck him down when his nephew William obtained Flanders and Henry thought that he would himself certainly lose the crown of the kingdom? He was regarded as the most blessed of kings. But he was assuredly the most wretched.

13. What can be said of Philip, the French king, and his son Louis, who reigned in our time, whose god was their stomach, a deadly enemy indeed? For they ate so much that they lost their strength in obesity and could not stand up. Philip died of obesity long ago.* Louis has now also died of obesity, while still a young man.* But what can be said of their happiness? Was not Philip often defeated by his own men? And was he not often put to flight by the vilest of people? Was not Louis driven from the battlefield by King Henry, and frequently put to flight, it appears, by his own men?

The Norwegian king recently captured his brother king in battle. He put out his eyes. He castrated him. He cut off his right foot. He beheaded his baby son. He hanged his bishop on the gallows.* Both kings were equal in misfortune.

14. But you will object, 'Why in your *History* do you extol King Henry with such lavish praise, while here you accuse him of such great crimes?' My answer to that is: I said that the king was great in wisdom, profound in counsel, famous for his far-sightedness, out-standing in arms, distinguished for his deeds, remarkable for his wealth, and yet everything that I have added here is only too true—would that it were false. But you will perhaps go on to say, 'He has already reigned for thirty-five years, and if you add it up, he has experienced far more good luck than bad.' Against this I say: not even a thousandth part of his good fortune can be used as evidence of his happiness. What seemed happy was always mingled with grief. When he conquered the king of France in battle, with what prolonged mental agitation did he obtain that brief joy? I say brief, because very soon another army rose up and brought him fresh agony of mind. You wonder at the length of his life and his reign, but a man of God has predicted that he will not reign for two years longer. Soon you will see the wretched end of a wretched life. I wish that—if it were possible—it might go away, but it will not go away. So do not regard these unhappy kings with wonder, but rather wonder at God, who alone is happy and gives happy kingdoms to His own.

15. The sixth section, which will be the last, considers the nobility of our realm, those who have recently been in power and are still powerful. But already they are nothing, they are nowhere, and it could be said, with hardly any exaggeration, that they never were. For now scarcely any of them is remembered. All memory of them has begun to fade, and soon there will be none. 'They will come to nothing, even as running water.'* Listen then, dear friend Walter, to this discourse on the famous men* we have seen with our own eyes, though it may be tedious to hear.

In our time there shone forth Archbishop Lanfranc, a philosopher and an outstanding man. To him there succeeded Anselm, phil-osopher and saintly man. After them we saw Ralph, held to be worthy of that high office. But afterwards William presided over Canterbury, whose praises cannot be spoken because there are none. At the present time Theobald, a man deserving of all praise.

There was also in our time Walkelin, bishop of Winchester. He was succeeded by William Giffard, a member of the nobility. These are dead and have come to nothing. Now there sits in their place Henry [of Blois], nephew of King Henry, who will be a new kind of monster, composed part pure and part corrupt, I mean part monk and part knight.*

There was also in our time Gundulf, bishop of Rochester. After him Ralph. After him Ernulf. Then John. All these are dead. Now Ascelin presides, soon to die.

In our time Maurice died, the bishop of London. After him Richard. After him Gilbert, the great philosopher. Now Robert, a man of great spirit. And these are dead.

At Bath John the physician, and Godfrey. Now Robert presides there. And already these are nothing.

At Worcester I saw Sampson, a most distinguished man. After him, Theulf. Now we see Simon there.

At Chester we saw Bishop Robert. Then another Robert, surnamed Pecche. Now Roger presides, soon to be nothing.

At Norwich Herbert presided, a kind and learned man, whose writings survive. To him succeeded Everard, a very cruel man, for which he was deposed. Now William presides there.

The first bishop of Ely was Hervey. To him succeeded Nigel.

The bishop of Salisbury was Osmund. He was succeeded by Roger, a great man in secular affairs. But now Jocelin.

At Exeter there presided William, recently dead and long since blind. Now his nephew [Robert].

In Chichester Ralph presided. In his place presides [Seffrid] Pelochin, a flatterer, for which he has now been deposed.

At Durham presided W[alcher], who was murdered. After him Ranulf, whose rapacity inflamed all England. To them succeeded Geoffrey. At the present time William.

We saw Gerard, archbishop of York. After him Thomas. After them Thurstan, praiseworthy in every way. But now William, treasurer of the same church.

At Lincoln in our time Remigius was bishop. To him succeeded Robert, a most merciful man. To them succeeded Alexander, a faithful and generous man.

So much for the bishops.

16. Did you not see Hugh, earl of Chester, and Richard his son, and

Ranulf their successor, and now another Ranulf? And these are all dead.* You saw the very evil man of whom I spoke earlier, who was also very knowing in secular affairs, I mean Robert, count of Meulan. And now his son Robert, of whom little can be said in praise.* Did you not see Henry, earl of Warwick, and his son Roger, who is still alive, men with base minds?* You saw Earl William of Warenne, and Robert, count of Bellême, and Robert, count of Mortain, of whom I spoke in the *History of the English*, and Simon, earl of Huntingdon, and Eustace, count of Boulogne,* and many others. Even the memory of them is wearisome. They who were so powerful and seemed to merit eager scrutiny, are now not fit to be mentioned. Even the parchment on which their names are inscribed is utterly lost, nor do we find eyes that would wish to read it. This letter is a witness to the names of the most powerful and of all those most worthy of remembrance, yet there may be no one, or scarcely anyone, to read it.

17. What can I recall of Aldwine, my lord, abbot of Ramsey, and his successor Bernard, and afterwards Reginald, a clever but harsh man, and now Walter, a fine gentleman? Where are they? Turold, abbot of Peterborough, and Ernulf, and Matthew, and Godric, and John, and Martin,* all of whom I have seen, are dead, and come to nothing.

But you ask why, at the end, after the dead, I speak of the living as also having come to nothing. The reason is this. Just as the dead have come to nothing, so the living will soon come to it—indeed, I may say, with some freedom, that they have already done so. For, as Cicero says, what is called 'life is death'.* It follows that to begin life is to begin death.

I omit some very famous men—Ralph Basset and his son Richard, justices of all England, and Geoffrey Ridel, justice of all England, and Geoffrey de Clinton,* justice of all England, and countless others to whom in the past it seemed a pleasure to devote one's service at great cost. But now they are dead, it seems worthless to devote the briefest written notice to them.

I omit also that man of famous memory, the venerable and Christian William de Glanville, my kinsman, who was such an enthusiastic cultivator of religion that he gave and conceded all the churches of his barony to God and the church of St Andrew the Apostle [Broomholm (Norf.)] and the monks of Cluny. He also tithed the greater part of his land for the health of his soul. But now his son Bartholomew has succeeded in his place, the heir of his character and his honour, for whom, by the graciousness of God, we hope for good things, to whom we also wish good things.*

18. Think, therefore, Walter, how this present life is nothing. For seeing that the most powerful, who strove their utmost to gain their riches, have accomplished nothing, lest we also accomplish nothing, let us seek another way of life, in which we may hope for and gain blessedness. Rise, brother, rise, and seek, because in this life you have never found what you sought. Was not King Alexander [the Great], a man, one might say, who was more than very powerful, finally destroyed by a little poison? He did not find what he sought. And was not Julius Caesar—a man of equal or greater power—after he had conquered everything, killed by pens?* What he sought he did not find.

Seek therefore what you will find, seek the life after life, since in this life there is no life. O great God, how rightly are we called mortals! For our death, which surrounds us while we live, is continual. But what is called death is the end of our death. For whatever we do, whatever we say, once it is done or said, it dies immediately. It is true that the memory of them, like that of the dead, survives for a while, but when that perishes it is like a second death, in which all our deeds and sayings are totally annihilated. Where is what I did yesterday? Where is what I said? They have come to nothing. Where are what I did and said on this day last year? They have been swallowed up by the everlasting death of oblivion. Let us therefore wish for the death of this death, since we may not escape this living death, except by the death of the body, which is the frontier midway between death and life.

19. But before I have completed this letter, it has been announced that the friend to whom I was writing has yielded to death's decree. O, the lot of mortals is lowliness at birth, wretchedness in life, hardship at death! O death, how speedy your advance, how unexpected your attack, how absolute your conquest! So may He who is the physician after death give you, Walter, the medicine of His lovingkindness, so that you may lay hold on the life of everlasting health. This cannot now be sent to you as a letter, but as an epitaph, a brief memorial, to be written with tears.*

I, Henry, who bear garlands to you, first brought epigrams, next the contests of love, and then medicinal herbs.* Now, Walter, I—a wholly different man from the Henry who offered three garlands—offer a funeral lament. Half of me has died, my ornament and light have perished; the shape and spirit of the man—a spirit which will remain unrivalled. This man's habitual disposition was to give great gifts, although he did so modestly, seeming to himself to have given less than he intended. This man's habitual disposition was to make the most lavish provision, but, in preparing his many gifts, he is fearful of their being too small. This man's habitual disposition was to give with a cheerful face, and to double the gift with equal joy. This man's habitual disposition was to give so freely that no gift needed to be asked; anticipating the request, he brought double gifts in his hand. He was unrivalled, having no equal or peer in his generosity. May the supreme grace of God be with him, and grant him thankful rest.

THE MIRACLES OF THE ENGLISH

1. I have determined in this book to deal with illustrious Englishmen, and what the omnipotence of the Deity has revealed through them in miracles, so that the temporal deeds of kings and peoples might be brought to a conclusion with the glorious works of the eternal God.

Whence it is important that the Godhead Himself be implored to concede to those who speak of Him, that they may speak according to His will. For he who does not speak truly about the truth will appear ungrateful and unfaithful to the truth itself, which is God. Simple people especially, and some clever ones in the name and under the guise of religion, seem to err in assenting to instant belief in miracles which are either fictitious or are not susceptible of certain proof; indeed, ordinary people for the sake of stupid novelty, and men in religion either for money, or so that their saint's resting-place may be improperly enriched, mendaciously and fraudulently go along with these customs. In addition, if they discover any anonymous record, they are so bold as to teach and proclaim it in the revered presence of God and the holy altar, neglecting the fear of the Lord.

However, if miracles are narrated to me in this way I do not openly contradict them unless they are obviously fictitious, nor give them constant affirmation unless I observe them to be fully corroborated by well-known proofs and trustworthy persons. In fact, in this little book I have added none, or nearly none, to the miracles which that man of the Lord, the venerable Bede, whose authority is completely secure, has written in his *History*. Although wonderful and magnificent men have lived in subsequent ages, yet their deeds lack either a known author or one so trustworthy as Bede, the servant of God. But the moderns do not shine any less than the ancients, as writings in churches dedicated to God in their name gloriously attest. And now, as I have promised, the flourishing and luminous activity of illustrious men shall be made public.

2. I dealt in the first book, entitled 'The Kingdom of the Romans', with the glorified passion of the most holy martyr Alban.* St

Germanus examined the venerable remains of his body and took away with him a small part, and placed there, to join that great man in his tomb, the relics of saints which he had brought with him. A long time afterwards, at the place [St Albans*] where the holy body was buried, the great king Offa* built a famous abbey which he endowed with many estates, and when the church was complete he moved the holy body into it.

In the time of the Normans, Paul, abbot of the same place, built a great new church. His successor, Abbot Richard, in the sixteenth year of the reign of King Henry [1115], and in the king's presence, had it dedicated by the reverend Robert, the famous bishop of Lincoln.* Later their successor, Abbot Geoffrey, in the twenty-ninth year of King Henry [1129], and in the presence of Alexander, the praiseworthy bishop of Lincoln, and an innumerable gathering of people, transferred the most holy body to a shrine that gleamed wonderfully with gold and jewels.

In addition to the miracles I have copied from Bede, much true written evidence is found in the same church. This church is regarded with such honour on account of the most holy protomartyr of the English, that it is free of the papal tax called 'Rome-scot',* from which no king, earl, archbishop, bishop, abbot, or anyone else is exempt. The abbot of that place has always had the privilege of exercising the same power as a bishop over the priests and laity in his land.* For Alban, the protomartyr of Britain, should be held in the highest veneration and exalted by the English people. He dedicated their first fruits to the Lord,* and 'as the healthful morning star'* he redeems them and always prays for them, though only as far as their sins allow. To the giver of whose eternal glory is due praise and honour. Amen.

3.* In my own time, after Abbot Symeon had begun a church of wonderful workmanship at Ely, Abbot Richard his successor, the last abbot of the place (for after that, bishops were established there), moved Æthelthryth's most holy body into the new church, and at the time the most trustworthy men found her body whole and of the most beautiful colour. I firmly support the truth of this.*

A certain man who had taken refuge at her church in order to become a monk, was dragged out by the king's agents and put into prison in London for the sake of money. It is said that his shackles were cut, at their thickest point, and he was miraculously freed, by the virgin Æthelthryth herself in her own person. It was impossible for any living person to have broken the shackles. So this man, called Bricstan, was received with his miraculous shackles by the revered queen, Matilda, and by all the clergy and people of London, in a triumphal procession. When he returned he was received with honour at the church of the blessed virgin Æthelthryth. His shackles hang at the present time by the altar, to be seen and touched with wonder by visitors.*

4. *The record of recent saints**

I have collected together in a continuous sequence almost all the miracles which the great author Bede included, though in his work they were scattered according to the different periods of time. On the subject of the illustrious men who have performed miracles since the age of Bede, I have decided to say nothing, although they are not inferior or more infrequent, but, as I said above, they lack either a known author or one so trustworthy as Bede, the servant of God. But recent saints do not shine any less brightly than the ancients. If anyone should wish to put this to the test of impartial enquiry, he should seek the churches dedicated in their names, where he will see the miraculous deeds* of these miraculous men.

5.* Who, making the journey to Canterbury's celebrated cathedral will not marvel as he reads of the many great achievements of the most holy father Dunstan,* and will not burst into thankful praise of the Holy of holies? Cherishing the splendid deeds and the splendid words of this great father would cause him to cry out, 'God is wonderful in His saints!'*

Who, beholding the church of Winchester and looking at the brilliant deeds of father Æthelwold,* will not praise the Father who alone works through him and his miracles? O how many churches this bishop established for God, how many communities he designated for the practice of the monastic life, how many fires of impiety he extinguished with the dew of the Holy Spirit? In that place you will also see the praises of the holy father Swithun,* who was the diligent and godly tutor of the mighty King Ecgberht and his son Æthelwulf. With the consent of Pope Leo, Æthelwulf, though in holy orders, was made king, and ruled the kingdom successfully.* In the third year of King Æthelberht, son of Æthelwulf, the saintly man departed with glory. In that place, too, he will observe the great miracles of Birinus, bishop of Dorchester, the cathedral that has now been moved to Lincoln.*

If you visit Sherborne [Dorset], you will behold the marvellous deeds of Aldhelm, bishop of that place, the cathedral that has now been moved to Salisbury.* You will see the great triumphs of the great father, and you will burst out in praise of God, the triumphant.

At Winchcombe [Glos.] you will read of the secret martyrdom of Kenelm.* He was the son of Cenwulf, the Mercian king, who died in the year of grace 819, having reigned for twenty-four years. The martyrdom of his son Kenelm was revealed from heaven to Pope Silvester II at Rome.

At Wenlock [Salop] you will see the virginal life of Mildburg. She was the daughter of Merewalh, son of King Penda, and Domne Eafe, daughter of Eormenred, son of King Eadbald of Kent. Her sister Mildgith lies in the country of the Northumbrians. You will find the chaste life of the third sister, Mildrith,* in the Isle of Thanet.

At Buckingham, on the river Ouse, you will see the wonderful life of Rumwold.*

You may see the praiseworthy life of Neot* beside the river just mentioned, that is, the Ouse, which flows down into Huntingdon-shire, where his most holy body rests. He shone forth in the time of King Alfred and Pope Marinus [I].

You will look at the revered life of Yvo* further on down the same river. For his glorious body was revealed there 400 years after his death in the time of the long-lived King Æthelred, who reigned for thirty-seven years, and not long before the time that I can remember.*

At Ramsey, which is situated in the fens further down the said river, you will discover both the bodies and the lives of Æthelred and Æthelberht.* They were the sons of Eormenred, son of Eadbald, king of Kent, who were secretly martyred and found by a great miracle.

At Peterborough, which is situated in most beautiful fens, there rest the two virgin saints, the sisters Cyneburh and Cyneswith, sisters of Kings Peada, Wulfhere and Æthelred. Their kinswoman, St Tibba* the virgin, also lies there.

St Guthlac rests in the same verdant fen, at Crowland [Lincs.]. He lived in the days of four kings of Mercia, namely, of Æthelred, son of Penda, and of Cenred, his kinsman, who both became monks, and of Ceolred, son of the mighty King Æthelred, and in the time of Æthelbald. He died in the year of grace 715.

St Werburg* lies at Chester, and from the many stories about her, I cannot avoid mentioning one that is outstanding and unique. For it is on record that a large flock of wild geese were devouring her growing corn, so she had them confined in a certain house, as if they were domestic geese. In the morning, when she called them, ready to send them out, she saw that one was missing. On enquiry, she heard that it had been eaten by the servants. 'Bring me', she said, 'the feathers and bones of the bird that has been eaten.' When they were brought to her, this bride of the high God commanded that it should be whole and should live. 'And it was done.'* Then she instructed the geese, which were cheering and crying out at the return of their lost companion, that none of their kind must ever, in all eternity, enter that field. They all departed in safety. And the virgin's command has been obeyed to the present day.

St Wulfhild,* spurning marriage with King Edgar in favour of a vow to God, was abbess of Barking [Essex], and is buried there. Anyone seeing the miracles of the holy virgin there will praise [Christ] the bridegroom of virgins.

Edith,* daughter of King Edgar, rests at Wilton [Wilts.], and the splendid miracles of this virgin are read in that place.

6.* In my concern to be brief, I have collected these from a great number of saints: who in all their various shrines in great Britain fitly tend their saving beams, which are like the lights of heaven.* I have omitted many whose names and deeds shine out in splendour in the churches dedicated to God in their names. Happy England, to be so arrayed with the beams of these great fathers.

But someone will ask, 'Whereas in ancient times so many saints were renowned for their numerous miracles, I am totally bewildered that in our own days no glimmer of a miracle is seen, nor is there any feeble reputation that has the strength to soar above those of the past. From this it seems that either stories about the past are greatly exaggerated, or the world is now utterly forsaken by God.' My reply is that I do not concede that our age is utterly forsaken by God, but it is greatly injured and sadly overshadowed by the darkness of sin. The Lord, however, knows His own,* and the high One dwells among the humble,* who are very few. Although miracles in our times are very rare, whenever they are done they are most glorious.

Therefore I am going to make public the glorious record of a man whose living spirit still survives today.

7. *St Wulfric, venerable priest**

In the county which is called Dorset, at a town which is called Haselbury, there lived a servant of God, by name Wulfric, by profession a priest, by way of life a hermit.* He always wore a hauberk next to his flesh to subdue his turbulent passions, and begged a new one from his earthly lord, since his own was almost worn out and torn in pieces by his sweat. He put on the new one, but was enraged at its length, because it might be seen below his garment. So he snatched up the shears and cut the soldered iron rings at the bottom and in the openings of the sleeves, as if it were linen cloth. The servant of God applied the shears a second time, in case there was any unevenness, cutting it through without delay or difficulty. Seeing this, his lord was filled with immeasurable joy and sank down at the holy man's feet. The man of the Lord was embarrassed, pulled him upright, and swore him not to tell anyone what he had seen. But it could not be kept secret. For many religious devotees rejoiced to have rings from the holy hauberk, and the famous story has travelled everywhere through all parts of the kingdom. I would not have included this miracle in this cautious and carefully researched work, except that Pope St Gregory gives the narrative of father Benedict and other saints,* partly from what he had heard from a fellow monk and partly from other extremely reliable witnesses. The story of Wulfric is attested by those who have seen parts of the hauberk, or visited his delightful presence, or heard his desirable speech, or have freely sought out the religious life and taken it up themselves, and it is also spread among all the people and is commonly known everywhere.

EPILOGUE

1. This is the year which holds the writer. The thirty-fifth year of the reign of the glorious and invincible Henry, king of the English. The sixty-ninth year from the arrival in England, in our own time, of the supreme Norman race. The 703rd year from the coming of the English into England. The 2,265th year from the coming of the Britons to settle in the same island. The 5,317th year from the beginning of the world. The year of grace 1135.*

2. This, then, is the year from which the writer of the *History* wished his age to be reckoned by posterity. But since I gave hope to those starting this book that they might turn back to moral purity,* this computation will show what point in Time we have reached. Already one millennium has passed since the Lord's incarnation. We are leading our lives, or—to put it more accurately—we are holding back death, in what is the 135th year of the second millennium.

3. Let us, however, think about what has become of those who lived in the first millennium around this time, around the 135th year. In those days, of course, Antoninus ruled Rome with his brother Lucius Aurelius, and Pius the Roman was pope. Lucius, who was of British birth, ruled this island, and not long after this time, while those emperors were still in power, he was the first of the British to become a Christian, and through him the whole of Britain was converted to faith in Christ.* For this he is worthy of eternal record.

But who were the other people who lived throughout the countries of the world at that time? Let our present kings and dukes, tyrants and princes, church leaders and earls, commanders and governors, magistrates and sheriffs, warlike and strong men—let them tell me: who were in command and held office at that time? And you, admirable Bishop Alexander, to whom I have dedicated our history, tell me what you know of the bishops of that time.

I ask myself: tell me, Henry, author of this *History*, tell me, who were the archdeacons of that time? What does it matter whether they were individually noble or ignoble, renowned or unknown, praiseworthy or disreputable, exalted or cast down, wise or foolish? If any of them undertook some labour for the sake of praise and glory, when now no record of him survives any more than of his horse or his ass, why then did the wretch torment his spirit in vain? What benefit was it to them, who came to this?

4. Now I speak to you who will be living in the third millennium, around the 135th year. Consider us, who at this moment seem to be renowned, because, miserable creatures, we think highly of ourselves. Reflect, I say, on what has become of us. Tell me, I pray, what gain has it been to us to have been great or famous? We had no fame at all, except in God. For if we are famed now in Him, we shall still be famed in your time, as lords of heaven and earth, worthy of praise, with our Lord God, by the thousands of thousands who are in the heavens. I, who will already be dust by your time, have made mention of you in this book, so long before you are to be born, so that if—as my soul strongly desires—it shall come about that this book comes into your hands, I beg you, in the incomprehensible mercy of God, to pray for me, poor wretch. In the same way, may those who will walk with God in the fourth and fifth millennia pray and petition for you, if indeed mortal man survives so long.

5. Someone will ask, 'Why do you talk in this way about future millennia when the conclusion of Time will come in our own epoch and we are in daily and trembling expectation of the end of the world?' This is my answer. The day on which you die is for you the end of the world. But Christ is the conclusion of Time. He did not choose the first part of Time for His coming, but the last, in which the law and the prophets and their meaning came to an end with the coming of what they signified.* But since no one knows the extent of Time except the Father of all, what I have written is my opinion, which I derived a long while ago from Herbert, bishop of Norwich, a very learned man.* He used to say, 'According to my judgement and what I can conclude by reason, truth will endure much longer than symbol, light than shadow, the thing signified than what signifies it, the time of grace than the time of law. If the symbol and shadow preceding and signalling the grace of Christ stretched, let us say, for 5,000 years, would the light and grace of Christ be so much the greater? We see the folly of the theory of those who thought that after the Lord's Passion the world would last only a thousand years, since Christ will come in the last age. Nor is the view of the Jews to be followed, which asserts that after 6,000 years from the beginning

of the world its sabbath will start in the seventh millennium, with their return to their land and their dominion over all the earth, to be followed after a little while by the end of the whole world. But rather I believe with good cause, on the authority of Jesus Christ, that the truth promised for many ages will endure much longer.' I agreed with the bishop when he said this, and still agree.

6. I have dwelt at some length on the question of the extent of Time. This was because we shall lie decaying in our tombs for such a long time that we shall necessarily lose the memory of all bodily activities, and therefore we should think about it in advance, in order to work hard at seeking the glory, honour, goodness, wealth, dignity, and prestige that are in God. When you have gained these things, you have them and will always have them. When you have gained the things of this world, they will flow away like water from a broken pitcher, and you have nothing.*

EXPLANATORY NOTES

The following abbreviations are used:

ASC   *The Anglo-Saxon Chronicle*, ed. and trans. D. Whitelock, D. C. Douglas, and S. I. Tucker (London, 1961).

Bede, *EH*   Bede, *The Ecclesiastical History of the English People*, ed. J. McClure and R. Collins (Oxford World's Classics, 1994).

EHD   *English Historical Documents 1042–1189*, ed. D. C. Douglas and G. W. Greenaway (2nd edn.: London and New York, 1981).

Gaimar   *L'Estoire des Engleis by Geffrei Gaimar*, ed. Alexander Bell (Oxford, 1960).

GS   *Gesta Stephani*, ed. and trans. K. R. Potter and R. H. C. Davis (Oxford, OMT, 1976).

HH   *Henry, Archdeacon of Huntingdon, Historia Anglorum: The History of the English People*, ed. and trans. D. Greenway (Oxford, OMT, 1996).

JW ii   *The Chronicle of John of Worcester*, ii, *The Annals from 450 to 1066*, ed. and trans. R. R. Darlington and P. McGurk (Oxford, OMT, 1995).

JW iii   *The Chronicle of John of Worcester*, iii, *The Annals from 1067 to 1140*, ed. and trans. P. McGurk (Oxford, OMT, 1998).

OMT   Oxford Medieval Texts.

OV   *The Ecclesiastical History of Orderic Vitalis*, ed. and trans. M. M. Chibnall, 6 vols. (Oxford, OMT, 1969-80).

WM *GR* i William of Malmesbury, *Gesta Regum Anglorum: The History of the English Kings*, i, ed. and trans. R. A. B. Mynors, R. M. Thomson, and M. Winterbottom (Oxford, OMT, 1998).

WM *HN* William of Malmesbury, *Historia Novella: The Contemporary History*, ed. and trans. Edmund King and K. R. Potter (Oxford, OMT, 1998).

I. PROLOGUE

The prologue contains Henry's statement of his moral purpose in writing the *History*. On prologues, see A. Gransden, 'Prologues in the Historiography of Twelfth-Century England', in her *Legends, Traditions and History in Medieval England* (London and Rio Grande, 1992), 125–51.

  3 *literature*: in this paragraph Henry draws on classical literature, quoting Horace (*Epistles* i. 2. 3–4), and introducing the four cardinal virtues—prudence, temperance, fortitude, and justice. It was not directly from Homer's *Iliad*, even in its abbreviated Latin version, that Henry knew of the Homeric heroes, but from his rhetorical training, in which discussion of their virtues and vices played a part.

3 *sacred history*: the Old Testament. In this paragraph Henry uses incidents and characters chiefly from Genesis, Exodus, Numbers, Samuel, Kings, and Chronicles.

4 *perpetual silence*: for the sentiments of this paragraph, cf. Sallust, *Catilina*, i. 1.

   Bishop Alexander: bishop of Lincoln, 1123–48; see above, Introduction, pp. xv–xvi.

   Venerable Bede . . . chronicles preserved in ancient libraries: for Henry's use of Bede and the Anglo-Saxon Chronicle, see above, Introduction, pp. xxii–xxiii.

   commence by calling on Him: this prayer takes the form of a twenty-hexameter poem. Its opening, 'O Adonai', recalls a prayer sung on 18 December. The divine name 'Adonai', deriving from the Hebrew word for 'master' or 'Lord', is applied in Christian liturgy to Jesus Christ.

5 *as the prophet attests*: Isa. 45: 7; the text is cited also below, IV. 37.

II. 1000–1087: THE COMING OF THE NORMANS

This book was written by c.1130. For the family relationships of the dukes of Normandy, the kings of England, and the kings of Scots, see the Genealogical Tables.

6 *daughter of Richard*: Emma, daughter of Duke Richard I (946–96), and sister of the current duke, Richard II (996–1026); see Genealogical Table I.

   the law of peoples: in Roman law, the law of peoples justifies warfare in self-defence and to avenge an injury. Here and below, c. 27, it is said to justify the Norman Conquest. It is also referred to below, IV. 21, relating to an incident in Stephen's reign.

   A certain man of God . . . confusion: referring to Archbishop Dunstan's prediction on his deathbed (d. 988), that because of their sins the English would suffer fearful daily misfortunes inflicted by foreign races. Henry relates the prediction to the Norman Conquest and also to an invasion by the Scots (either that of 1076 or that of 1093).

   In addition . . . and garments: this 'prediction', not found in any other source, reflects Henry's distaste for the fashions of his own day.

7 *in my childhood . . . old men*: as a child in the 1090s Henry may have heard stories from old men whose fathers or grandfathers had been eyewitnesses. The recollection shows that Henry spoke English as a boy.

8 *like a reed-bed . . . west wind*: this simile, which suggests Henry's familiarity with the fenland landscape, is used also below, IV. 34.

   'I will turn . . . into mourning': Tobit 2: 6; Amos 8: 10.

9 *messengers*: this information is not found elsewhere. In 1009, in face of the Danish threat, it would have been desirable for Æthelred to ensure that the Danes did not find shelter or support in Normandy.

10 *Mireneheued, that is 'ant's head'*: ASC has *myran heafod*, correctly understood in JW ii. 466 as 'mare's head'. But Henry takes *myre* to be the same as Middle English *mire*, 'ant'.

the previous book: a reference to Henry's description of the fenland and its churches, HH, pp. 321–3.

tossing them . . . their lances: this gruesome image is used again below, IV. 6.

And withdrawing . . . whole army: the story is known only from this passage. Balsham is south of the Gog Magog hills, and about 8 miles south-east of Cambridge. It was within the area of Henry's father's archdeaconry. The Anglo-Saxon church tower at Balsham no longer exists: it may have been one of a type of stone church tower that had a defensive function.

The river Ouse . . . beasts and fish: another passage based on Henry's local knowledge.

11 *Northumbria*: at this period the southern part of Northumbria reached the river Humber and included York.

Lindsey . . . the Five Boroughs: Lindsey was the northern division of Lincolnshire; the Five Boroughs were the Danish strongholds of Leicester, Nottingham, Derby, Stamford, and Lincoln.

13 *histories of the ancients*: referring to the lengthy annal *ASC* 1016, summarized in the following paragraph. Cf. also 1 Kgs. 15: 7.

14 *'the last day of the war and of the Danes'*: cf. Vergil, *Aeneid*, ix. 759.

between the dragon and . . . the 'Standard': the dragon was the banner of Wessex and the 'Standard' was the king's personal ensign.

15 *'Flee, Englishmen . . . Edmund is dead'*: this story of Eadric's treachery, not found in *ASC*, is told in JW ii. 487–9 and WM *GR* i. 315 of the earlier battle of Sherston. Only Henry gives Eadric's words in English. C. E. Wright, *The Cultivation of Saga in Anglo-Saxon England* (Edinburgh and London, 1939), 186–91, argues that this account derives from English narrative or saga.

in Alney and began the duel: Alney is an island in the river Severn in Gloucestershire. The story of the duel is not found in *ASC* or JW. In WM *GR* i. 317–19, Edmund suggests single combat, but Cnut declines. In Gaimar, vv. 4251–352, the setting is Deerhurst in Gloucestershire. See Wright, *Cultivation of Saga*, 191–8. The duel as a method of trial which revealed the judgement of God was introduced with the Norman Conquest: see R. Bartlett, *Trial by Fire and Water: The Medieval Judicial Ordeal* (Oxford, 1986), 103–26.

This is how he was killed: the following story of Edmund's murder is told in different versions by two other writers of Henry's time, William of

Malmesbury, WM *GR* i. 319, and Gaimar, vv. 4403–24, and by Walter Map, writing in the 1180s or 1190s (*De Nugis Curialium*, ed. and trans. M. R. James, C. N. L. Brooke, and R. A. B. Mynors (Oxford, OMT, 1983), 429–31). See Wright, *Cultivation of Saga*, 198–206.

15 *Eadric came to King Cnut*: the following story is found variously in WM *GR* i. 321, Gaimar vv. 4441–78, and Walter Map, *De Nugis*, 431–3. For a suggestion that the common source of this and the previous story is a saga-cycle about Ealdorman Eadric, see Wright, *Cultivation of Saga*, 206–12.

16 *against the Wends*: Henry is the only source for the campaign against the Wends, the Slav peoples on the southern shores of the Baltic, and for Godwine's participation. See M. K. Lawson, *Cnut: The Danes in England in the Early Eleventh Century* (London and New York, 1993), 91.

17 *Duke Richard II ... Robert for eight years*: Duke Richard II was the brother, not (as Henry says) the father of Emma. He died in 1026, not 1024. Richard III, his eldest son, died in 1027, and Robert I, Richard II's younger son, in 1035.

Robert ... succeeded by his son Henry: Robert the Pious died on 20 July 1031.

Robert duke ... at a tender age: Henry follows the incorrect dating of *ASC* 1031. In fact Duke Robert died in 1035, when his illegitimate son William was aged 8.

Rome-scot: an annual tax from England to the pope, originally a free-will gift from kings. By the eleventh century it was levied at 1d from house-holders, and as it was paid on St Peter's day, 1 August, it was also known as Peter's Pence.

marriage to the Roman emperor: the marriage between Cnut's daughter Gunhild and Henry (later Emperor Henry III), the son of the Holy Roman Emperor Conrad II, took place in 1036, the year after Cnut's death. It is not mentioned in *ASC* or JW, but appears in WM *GR* i. 339, with the interesting note that 'the wedding ceremony ... even in our own day is still the subject of popular song'. Henry's knowledge of it may have derived from a traditional ballad.

as the tide was coming in: this is the first written account of Cnut's attempt to turn back the tide. It appears in a slightly different form in Gaimar, vv. 4693–722, where it is placed at Westminster, on the Thames, not at the sea. For discussion, see Lawson, *Cnut*, 133–8.

18 *Normandy's ... royal treasury*: this anachronistic statement reflects Henry's observation of the French king's assertion of feudal overlordship of Normandy in the twelfth century; see David Bates, *Normandy Before 1066* (London and New York, 1982), 61.

every port had rendered eight marks of silver for sixteen ships: a mistranslation of *ASC* 1040, 'sixty-two ships should be paid for at eight marks to each rowlock'.

19 *He had been honourable . . . once a day*: this passage has no parallel in any other source.

Alfred, the first-born son of Æthelred: in fact, Alfred was the younger of the two surviving sons of Æthelred and Emma, and was killed at Ely not in 1042 but in 1036, at the time that his elder brother, Edward, attempted an invasion of England; for this event, its context, and sources, see Keynes, 'The Æthelings in Normandy', *Anglo-Norman Studies*, 13 (1991), 173–205, at 195–6, and cf. F. Barlow, *Edward the Confessor* (London, 1970), 45–6. The following account of Alfred's death was written *c.* 1140, about ten years after most of the rest of the book and at the same time as the Conqueror's speech before Hastings, below, II. 29. It was inserted at the wrong point, after the death of King Harthacnut, instead of after the death of Cnut. Later in the narrative (II. 27), Henry gives as one of the reasons for the Norman Conquest the desire by Duke William to avenge his murdered kinsman Alfred, mentioned also in the Conqueror's speech (II. 29).

20 *Siward . . . in his place*: Siward was never archbishop, but was assistant to Archbishop Eadsige.

Val-ès-Dunes: at this battle in 1047, to the south-west of Caen, the French king gave William crucial help in defeating the rebellious Norman nobles.

Beorn: earl of the east midlands, nephew of King Cnut and brother of Swein, king of Denmark (1047–76).

successor Siward: Siward was the archbishop's assistant, not his successor.

21 *Swegn his son*: Swegn was not with Godwine, but had gone from Bruges to Jerusalem and was to die on the return journey.

'Northmouth': the northern mouth of the Kentish river Stour.

Around this time Siward . . . or my son: Siward's son was Osbeorn (*ASC* 1054). Henry's account of Osbeorn's death probably derives from a *Siwards Saga*, perhaps preserved in oral tradition in the locality of Huntingdon, where Siward held some east midland estates. This story and that of Siward's own death (below, c. 24) are discussed by Wright, *Cultivation of Saga*, 127–35, 266–70.

22 *tasted endless death*: *ASC* 1053 C, D, reports that Godwine died, having been 'taken ill while sitting with the king at dinner at Winchester'. The embellished story told here by Henry is shared by WM *GR* i. 355. There seems to be an allusion to the Last Supper, and the piece of bread given by Christ to Judas Iscariot (John 13: 23–7). 'Windsor', the scene in Henry's version, may be a mere slip for 'Winchester', found in *ASC* and WM *GR*. See Wright, *Cultivation of Saga*, 233–6, 296–8.

Ralph the chamberlain: no earlier source mentions Ralph, the chamberlain, whose death is referred to again, below, II. 29; his identity is unknown.

gave up his spirit with honour: Wright, *Cultivation of Saga*, 128–35, argues

that Henry's account of Siward's last words and death derives from a lost
Siwards Saga; cf. above, II. 22.

22 *Waltheof . . . small boy*: neither *ASC* nor JW mentions Waltheof at this
point. Henry may have guessed that Waltheof was still a boy, or known
it from local tradition in the Huntingdon area. Waltheof probably
succeeded to the counties of Huntingdon and Northampton on Tosti's
banishment in October 1065.

23 *Now Harold . . . perjury*: the story of Harold's journey and oath is not
found in *ASC* or JW, but has a Norman origin, occurring in various early
versions, all discussed by Barlow, *Edward the Confessor*, 220–9. Harold's
visit to Normandy took place in the summer of 1064 or 1065, but Henry
seems to place it in 1062. Henry is alone in saying that Harold had set out
for Flanders. For a discussion of the identity of William's daughter and
the various accounts of her betrothals, see F. Barlow, *William Rufus*
(London, 1983), 442–3.

It happened . . . outlawed and exiled: this passage is not paralleled in any
other source. In fact Tosti, the third son of Godwine, was younger than
Harold, the second son.

24 *usurped the crown of the kingdom*: *ASC* says, 'Earl Harold succeeded to the
realm of England, just as the king had granted it to him, and as he had
been chosen to the position.' The idea of Harold's usurpation depends
on the Norman story of the oath, told above, II. 25.

murdered his kinsman Alfred: for the murder of Alfred, and the accusation
against Godwine, see above, II. 20.

the law of peoples: cf. above, II. 1.

25 *leaders . . . his word*: Henry is the first writer to describe William Fitz-
Osbern's ruse.

The site . . . the city: the battle was fought at Fulford, 2 miles south of the
centre of York. This sentence suggests that Henry had visited York,
about 80 miles north of Lincoln.

Mars: the god of war.

single Norwegian: the following story does not appear in eleventh-century
sources. It was known to William of Malmesbury, WM *GR* i. 421, and
was added in the late twelfth century to *ASC*, version C.

on the same day: the battle of Stamford Bridge was fought on 25 September and Duke William landed on 28 or 29 September.

Hastings: for detailed discussion of the battle and the background, see S.
Morillo, *The Battle of Hastings: Sources and Interpretations* (Woodbridge,
1996).

a speech: Henry composed and inserted this speech, *c.*1140. There are
parallels in the speech at the battle of the Standard in 1138, which Henry
also wrote *c.*1140 (below, IV. 8). For the intellectual background to the
ideas of 'the Norman achievement', see R. H. C. Davis, *The Normans and*

their Myth (London, 1976), 49–69. The elements of twelfth-century battle-speeches are analysed by J. R. E. Bliese, 'Rhetoric and Morale: A Study of Battle Orations from the Central Middle Ages', *Journal of Medieval History*, 15 (1989), 201–26.

26 *Hasting*: the conquests made by the Norse leader Hasting form the main topic of book I of Dudo of Saint-Quentin's *Customs and Acts of the First Norman Dukes*; see trans. by E. Christiansen, *History of the Normans* (Woodbridge, 1998).

Rou, my ancestor: Rollo, traditionally the first 'duke' of Normandy from 911. Henry's use of the French, 'Rou', suggests that he used a French vernacular source, possibly based on Dudo's work.

victor of angels: in this otherwise unknown story about Duke Richard II, there is probably an allusion to the archangel Raphael catching and binding a demon, in Tobit 8: 3.

Ralph: cf. above, II. 24, where the death of Ralph the chamberlain is also reported.

27 *the oath he made to me*: see above, II. 25.

my kinsman Alfred: Alfred was the son of William's grandfather's sister; for his murder, see above, II. 20, 27.

Taillefer: versions of the story of the juggler appear also in two verse narratives: the Latin *Carmen de Hastingae Proelio of Guy Bishop of Amiens*, ed. and trans. F. Barlow (Oxford, OMT, 1999), 24–5, and the French Gaimar, vv. 5261–99. Henry's use of the French form *Taillefer* (meaning 'iron-cutter') suggests that his source for the story was French, perhaps a song or a poem.

into the air: Henry and other chroniclers seem to have been inspired by the scenes of archers aiming upwards in the lower border of the Bayeux Tapestry: *The Bayeux Tapestry*, ed. F. M. Stenton (2nd edn.; London, 1965), nos. 70–1.

28 *struck in the eye*: both Henry and William of Malmesbury (WM *GR* i. 455) seem to have been influenced by scenes nos. 71–2 in the Bayeux Tapestry; see also D. Bernstein, 'The Blinding of Harold and the Meaning of the Bayeux Tapestry', *Anglo-Norman Studies*, 5 (1983), 40–64.

a change . . . the Most High: Ps. 77: 10.

the comet: Halley's comet, which is particularly large and active, has an orbit of *c.*76 years and was visible in 1066. Henry quotes an anonymous Latin couplet.

St Calixtus: a mistake, as the feast of Calixtus is 14 October but the battle took place on 14 September.

29 *castle . . . survives today*: the castle at Ely is not mentioned in *ASC*. Henry's knowledge of it may be accounted for by the fact that his father's archdeaconry had included Ely. Today it is probably to be identified with the motte and bailey in the Park at Ely ('Cherry Hill').

30 *cursed his son Robert*: the only other source to mention the curse is the
    'Chronicle of Hyde', in *Liber Monasterii de Hyde*, ed. E. Edwards (Rolls
    Series, 1866), 297. The best account of the career of William's eldest son,
    Robert Curthose, is still C. W. David, *Robert Curthose Duke of Normandy*
    (Cambridge, Mass., 1920).

    Urban was made pope at Rome: Gregory VII died in 1085, to be succeeded
    in the following year by Victor III, who died in 1087. Urban II was
    elected in 1088 and died in 1099. Henry was probably misled by the
    compression of these events in the Norman annals.

    kept among the treasures: Henry adds to his translation of *ASC* 1085 the
    comment about the keeping of the records of the survey, i.e. Domesday
    Book, in the royal treasury at Winchester. His information on this point
    doubtless came from Bishop Alexander, nephew of Henry I's first minis-
    ter, Bishop Roger of Salisbury; cf. other details about the royal treasury
    below, II. 40, IV. 5, and V. 9.

    not yet finished: like the main portion of this book, this was written *c.*1130.
    The Norman church of St Paul's replaced the Anglo-Saxon one,
    mentioned above, II. 8, 24.

    clothed . . . arms of manhood: the ceremony of giving arms to a young
    warrior to make him a knight on coming of age. Henry was 18 in 1086.
    For similar occasions, see below, IV. 29.

31 *In King William's twenty-first year . . . Sicily and Antioch*: Henry restates
    the theme of God's punishment of the faithless inhabitants of Britain and
    also delivers a penetrating judgement on the Norman character and
    achievement. Apulia and Calabria were acquired by Normans in 1059
    and Sicily by 1072; see Davis, *The Normans and their Myth*, 71–100.
    Antioch was taken by the crusaders in 1098 and formed Bohemond's
    principality. The basis of the rest of this chapter and c. 39 is the obituary
    of William I in *ASC*.

    'Whence it may be had . . . they must': Juvenal, *Satires*, xiv. 207, quoted in
    ASC.

33 *took the land away from him*: not found in *ASC*, this refers to the western
    peninsula of Normandy, the Cotentin.

    In the treasury . . . and hangings: this information probably came to
    Henry from his sources at court, principally Bishop Alexander; cf.
    above, II. 36.

    there were present: the list of bishops that follows is possibly drawn from
    the witness-list of a royal charter for Lincoln cathedral, now lost.

    justice and ruler of all England: the description should probably apply to
    William of Saint-Calais, bishop of Durham, not to Odo of Bayeux; see
    Barlow, *William Rufus*, 61 n. 35, and 67–8.

    Remigius, bishop of Lincoln: for Remigius's career, see D. Bates, *Bishop
    Remigius of Lincoln 1067–1092* (Lincoln Cathedral Publications, 1992).
    See also below, V. 3–4.

a few words: the following account of Remigius is Henry's own record.

34 *Lindsey*: the division of the county of Lincolnshire in which the city of Lincoln was situated was adjacent to the diocese of York. For the dispute, see Bates, *Remigius*, 20–1, 34.

treason: Bates, *Remigius*, 13–15, discusses this mysterious reference, possibly to the revolt against Rufus by Bishops Odo of Bayeux and William of Durham in 1088 (below, III. 1).

hot iron: one of the types of trial by ordeal. If the accused's burns were healing cleanly three days after handling red-hot iron, innocence was proved. The accused's part might be taken by a representative, as in the case of Remigius. On the subject of ordeal, see Bartlett, *Trial by Fire and Water*.

it was said: the following couplet is unlikely to be Henry's work, and its position may suggest that it came to hand after he had completed the book. For the comet in 1066, see above, II. 30; and for the omen of war and revolution, cf. Lucan, *Civil War*, i. 528–9, 'the hair of the comet . . . which portends change to monarchs'.

III. 1087–1135: THE KINGDOM OF THE NORMANS

This book, down to 1129 (c. 40), was written by *c.*1133. The rest of the book was certainly complete by *c.*1140. For the family relationships of the dukes of Normandy, the kings of England, and the kings of Scots, see the Genealogical Tables.

35 *I have either seen . . . did see them*: Henry was born *c.*1088, around the time of the first events of this book.

5,000: a misreading of *ASC*'s '500'.

37 *Bloet . . . agreeable in conversation*: Henry adds to *ASC* Bloet's surname and a personal note on his appearance and character. For Bloet, in whose household Henry was brought up, see Introduction, p. xv.

He regretted . . . behaved correctly: Henry's own account of the settlement of the dispute over the boundaries of the archbishopric of York, based on personal knowledge.

39 *the crusade*: for the most part, the account of the First Crusade that follows is drawn, directly or indirectly, from *Gesta Francorum*, ed. and trans. R. M. T. Hill, *The Deeds of the Franks and other Pilgrims to Jerusalem* (Oxford, OMT, 1979). There are also some echoes of material found in other crusading sources. Several passages, especially in the battle-scenes, represent Henry's embellishments, written in a colourful, rhetorical style, but perhaps based on a lost source such as a narrative poem. For the surviving sources, see S. Edgington, 'The First Crusade: Reviewing the Evidence', in Jonathan Phillips (ed.), *The First Crusade: Origins and Impact* (Manchester, 1997), 57–77.

40 *battle is waged*: the battle of Dorylaeum, 1 July 1097.

42 *Suliman*: Kilij Arslan Ibn-Sulaiman was son of Sulaiman, Selchükid of Rum, and is called 'Suliman' (Solomon) in all the western chronicles.

43 *victory to His people*: cf. 2 Macc. 10: 28; 1 Cor. 15: 57; Ps. 29: 11.

44 *the sand of the sea*: cf. Ps. 78: 27.

the sons of God . . . the devil: cf. 1 John 3: 10.

45 *George, Mercurius, and Demetrius*: the cults of these three warrior saints originated in the Greek Church.

His name only was exalted: Ps. 148: 13.

47 *took the city*: the siege of Jerusalem is here drastically abbreviated. As told in *Deeds of the Franks*, cc. 38–9, pp. 89–93, the siege was long and difficult, and the city was not taken until 15 July.

refused it: the story of the offering and refusal of the crown is a later invention, not found in the earliest accounts, though it was known also to William of Malmesbury, WM *GR* i. 703.

pledge . . . Jerusalem: William paid Robert 10,000 marks towards his crusading costs, in return for custody of the duchy for three years.

48 *only half large enough*: Henry is the sole source for this saying.

The sailors . . . in the waves: the scene is not in *ASC*. A similar story appears in WM *GR* i. 565–7 and Gaimar, vv. 5825–32.

49 *in his own hands . . . let out for rent*: after the death of a bishop or abbot a king was permitted to take the revenues of their estates. By delaying the appointment of successors, Rufus and other kings made exorbitant profits and impoverished the churches.

debauchery: on the suspicions shared by Eadmer, William of Malmesbury, and Orderic Vitalis that homosexuality and promiscuity were rife at Rufus's court, see Barlow, *William Rufus*, 102–10.

amendment of laws and customs: the coronation charter, in which Henry I made fourteen promises, is printed in *EHD*, 432–4.

50 *Robert of Bellême*: see below, V. 11.

forbade English priests to have wives: the prohibition of clerical marriage concerned Henry personally; for his own marriage, see Introduction, p. xiv. Councils summoned by archbishops and attended by the bishops and senior clergy, were used to publicize church laws and check up on clergy discipline.

51 *Tinchebrai*: the following account of the battle of Tinchebrai (Sept. 1106) is independent of any other source; its accuracy is confirmed by the fuller account in OV, vi. 89–91.

the bugles . . . harsh calls: cf. Vergil, *Aeneid*, viii. 2.

The Lord . . . perpetual imprisonment: see c. 18 above, for Robert's supposed refusal of the crown of Jerusalem, which in Henry's eyes doomed him. After Tinchebrai he was imprisoned for the remainder of his life, finally dying in 1134; cf. below, V. 12.

52 *exalts . . . down the mighty*: Luke 1: 52 (the canticle, *Magnificat*).

wisdom, victory, and wealth: God's three gifts to Henry I reappear in the king's obituary, below, IV. 1.

Henry . . . in marriage: the emperor ruled the remnant of the Roman empire in the west (known as the Holy Roman Empire), which was centred in western Germany. Matilda was the king's only legitimate daughter.

in a manner . . . fitting: the first of three waspish comments about the empress; for the others, see below, III. 41, 'the pomp that befitted such a great heroine', and III. 43, 'the machinations of none other than the king's daughter'.

I have said this: the following two-line elegy is Henry's pious memorial to his father, Nicholas, first archdeacon of Huntingdon, for whom see below, V. 4, and above, Introduction, p. xiv. Nicholas died on 13 March 1110.

53 *May his soul rest in peace, Amen*: Henry's prayer for the repose of his father's soul is a quotation from the text of the funeral Mass.

a great dispute . . . Ralph and Thurstan: Thurstan denied that York was subordinate to Canterbury, and avoided promising obedience to Ralph by having himself consecrated as archbishop at Reims in 1119. For the history of the long-running dispute, see F. Barlow, *The English Church 1066–1154* (London and New York, 1979), 37–46.

William his son: Henry I's only legitimate son and therefore his heir.

St Albans: the dedication is also mentioned below, VI. 2.

54 *he died*: Henry gives a more detailed account of his death below, V. 7–8.

The wisdom . . . foolishness with God: 1 Cor. 3: 19.

I have said this: Henry's poem is of six lines in elegiac metre.

the French king: for the battle of Brémule, fought on 20 August 1119, this is one of four independent sources (the others are: OV, vi. 235–43; Suger, *Vie de Louis VI le Gros*, ed. H. Waquet (Paris, 1929), c. 26, pp. 196–8; 'Chronicle of Hyde', in *Liber Monasterii de Hyde*, ed. E. Edwards (Rolls Series, 1866), 317–18).

55 *I have written in hexameters*: for Henry, the victory was an event of major historical significance, fit to be celebrated in eight hexameters, the 'heroic' metre.

Noyon: Brémule is close to Noyon-sur-Andelle, south-east of Rouen.

56 *shipwrecked*: the king's only male heir, William, and two illegitimate children were drowned in the sinking of the *White Ship* of Barfleur; see also below, V. 5. The fullest account is OV, vi. 295–301, where Orderic blames the sailors' drunkenness for the disaster. With only the Empress Matilda left of Henry I's legitimate children, his nephew, William Clito ('clito' is Latin for 'prince'), the son of Robert Curthose, now had a strong claim to the throne; see below, III. 37.

56 *I have written of it*: Henry's poem is an eight-line elegy.

elegiacs: Henry's poem is of ten lines.

57 *Windsor . . . Durham*: Henry is the only source for the royal visits to Windsor and to Durham.

his life ended: only Henry mentions Ranulf's illness and gives the circumstantial detail of the place and cause of death (to which he refers again below, V. 9). If the illness involved physical deformity, this may explain why, alone of Henry I's chancellors, he did not gain a bishopric. See J. A. Green, *The Government of England Under Henry I* (Cambridge, 1986), 28, 160, 179 n.

men and beasts: Henry I had a park at his palace of Woodstock (Oxon.), where he kept exotic animals, such as lions, leopards, lynxes, camels, and a porcupine (WM *GR* i. 741).

epitaph: another eight-line elegy by Henry. Below, V. 2, Henry retells the story of the bishop's death with details that suggest he may have been present.

second to the king: for Roger's career, see Green, *Government Under Henry I*, 273–4.

58 *council in London*: as papal legate, John of Crema was the pope's personal representative and had the power to call church councils and promulgate ecclesiastical legislation.

Moses, God's scribe: Moses was thought to be the writer of the Pentateuch. See Genesis for the examples of vice that follow: Lot, 19: 30–8; Reuben, 49: 4; Simeon and Levi, 49: 5–7; Joseph's brothers, 37: 12–36.

a true law of history: this expression derives from Jerome, quoted by Bede, *EH*, 5, 361.

a whore: Henry, who, as a married archdeacon, had a close interest in the issue of clerical marriage, is the only source for this defamatory story.

I have said in hexameters: eleven hexameter lines. Bishop Alexander was the patron of the *History*, and the subject of seven hexameters above, I. 5; and see Introduction, pp. xv–xvi.

59 *steadfast faith . . . correction*: these phrases are reused below, IV. 40.

Woodstock: Henry is the only source for the king's stay at Woodstock during Lent and Easter 1127.

Charles, count of Flanders . . . at Bruges: Count Charles was murdered in the church of St Donatian in Bruges on 2 March 1127.

Flanders to William, your nephew and enemy: William Clito, the son of Robert Curthose, had a claim to Flanders through his grandmother, Matilda, daughter of the count of Flanders (see Genealogical Table I). After the death of Henry I's son William in 1120, Clito was considered by some, including Henry of Huntingdon, to be the rightful heir to the crown of England: see below, V. 5.

council in London: Henry is the only source for this royal council.

Winchester: Henry is the only source for the king's stay at Winchester.

Epernon for eight days: Henry is the only source for this invasion into French territory. Epernon is 15 miles north-east of Chartres.

60 *origin . . . the Frankish kingdom*: the Trojan origin myth and the genealogy from Faramund that follow are derived ultimately from a compilation of Frankish history, such as the *Liber Historiae Francorum*. Cf. WM *GR* i. 99–103.

a monk at the end: in fact, Philip I did not become a monk.

61 *present time*: Louis VI was consecrated as king on 3 August 1108 and died on 1 August 1137.

a pitched battle: this must refer to the battle of Axspoele, 21 June 1128. Henry is the only English chronicler to refer to this battle.

died: William Clito died at the siege of Aalst, which began on 12 July 1128; see OV, vi. 375–7.

Galo the versifier . . . an equal god: having given a garbled version of the first 2 lines of the epitaph, Henry's memory failed. The text of the twelve-line elegy is known from another source. The poet was probably Galo, a member of the poetic circle of Baudri of Bourgueil. See HH, 836–8.

his son . . . as king: Henry is the only English chronicler to mention this event. It was a common practice for medieval kings to have their heirs crowned in their lifetime; cf. below, IV. 32, for King Stephen's attempt to have his son Eustace crowned.

present at this council: possibly this list represents Henry's personal observation.

62 *the king . . . released them*: the king collected fines from married arch-deacons and priests for licences to continue in their marriages; cf. *ASC*.

books of Moses and Kings . . . go unpunished: the only remotely similar texts are Lev. 18: 25 and Deut. 18: 12.

Damascus: it is possible that Henry (who reported the beginning of the expedition above, c. 39) heard of the disaster at Damascus from an eye-witness, perhaps Saher of Archelle, a Lincolnshire landowner (see HH, pp. xcix–c).

a broken neck: Henry is the only English chronicler to mention the accident, which occurred in 1131.

nothing: this is the end of Henry's first and second versions of the *History*, completed by *c.*1133.

treason: Henry is the only English source for the trial of Geoffrey de Clinton, though it is mentioned in OV, iv. 277.

63 *Dunstable . . . Woodstock*: Henry is the only source for the royal courts at Dunstable and Woodstock.

63 *assembly at London*: Henry may well have been present at this council at London in 1132, for which he is the only narrative source.

ill at Windsor: Henry is the only source for this.

council at London: Henry is the only source for this council in 1133, and may have been present.

Oxford . . . Winchester: Henry is the only source for these two royal visits.

64 *Lyons*: Lyons-la-Forêt is in a forest *c.*18 miles east of Rouen.

lampreys: small eel-like vertebrates, found predominantly in freshwater, eaten as a delicacy in the Middle Ages (though not easily digestible). Henry is the first writer to give lampreys as the cause of the king's death.

We always strive . . . is refused: Ovid, *Amores*, iii. 4. 17.

aged body: he was 68 when he died.

a memorial, if he has deserved it: the sentiments of this ten-line elegy are belied by the bitter obituary (version A) at the beginning of the next book.

IV. 1135–1154: THE PRESENT TIME

This book was written in at least four sections: down to 1138 (c. 9) was complete by *c.*1140; to 1146 (c. 25) by *c.*1147; to 1149 (c. 28) by *c.*1149; to 1154 (c. 40) by *c.*1155. It begins with an obituary of Henry, written before *c.*1140 (version A), which was so harsh that it had to be modified by the author *c.*1153 (version B), when it became clear that Henry I's grandson, Henry II, would succeed Stephen as king. For a modern narrative and analysis of Stephen's reign and the sources, see R. H. C. Davis, *King Stephen, 1135–1154* (3rd edn.; London and New York, 1990). For the family relationships of the dukes of Normandy, the kings of England, and the kings of Scots, see the Genealogical Tables.

65 *three brilliant qualities*: God's three gifts to Henry I—wisdom, victory, and wealth—are first mentioned above, III. 26.

Version A: written before *c.*1140.

the count of Mortain: William, count of Mortain, was Henry I's cousin (see Genealogical Table I). He had been imprisoned since his capture at Tinchebrai in 1106 (above, III. 25, 26). Henry is the only chronicler to state that he suffered blinding: this may be true, as it was indeed a punishment favoured by Henry I in cases of treason.

King Solomon: Solomon 'loved many foreign women', and had 700 wives and 300 concubines; 1 Kgs. 11: 1, 3. Henry I was the father of at least twenty-one illegitimate children.

Version B: a revision composed *c.*1153, when it was clear that Henry II was going to succeed Stephen. The length of the substituted passage is exactly the same as Version A—sixty words—suggesting that in his autograph copy Henry made an erasure and wrote over it.

66 *mad treacheries*: an echo of Lucan, *Civil War*, ii. 544.

Stephen . . . of Blois: Theobald was the second and Stephen the third son of Stephen, count of Blois (for whom see above, III. 5, 6, 8, 13), and Adela, daughter of King William I (see Genealogical Table I).

oath . . . King Henry: at III. 37, above, Henry omitted to mention the oath to Matilda demanded by the king at the Christmas court in 1126.

tried God's patience: cf. Ps. 78: 18, 41, 56.

the one who had struck . . . beyond a year: the biblical reference is inaccurate: the man who struck Jeremiah was Pashhur, Jer. 20: 2, whereas Jeremiah's prophecy of death within a year related to Hananiah, Jer. 28: 15–17.

Roger . . . of Salisbury: for Roger, see above, III. 35. For his arrest and death, see below, IV. 10–11.

in the twinkling of an eye: 1 Cor. 15: 52.

stench: on the moral criticism implied in the statement that the body stank, the opposite of the 'odour of sanctity', see R. Morse, *Truth and Convention in the Middle Ages* (Cambridge, 1991), 1–2.

67 *buried King Henry*: the burial took place on 5 January 1136.

these: King Stephen's two 'charters of liberties', one given at London and the second at Oxford, are printed in translation in *EHD*, 434–6.

canonical election: in church law the cathedral clergy had the right to choose their bishop, though the king's approval was necessary to secure the restoration of the bishopric's revenues which he enjoyed during vacancies; cf. above, III. 22.

the woodlands . . . innocent party: the introduction by William I of royal forests and special laws to protect them (above, II. 39) criminalized hunting, the cutting of trees, pasturing of animals, and new ploughing within prohibited areas, even where settlements were already in existence, and gave the king the monopoly of hunting deer and boar throughout the country. The classification of land as 'waste' meant appropriation to the Crown.

Danegeld . . . remit for all time: the promise is not contained in either charter, but that it was made by Stephen is confirmed by JW iii. 203.

68 *Norwich castle*: Hugh Bigod's taking of Norwich castle is not otherwise recorded. Henry may have heard of it from his kinsman, William de Glanville, a Norfolk tenant (son of Robert de Glanville, for whom see Introduction, p. xiv).

Brampton . . . Huntingdon: Henry is the only source for the visit to Brampton, of which presumably he knew from local knowledge.

69 *Dunstable at Christmas*: this occasion is not otherwise recorded.

Alexander . . . with him: Henry is the only source to mention that Bishop Alexander accompanied the king to Normandy.

69 *Eustace his son*: Eustace, who was born *c.*1130, was betrothed in 1140 to Constance, the daughter of King Louis VI, below, IV. 10. At the end of 1146 or the beginning of 1147 he was knighted by his father, who also gave him the title and honour of count of Boulogne. The Church refused Stephen's request to crown him in 1152 (below, c. 32), and he died in August 1153 (below, c. 35).

the two last: this reference to the years 1139 and 1140 indicates that the passage was not completed before 1140.

70 *queen*: Stephen's wife, Matilda (see Genealogical Table I).

urged them on as follows: the battle of the Standard took place on 22 August 1138. The rhetoric of this battle-speech may be compared with that of the Conqueror's speech before Hastings (above, II. 29), composed about the same time, *c.*1140. Ailred of Rievaulx drew on Henry's *History* for his account of the battle; he put a similar speech into the mouth of Walter Espec, a Yorkshire baron: 'Relatio de Standardo', *Chronicles of the Reigns of Stephen, Henry II and Richard I*, ed. R. Howlett (Rolls series, 1886), ii. 181–99.

72 *Albani*: the Albani are the inhabitants of Albany, a term for Scotland which is found also in *GS*, 55. The Albani are mentioned in the ninth-century *Historia Brittonum*, which was used and developed by Geoffrey of Monmouth. He derived Albany from Albanectus, son of Brutus: *Geoffrey of Monmouth: The History of the Kings of Britain*, trans. L. Thorpe (Harmondsworth, 1966), 75. The true derivation is from the Celtic word for Scotland, Alban.

the battle: the following account of the battle of the Standard is fuller than any other, and alone gives the information about King David's son Henry and his mounted force. Prince Henry was earl of Huntingdon (above, IV. 4).

11,000 Scots: statistics in medieval chronicles are unreliable, and this figure should be taken to mean 'a great many'.

73 *Canterbury*: this marks the end of Henry's third version of the *History*, completed *c.*1140.

Leeds . . . after Christmas: Henry is the only source for this.

Vulcan: the god of fire. 'Mars and Vulcan', here and below, IV. 29, is a rhetorical term for sword and flame.

this Henry . . . the enemy: Henry is the only source for this incident.

Devizes: *GS*, 79, says that Alexander was also taken to Devizes. For a full discussion of the whole affair, see E. J. Kealey, *Roger of Salisbury, Viceroy of England* (Berkeley, Los Angeles, and London, 1972), 173–208.

Eustace: JW iii. 285 dates the betrothal to February 1140.

74 *council at Winchester*: WM *HN*, 51–9, gives a very full account of the council, which began on 29 August 1139. For Henry of Blois's career, see F. Barlow, *The English Church 1066–1154* (London and New York, 1979), 87–8.

royal crown-wearings: these impressive ceremonies, introduced by William the Conqueror, were held at the major festivals of Christmas, Easter, and Whitsun.

75 *elegiac verses*: the poem of eighteen lines expresses Henry's bitterness and sorrow over the civil war and breakdown of law and order.

Lincoln . . . by deceit: Ranulf had a hereditary claim to the office of sheriff and hence to the custody of Lincoln castle.

battle: Henry's narrative of the battle of Lincoln is probably the fullest contemporary account and is doubtless based on local knowledge.

76 *prepare my way*: cf. Isa. 40: 3.

young man: in 1141 Ranulf was not young, having been born, like Earl Robert, before 1100.

judges the peoples with equity: Ps. 67: 4.

from His high dwelling . . . look down: Deut. 26: 15.

no hope in flight: cf. Sallust, *Catilina*, lviii. 16.

your opponents: the comments on individuals that follow, although they are put into the mouth of Earl Robert and presumably are intended as character assassination rather than accurate portrait, may well represent, albeit with some exaggeration, Henry's view, as a member of Bishop Alexander's circle.

77 *Alan, duke of the Bretons*: Alan III (the 'Black'), count of Brittany and lord of Richmond. Bishop Alexander had an old hatred for Alan: the animosity between them precipitated the brawl among their men that immediately preceded Alexander's arrest in 1139.

the count of Meulan: Waleran was deeply implicated in persuading Stephen to arrest the bishops, and in instigating the brawl that was the pretext for the arrest.

set aside his daughter: John of Salisbury, *Historia Pontificalis: Memoirs of the Papal Court*, ed. and trans. M. M. Chibnall (Oxford, OMT, 1986), 84, reports Hugh Bigod's sworn testimony, before Archbishop William in December 1135, that King Henry, on his deathbed, had changed his mind and designated Stephen as his heir: this evidence was used at Rome in 1139, when Henry may have been present.

That earl: William III de Warenne, earl of Surrey, dismissively referred to as 'the man from Warenne', below, IV. 18.

fugitive William of Ypres: a grandson of Robert the Frisian, count of Flanders, William was a 'fugitive' because he had been banished from Flanders in 1133; he had lands in Kent, and as Stephen's mercenary captain he was one of his most consistently loyal supporters.

78 *seething in a great sea of troubles*: cf. Vergil, *Aeneid*, viii. 19.

a candle . . . broke in pieces: at Mass on the feast of the Purification of the Blessed Virgin, 2 February (Candlemas), candles held by the congregation are blessed. Similar stories appear in *GS*, 111–13, and OV, vi. 545.

78 *the pyx . . . fell*: this is not found elsewhere, and presumably came to Henry from the first-hand testimony of Bishop Alexander. A pyx is a container for the consecrated bread at Mass.

Baldwin: Baldwin Fitz Gilbert of Clare, the son of Gilbert Fitz Richard of Clare, and lord of Bourne, Lincs. Two MSS of the *History* have line-drawings of the scene as Baldwin addressed the royal troops.

80 *blare of trumpets*: cf. Lucan, *Civil War*, i. 237.

in the twinkling of an eye: 1 Cor. 15: 52.

hissing: the sound of arrows moving through the air.

all against him, he against all: cf. Gen. 16: 12.

William of Cahagnes: only Henry gives the name of the king's captor. William was probably a tenant of the bishop of Lincoln and belonged to an east-midland family that came originally from Cahagnes in Normandy. From the thirteenth century the family name was spelt with a K; cf. John Maynard Keynes and the place Milton Keynes.

81 *Richard Fitz Urse*: his son Reginald Fitz Urse was to become infamous in 1170 as one of the murderers of Archbishop Thomas Becket.

received as Lady: a preliminary to being crowned at Westminster, but Matilda's arrogance was to lead to her expulsion before the ceremony could take place: see below, and Davis, *King Stephen*, 52–7.

82 *resembled the snow*: Henry is the only writer to mention the camouflage clothing.

law of peoples: cf. above, II. 1.

den of thieves: Matt. 21: 13.

seeking . . . now dead: the powers of a legate, in this case Bishop Henry of Winchester, ceased on the death of the pope who had appointed him.

83 *Lincoln . . . business unfinished*: Henry alone reports this aborted siege of Lincoln.

he died: Geoffrey was besieging Burwell (in east Cambs., 4 miles north-west of Newmarket) when he received a fatal wound in the head.

God was asleep, He was aroused: the allusion is to the Psalms, especially Pss. 78: 65 and 121: 4. *ASC*, under the year 1137, says: 'they said openly that Christ and his saints were asleep.'

84 *Indeed, in the same year . . . for evermore*: none of the material in this paragraph appears in any other source. For the casting of lots at sea, cf. Jonah 1: 7.

his church: for the architectural history of Lincoln minster during the period, see R. Gem, 'Lincoln Minster: ecclesia pulchra, ecclesia fortis', *Medieval Art and Architecture at Lincoln Cathedral* (British Archaeological Association, 1986), 9–28.

85 *King Stephen . . . dared to do so*: Henry is the only contemporary source for this crown-wearing at Lincoln, and for the superstition.

not fearful of danger: this marks the end of the fourth version of the *History*, completed *c.*1147.

the Virgin of virgins: Lincoln minster is dedicated to the Blessed Virgin; cf. above, II. 41. *GS*, 199, gives a much briefer account of Earl Ranulf's attack on Lincoln in 1147.

took the Cross: i.e. became crusaders. Henry is well informed on the Second Crusade, perhaps from Saher of Archelle (cf. above, p. 133). For a modern narrative, see H. E. Mayer, *The Crusades*, 2nd edn., trans. J. Gillingham (Oxford, 1988), 93–106.

Moses: cf. above, III. 36.

86 *God despised them*: Ps. 53: 5.

God resists . . . the humble: Jas. 4: 6; 1 Pet. 5: 5.

England: it is not quite true that the English formed a majority of the forces at Lisbon; the combined forces from Boulogne, Flanders, and Cologne probably outnumbered them.

spiritual cheer: this marks the end of the fifth version of the *History*, completed *c.*1149. For Robert de Chesney as archdeacon of Leicester, see also below, V. 4.

Henry: this is the first notice in the *History* of the future Henry II, son of Empress Matilda and Count Geoffrey of Anjou, and nephew of the king of Scots (see Genealogical Tables I and II). He was born in March 1133 and thus was 16 years of age at the time of his knighting.

87 *council in London*: Henry is the only chronicler to notice this council, at which he may have been present in the entourage of Bishop Robert of Lincoln.

appeals: the growing practice of taking ecclesiastical law-suits to the pope was not welcomed by defendants, who feared the expense, or by the English church courts, who saw a diminution of their own jurisdiction.

88 *death*: Geoffrey died on 7 September 1151.

Henry: Henry succeeded as count of Anjou, Maine, and Touraine. Unknown to Henry of Huntingdon, he had become duke of Normandy earlier, between November 1149 and March 1150, when his father abdicated the duchy in his favour.

married her: Eleanor of Aquitaine was the heiress of William, count of Poitou and duke of Aquitaine (see family-tree in W. L. Warren, *Henry II* (London, 1973), 43). Louis VII's divorce from Eleanor had taken place in March 1152; Duke Henry married her around 18 May and thus gained Aquitaine and Poitou.

royal crown: for the practice of crowning the king's heir during his lifetime, cf. above, III. 40.

88 *summoned there*: Henry's is one of only two contemporary accounts of this meeting, at which he was possibly present.

Newbury ... assault: Henry is the only contemporary chronicler to mention the siege and taking of Newbury.

89 *these words*: the following poem, consisting of thirty-one hexameters, is the longest in the *History*. For the personification of a country, and its dialogue with the leader, cf. Lucan, *Civil War*, i. 185–203 (Caesar at the Rubicon).

90 *like a reed-bed ... west wind*: the same image is used above, II. 3.

Jordan ... King Stephen: from *GS*, 233, it is clear that Jordan was a traitor who handed over the castle to Duke Henry.

retired far away from them: cf. Ps. 10: 1.

squalls ... tempestuous gales: extreme weather conditions in late January and early February 1153.

92 *young men*: Eustace was aged about 23 at the time of his death. Simon of Senlis, however, was at least 40, having been born some time before 1113.

93 *creator alike of peace and woe*: Isa. 45: 7, quoted also above, I. 5.

heir to the kingdom: the treaty of Winchester is detailed in a royal charter issued at Westminster in November 1153: printed in translation, *EHD*, 436–9.

Oxford: Henry is the only authority for the meeting at Oxford.

94 *Dunstable*: Henry is the sole chronicler to record this meeting.

his second visit to England: it was his second visit as an adult; for the first, in 1149, see above, c. 29. He had been to England as a boy in 1142–3 and 1146–7.

sons of men ... a sharp sword: Ps. 57: 4.

95 *hexameters*: a final poem of twenty lines.

steadfast faith ... correction: these phrases are reused from above, III. 36, the eulogy on Bishop Alexander.

96 *a new book*: Henry of Huntingdon died sometime between 1156 and 1164. If he wrote any of the next book it has failed to survive.

V. ON CONTEMPT FOR THE WORLD

This is Henry's most sophisticated piece of writing, composed in the form of a letter, in which his personal reminiscences ('drawn from my own experience') are presented rhetorically and are decorated with classical allusions, imaginary dialogue, and poetry. The piece consists of a series of vivid character-sketches of virtually all the great men of Henry's times, both lay and ecclesiastical, arranged to illustrate six aspects of worldliness and its penalties. Originally drafted in 1135, and appearing first *c.*1140 in the third version of the *History*, it received some slight revision for the fourth version, *c.*1146, when Henry brought up to date the lists of clergy in cc. 3–4 and 15.

97 *Walter*: the addressee, who died before the completion of this piece, was probably the man who was archdeacon of Leicester and left office some time after *c.*1133; see *Fasti Ecclesiae Anglicanae 1066–1300*, iii, *Lincoln*, comp. D. E. Greenway (London, 1977), 32–3.

epigrammatic verse . . . poem on love: all eight books of poems on love are lost, but two of the eight books of epigrams survive (see HH, pp. cxii–cxiv, 805–25).

98 *Robert [Bloet], our bishop*: see Introduction, p. xv.

Orestes: son of Agamemnon and Clytemnestra, who avenged his father's death by slaying his mother and her lover, and was driven mad by the Furies.

Thersites: a Greek in the siege of Troy, famous for his ugliness and his biting tongue.

99 *died*: the details of Bloet's death, which occurred on 10 January 1123, suggest that Henry may himself have been present on the occasion. See also above, III. 34, with an epitaph.

Cursed . . . arm: Jer. 17: 5.

the father of the fatherless: Ps. 68: 5.

Remigius: for his career, see note above, p. 128. The present passage is the only direct source for Remigius's presence at the battle of Hastings.

a few words: the following account of the clergy of Lincoln cathedral between 1072 and *c.*1146 is the most detailed to survive for any Anglo-Norman cathedral, and forms the basis for the early lists of deans, precentors, masters of the schools, treasurers, and archdeacons in *Fasti Ecclesiae Anglicanae 1066–1300*, iii, *Lincoln*.

100 *the richest . . . of England*: the earliest documentary evidence for the wealth of the archdeaconry of Lincoln is the papal taxation of 1291, when Lincoln was indeed by far the wealthiest of all the English archdeaconries.

Nicholas: father of Henry of Huntingdon; see Introduction, p. xiv.

Walter: probably the addressee of this letter; see above.

other virtuous clergy: in addition to the dignitaries (i.e. office-holders) named above, there were at any one time at Lincoln cathedral in this period around thirty ordinary canons.

101 *fuel for the fire*: cf. Isa. 9: 5; Ezek. 21: 32.

Not so the wicked, not so: Ps. 1: 4.

bellies of fishes: cf. Jonah 2: 1.

bottom of the ocean: for the drowning of William, the king's son and heir, in the *White Ship* in 1120, cf. above, III. 32, with a poem on the tragedy.

a change . . . the Most High: Ps. 77: 10.

102 *king's sole heir*: reflecting the view of Bishops Alexander of Lincoln and

Roger of Salisbury, Henry saw William Clito, son of the Conqueror's eldest son, Robert Curthose, as the rightful heir to the crown after Henry I's only legitimate son, William, was drowned in 1120. See W. Hollister, 'The Anglo-Norman Succession Debate of 1126: Prelude to Stephen's Anarchy', *Journal of Medieval History*, 1 (1975), 19–41, esp. pp. 25 and 28–9.

102	*perished*: William Clito died in 1128; see above, III. 39, where Henry gives a fuller account than any other English source.

Simon . . . King William: Robert Bloet was chancellor to William Rufus from 1091 to 1094, that is, before his consecration as bishop. Simon was dean of Lincoln between *c.*1113 and *c.*1123. The following passage is the only source for Simon's parentage, character, and fall from royal favour.

103	*more precious . . . compared with it*: Prov. 3: 15.

The wisdom . . . with God: 1 Cor. 3: 19.

Robert, count of Meulan: the following passage is an expanded reworking of the account given of Robert's death above, III. 30.

England . . . Normandy . . . France: he possessed, among other territories, the honours of Leicester in England, Beaumont-le-Roger and Ivry in Normandy, and Meulan in France (between Rouen and Paris).

his death: Robert died on 5 June 1118.

his sons: he had twin sons: while Robert succeeded to his English properties and the earldom of Leicester, Waleran inherited Meulan and the Norman and French estates. For their careers, see D. Crouch, *The Beaumont Twins* (Cambridge, 1986).

104	*Gilbert . . . bishop of London*: a biblical scholar, he was bishop of London 1127–34.

strange circumstances: a more detailed account of the strange death of Ranulf the chancellor, in 1123, is given above, III. 34.

I have made . . . the earth: 2 Sam. 7: 9.

Thomas: Henry is the only English chronicler to mention the sadistic cruelties of Thomas of Marle, who is called 'the most evil man of this generation' in the contemporary Memoirs of Guibert of Nogent (*Self and Society in Medieval France*, ed. J. F. Benton (Toronto, 1984), 170, and cf. 184–8 and 198–205).

105	*The sorrows . . . encompassed me*: Ps. 18: 5.

Your death . . . your life: Ovid, *Amores*, ii. 10. 38.

Robert of Bellême: for an assessment of his career and of Henry's accusations, see K. Thompson, 'Robert of Bellême Reconsidered', *Anglo-Norman Studies*, 13 (1991), 263–86. See also above, III. 20, 24, 25, 28.

a Pluto, a Megaera, a Cerberus: Pluto, the king of the underworld; Megaera, one of the Furies; Cerberus, the three-headed monster.

the day of his death: Robert was captured in 1112 and kept in captivity first at Cherbourg and then at Wareham; in 1118 there was a false report of his death, but he lived on until after 1130; see Thompson, 'Robert of Bellême', 279 and n. 80.

106 *Robert . . . until he died*: cf. above, III. 25. The following reflections on Henry I may be compared with version A of the obituary, above, IV. 1.

Philip . . . long ago: Philip I died on 5 August 1108.

Louis . . . a young man: Louis VI ('le Gros') died on 1 August 1137, not a young man, as stated here, but aged 54.

107 *The Norwegian king . . . on the gallows*: Henry's account of Harald Gille, who took the kingdom of Norway in 1135 from King Magnus IV, is largely substantiated by Scandinavian sources. As Lincoln had strong trading ties with Norway, Henry may have heard the stories from merchants.

They will . . . running water: Ps. 58: 7; cf. below, VII. 6.

famous men: for the dates of the bishops named below, see *Handbook of British Chronology*, 3rd edn., ed. E. B. Fryde, D. E. Greenway, S. Porter, and I. Roy (London, 1986).

108 *part monk and part knight*: he was a Benedictine monk, but resembled a knight in his worldliness and social status: he was a grandson of the Conqueror and brother of King Stephen (see Genealogical Table I).

109 *Hugh, earl . . . all dead*: Hugh of Avranches, earl of Chester, from 1071, died in 1101; Richard, son of Hugh, became earl in 1101 and died in the *White Ship*, in 1120; Ranulf I, nephew of Hugh, became earl in 1121 and died in 1129; the last named, Ranulf, son of Ranulf, became earl in 1129 and did not die until December 1153.

Robert, count . . . in praise: see above, V. 7–8.

Henry, earl . . . base minds: Henry de Beaumont, earl of Warwick 1088–1119; his son Roger was earl 1123–53.

Earl William . . . of Boulogne: for these men, see above, IV. 15 note, 18 (Warenne), III. 20, 24, 25, 28, and V. 11 (Bellême), III. 1 (Mortain), IV. 15, 18, 35 (Huntingdon), III. 1, 5 (Boulogne).

Aldwine . . . Martin: for the abbots of Ramsey and Peterborough, see *The Heads of Religious Houses, England and Wales*, i, *940–1216*, ed. D. Knowles, C. N. L. Brooke, and V. C. M. London (2nd edn.; Cambridge, 2001), 60, 62, 253.

life is death: Cicero, *Tusculan Disputations*, i. 31. 75.

Ralph Basset . . . de Clinton: brief accounts of all these judges' careers are found in J. A. Green, *The Government of England Under Henry I* (Cambridge, 1986), biographical appendix.

110 *I omit also . . . good things*: this passage, referring to the author's kinsmen, survives in only one manuscript. For the Glanville family, see Introduction, p. xiv. William de Glanville founded Broomholm *c*.1113; his son Bartholomew occurs from 1140 and died in 1180.

110 *pens*: the spike-like 'stilus', used for writing on wax tablets, was very
     similar to a slender dagger (a stiletto).

     tears: a poem follows, of sixteen lines in elegiac metre.

111 *herbs*: in addition to the epigrams and the poem on love (above, Preface),
     we learn here of another lost work by Henry, on herbs (see HH,
     pp. cxiv–cxv).

VI. THE MIRACLES OF THE ENGLISH

The section printed below consists of cc. 1–2, 33, and 51–4 of book ix of the
History, 'The Miracles of the English', dealing with the saints of England,
which was completed by *c.*1140. The selected passages are the parts of book ix
that are not drawn from Bede, *EH*. They reflect Archdeacon Henry's attitude
towards the authentication of saints and miracles and his enthusiasm for pilgrimage to their shrines. For the Anglo-Saxon background, see D. Rollason,
Saints and Relics in Anglo-Saxon England (Oxford, 1989). Accounts of all the
saints named below will be found in D. H. Farmer, *Oxford Dictionary of Saints*
(3rd edn.; Oxford, 1992).

112 *first book . . . Alban*: HH, 57–9. Bede, *EH*, 16–19, put Alban's martyrdom
     in the time of the persecution of Christians ordered by Emperor Diocle-
     tian in 303–5; ibid. 364.

113 *St Albans*: St Albans, Herts., was within the diocese of Lincoln and
     Henry's archdeaconry of Huntingdon; see Introduction, p. xvii.

     Offa: king of Mercia 757–96.

     dedicated . . . bishop of Lincoln: the dedication is also mentioned above,
     III. 29.

     Rome-scot: see above, II. 16 note (p. 124).

     same power . . . in his land: an ancient power confirmed by Pope Calixtus
     II in 1122.

     first fruits to the Lord: cf. Exod. 22: 29.

     as the healthful morning star: Ecclus. 50: 6.

     3: this is c. 33 of book ix, HH, 663.

     In my own time . . . of this: also called Etheldreda or Audrey, Æthelthryth
     had founded the church at Ely in 673 and died in 679 (see Bede, *EH*,
     202–5, 406). Before 1109, when the bishopric was set up there, Ely
     belonged to the bishopric of Lincoln and to Henry's father Nicholas's
     archdeaconry of Huntingdon. Nicholas (just possibly accompanied by
     Henry) was among those who inspected Æthelthryth's body at the
     reburial in Ely in 1106. With the establishment of the new bishopric, the
     abbey became a cathedral priory and was ruled by a prior rather than an
     abbot.

114 *A certain man . . . by visitors*: a longer and more detailed version of this

story appears in OV iii. 347–59. The date was between 28 September
1115 and 5 August 1116. Bricstan was charged with theft and tried at
Huntingdon before being imprisoned in London.

The record of recent saints: this is c. 51 of book ix, HH, 687.

see the miraculous deeds: Henry was encouraging his audience to visit the
shrines and look at pictorial representations, in the form of paintings,
sculptures, or stained glass, as well as read the lives of the saints. Of the
sixteen shrines featured in the following paragraphs, six were in Henry's
locality—Buckingham, St Neots, St Ives, Ramsey, Peterborough, and
Crowland. For a map of the resting-places of the Anglo-Saxon saints, see
David Hill, *An Atlas of Anglo-Saxon England* (Oxford, 1981), no. 245.

5: this is c. 52 of book ix, HH, 689–95.

Dunstan: archbishop of Canterbury 959–88.

God . . . His saints: Ps. 68: 35.

Æthelwold: bishop of Winchester 963–84.

Swithun: bishop of Winchester from 852 or 853 to *c.*865.

the consent . . . kingdom successfully: the story that Æthelwulf was in
subdeacon's orders and had Pope Leo's consent to become king is a
twelfth-century legend.

115 *Birinus . . . Lincoln*: Birinus was bishop of Dorchester 634–*c.*650. For
the move from Dorchester to Lincoln, see above, II. 41.

Aldhelm . . . Salisbury: Aldhelm was bishop of Sherborne *c.*705–709. The
cathedral was removed to Salisbury in 1075.

Kenelm: he died *c.*811.

Milburg . . . Mildgith . . . Mildrith: these three sisters died in the early
eighth century.

Rumwold: he allegedly died when three days old, some time in the middle
of the seventh century.

Neot: he died *c.*877. The place is St Neots, Huntingdonshire.

Yvo: he supposedly died in Persia in 600 and his body was found in 1001
or 1002 in Huntingdonshire, at St Ives.

I can remember: for Henry's earliest recollections, see above, Introduction, p. xxiii.

Æthelred and Æthelberht: the two princes supposedly died in the late
seventh century.

Cyneburh . . . Cyneswith . . . Tibba: these three women belong to the later
seventh century.

116 *Werburg*: she died *c.*700.

And it was done: Gen. 1: 7, 9, 11, etc.

Wulfhild: she died *c.*1000.

Edith: she died before 988.

116 6: this is c. 53 of book ix, HH, 695.

    the lights of heaven: cf. Gen. 1: 14; Ezek. 32: 8.

    knows His own: cf. John 10: 14.

    the high One . . . the humble: cf. Ps. 113: 4–6.

117 *St Wulfric, venerable priest*: this is c. 54, the final chapter, of book ix, HH, 697.

    Wulfric . . . a hermit: Wulfric of Haselbury (which is in Somerset, not Dorset) became an anchorite in 1125 and died in 1155. Henry's account, completed by c. 1140, is the first written notice of his life, pre-dating by at least forty years the first *Life of Wulfric*, which was written by John of Ford in the 1180s.

    Pope St Gregory . . . other saints: in his *Dialogues* Gregory the Great (pope 590–604) related the lives and miracles of numerous Italian saints, including St Benedict, the founder of western monasticism.

VII. EPILOGUE

Originally written in 1130 and revised in 1135, the Epilogue contains Henry's reflections on Time. He looks back at the first millennium, then turns to address his readers in the third millennium, and discusses the question of the end of the world.

118 *The 703rd year . . . year of grace 1135*: some of these calculations are difficult. The 703rd year from 1135 takes us back to the year 432; but the first English invasion is dated 455 in *ASC*. Nor is it possible to reconcile the 2,265th year from the coming of the Britons with the standard medieval calculations that were derived from Bede. On Bede's calculation also, the number of years from the Creation to the Nativity, 3,952 ('The Greater Chronicle', in Bede, *EH*, 307), the year 1135 would be the 5,087th since the Creation, rather than Henry's 5,317th.

    they might . . . moral purity: this is a reference back to the Prologue, above, I. 4.

    Lucius . . . faith in Christ: Bede, *EH*, 14.

119 *the law . . . they signified*: cf. Luke 16: 16.

    Herbert . . . learned man: Herbert Losinga, bishop of Norwich 1091–1119, was a well-known teacher: see F. Barlow, *The English Church 1066–1154* (London and New York, 1979), 68–9, 240–5.

120 *flow away . . . have nothing*: cf. Ps. 58: 7.

GLOSSARY

ætheling Old English for 'prince of the royal house'; Latin 'clito'

archdeacon chief clergyman of a district, or 'archdeaconry', which usually corresponded to an English county; he was responsible to the bishop of the *diocese* for the discipline of clergy and people

Danegeld or **geld** army tax, assessed on *hides* of land, introduced in 1012 and finally abandoned in 1162

diocese area whose churches, clergy, and congregations came under the authority of a bishop

ealdorman term used before the early eleventh century for chief officer of one or more English counties on behalf of the king: he acted as the leader of the local army, the president of the local courts, and collector of *geld*

earl the word replaced *ealdorman* in the early eleventh century. After 1066 the office of earl tended to become hereditary, on the model of the French count, and by *c.*1100 it was largely a position of prestige, its public functions having been entrusted in each county to the *sheriff*

fealty sworn loyalty owed to a lord by his subordinates (and see *homage*)

hauberk coat of armour formed of chain mail and reaching below the knees

hide measurement of land, originally without fixed acreage; defined by Bede (*EH*, 84, 379) as the amount of land supporting one peasant family, though by the eleventh century a hide might support eight or more families. Henry defined it as 'the land that can be cultivated annually by one plough' (above, II. 4, 36). In the later twelfth century it was often measured at 120 acres

homage ceremony introduced by the Normans, in which a subordinate or tenant pledged loyalty and service to his lord in return for protection and a landed tenancy

mark unit of money, two-thirds of £1, or 13s 4d.

sheriff royal official in charge of the shire, or county; initially subordinate to the *ealdorman* but becoming increasingly important, especially after 1066

simony buying and selling of church appointments, forbidden by church law

thegn Anglo-Saxon landowner of high status, belonging to the social class from which *ealdormen* and *sheriffs* might be drawn

witan Old English for 'wise men', i.e. a meeting of the king's council

INDEX

(All kings are of England unless otherwise stated)

American Literature

British and Irish Literature

Children's Literature

Classics and Ancient Literature

Colonial Literature

Eastern Literature

European Literature

Gothic Literature

History

Medieval Literature

Oxford English Drama

Poetry

Philosophy

Politics

Religion

The Oxford Shakespeare

A complete list of Oxford World's Classics, including Authors in Context, Oxford English Drama, and the Oxford Shakespeare, is available in the UK from the Marketing Services Department, Oxford University Press, Great Clarendon Street, Oxford OX2 6DP, or visit the website at www.oup.com/uk/worldsclassics.

In the USA, visit www.oup.com/us/owc for a complete title list.

Oxford World's Classics are available from all good bookshops. In case of difficulty, customers in the UK should contact Oxford University Press Bookshop, 116 High Street, Oxford OX1 4BR.

A SELECTION OF   OXFORD WORLD'S CLASSICS

The Anglo-Saxon World

Beowulf

Lancelot of the Lake

The Paston Letters

Sir Gawain and the Green Knight

Tales of the Elders of Ireland

York Mystery Plays

GEOFFREY CHAUCER   The Canterbury Tales
                          Troilus and Criseyde

HENRY OF HUNTINGDON   The History of the English People
                          1000–1154

JOCELIN OF BRAKELOND   Chronicle of the Abbey of Bury
                          St Edmunds

GUILLAUME DE LORRIS   The Romance of the Rose
and JEAN DE MEUN

WILLIAM LANGLAND   Piers Plowman

SIR THOMAS MALORY   Le Morte Darthur

Bhagavad Gita

The Bible Authorized King James Version
  With Apocrypha

Dhammapada

Dharmasūtras

The Koran

The Pañcatantra

The Sauptikaparvan (from the
  Mahabharata)

The Tale of Sinuhe and Other Ancient
  Egyptian Poems

The Qur'an

Upaniṣads

ANSELM OF CANTERBURY The Major Works

THOMAS AQUINAS **Selected Philosophical Writings**

AUGUSTINE **The Confessions**
  On Christian Teaching

BEDE **The Ecclesiastical History**

HEMACANDRA **The Lives of the Jain Elders**

KĀLIDĀSA **The Recognition of Śakuntalā**

MANJHAN **Madhumalati**

ŚĀNTIDEVA **The Bodhicaryàvatàra**

Classical Literary Criticism

The First Philosophers: The Presocratics
and the Sophists

Greek Lyric Poetry

Myths from Mesopotamia

APOLLODORUS   The Library of Greek Mythology

APOLLONIUS OF RHODES   Jason and the Golden Fleece

APULEIUS   The Golden Ass

ARISTOPHANES   Birds and Other Plays

ARISTOTLE   The Nicomachean Ethics
Physics
Politics

BOETHIUS   The Consolation of Philosophy

CAESAR   The Civil War
The Gallic War

CATULLUS   The Poems of Catullus

CICERO   Defence Speeches
The Nature of the Gods
On Obligations
Political Speeches
The Republic and The Laws

EURIPIDES   Bacchae and Other Plays
Heracles and Other Plays
Medea and Other Plays
Orestes and Other Plays
The Trojan Women and Other Plays

HERODOTUS   The Histories

HOMER   The Iliad
The Odyssey